The Faber Pocket Guide to Ballet

Deborah Bull is a former principal dancer with The Royal
Ballet. Noted for her performances in works by MacMillan
and Forsythe, she remains involved with the life of the Royal
Opera House while also pursuing a career as a writer and
broadcaster. In 2002 she wrote and presented the award-
winning *The Dancer's Body*, a 3-part series for the BBC, and is
the author of *The Vitality Plan* (1998) and *Dancing Away*
(1998).

Luke Jennings is a leading ballet critic and has written
extensively about dance and contemporary culture for the
New Yorker and in the UK press. He is also an award-winning
documentary film-maker and the author of several novels –
Breach Candy (1993), *Atlantic* (1995), *Beauty Story* (1998).

D0012530

in the same series

A POCKET GUIDE TO ALAN AYCKBOURN'S PLAYS
Paul Allen

A POCKET GUIDE TO IBSEN, CHEKHOV AND STRINDBERG
Michael Pennington and Stephen Unwin

THE FABER POCKET GUIDE TO OPERA
Rupert Christiansen

A POCKET GUIDE TO SHAKESPEARE'S PLAYS
Kenneth McLeish and Stephen Unwin

A POCKET GUIDE TO 20TH CENTURY THEATRE
Stephen Unwin with Carole Woddis

THE FABER POCKET GUIDE TO

Ballet

Deborah Bull and Luke Jennings

faber and faber

First published in 2004
by Faber and Faber Limited
3 Queen Square London WC1N 3AU

Typeset by Faber and Faber in Jansen
Printed in England by Bookmarque Ltd, Croydon

A CIP record for this book
is available from the British Library

ISBN 0–571–20724–3

10 9 8 7 6 5 4 3 2 1

Contents

Acknowledgements

My grateful thanks to Luke Jennings, for agreeing to collaborate with me on this book; Belinda Matthews for believing in it; Pat Kavanagh for her unfailing wisdom; Kate Bettley, Phyllida Ritter, Philippa Rooke, Umber Salam and all my colleagues at the Royal Opera House for their support; and my telly boys, for making me smile.

Deborah Bull

My thanks are due to the archive department of the Royal Opera House, Covent Garden, and to Geoffrey Whitlock, who gave me access to his Soviet ballet files. *The Oxford Dictionary of Dance* by Judith Mackrell and Debra Craine proved an invaluable resource, and I am indebted to Sally Banes for her insights (in her excellent *Dancing Women*) concerning *The Firebird* and *Rodeo*).

Luke Jennings

Introduction

Throughout my career with The Royal Ballet, I was constantly asked by my friends and my family for more information about the ballets they were watching me dance. What's it about? When was it created? Does it have a story? What should I look out for? I longed to find a book that would answer their questions, solve my Christmas-present problems for all time, and let me get on with my dancing. But while there are many wonderful ballet books both in and out of print, the one I was looking for didn't seem to exist. Perhaps there was room on the shelf for one more: a companionable pocket guide designed to help both first-timers and aficionados get more out of an evening at the ballet.

Thinking about the book, I turned to Luke Jennings, a dance writer and critic whom I have long admired. Together, we decided to create a ballet guide offering two separate perspectives: Luke would write the factual, historical and analytical core of the book, while I would contribute the performer's view – the View from the Wings.

Whilst a ballet performance can certainly be enjoyed with little or no knowledge, I've always found the ballet to be one of those experiences that is greatly enhanced by a little inside information. Our aim in this book has been to provide that inside information when it's needed: in advance of the performance. Printed programmes are often packed with fact and opinion, but most people don't get the chance to open them until five minutes before curtain-up. The result is always the same: row after row of audience members desperately speed-reading the plot synopsis as the house lights fade.

So dip in at random or trace the development of ballet from cover to cover. Either way, we hope the unusual combination of anecdote and analysis will add to your enjoyment of this art without words and, perhaps, tempt you to try ballets which otherwise might not have seemed worth the price of a ticket. To every ballet-goer – past, present or future – this book's for you.

Deborah Bull

I have a particular memory of Deborah on stage, dynamically cleaving through William Forsythe's *in the middle, somewhat elevated*. That was in 1992, and it was a great pleasure, exactly a decade later, to sit down with her and plan this book. The first challenge that we faced was how to slice the immense cake that is the international dance repertoire. In the end we agreed to be guided by a simple principle: to confine ourselves to works that readers might expect to see performed by the leading classical ballet companies. The art-form as we know it today came into being with the Romantic movement of the 1830s – the earliest ballets that are still performed were created in that era – and so that is where we've taken up the story.

Within the framework of a pocket guide, inevitably, it has been impossible to detail the entire ballet canon. We have included, I hope, all the most important works, but the book spans a century and three quarters of classical dancing and ultimately the choices that we made were personal ones – as are the opinions we express. The hardest decision of all, given the ever-evolving nature of the art-form, was which present-day ballets to describe. We can only guess which will stand the test of time. In consequence the more recent pieces that we have chosen are not necessarily 'the best', but those which, in our view, most clearly exemplify the various currents in present-day choreographic thought.

For readers wishing to take their researches a stage further, the quarterly *Dance Now* is unbeatable in the quality of its coverage. For a balletic overview, *Secret Muses* (Julie Kavanagh's biography of Frederick Ashton) or *Writing in the Dark* (Arlene Croce's essays from *The New Yorker*) would both be excellent starting points.

Luke Jennings

Prelude

Classical ballet was born of the court entertainments of the Italian Renaissance. Elaborately costumed and performed exclusively by the nobility, these entertainments were a formal expression of the aristocratic world-view. The fashion for them spread to France; Louis XIV was an enthusiastic performer, and as a young man took part in ballets to music by Lully and other composers.

The demands of the ballet soon began to exceed the skills of amateur performers. Acrobats and grotesques were called for – roles from which aristocrats were excluded by lack of training and by social position – and travelling players joined the amateurs' ranks. In 1671 Louis XIV established the first dance school, at the Académie Royale de Musique in Paris, and ballet began to migrate from the court to the theatre. Steps and movements were codified, and professional dancers built up a repertoire of technical feats – *jetés*, *pirouettes*, *entrechats* and *cabrioles* – distancing themselves from the amateurs and acquiring considerable status in the process.

In 1713 Louis established a permanent dance company at the Paris Opéra. There, the first true stars of the ballet were created. The most celebrated of these was a Florentine named Gaetano Vestris (1728–1808). Brilliant, vain and demanding in equal part, he became known as Le Dieu de la Danse. Like Vestris, many dancers of the day were Italian-born. The Italian tradition was older than the French, and Italian schooling, such as that offered by the Scala Theatre in Milan, was highly regarded. The Opéra, however, was viewed as the centre of the eighteenth-century ballet world, and the best Italian dancers made their way to Paris.

The eighteenth century saw ballet's gradual evolution from a minor form (usually in the service of vocal music or poetry) to an expressive art in its own right. Drawing on the physical vocabulary of the dramatic theatre and the commedia dell'arte, choreographers sought ways of telling stories purely through dance and movement. The most influential of these modernisers was Jean-Georges Noverre, who became chief ballet-master at the Opéra in 1776. Noverre strove to replace ballet's often cumbersome formality with naturalistic drama, and is credited with the creation of the *ballet d'action*, in which music, costume and steps are all subordinated to plot.

With these developments the art-form grew in popularity, and London, Vienna, Berlin, Stuttgart and Prague all became regular ports of call for the French and Italian dance stars. In Russia, the Empress Catherine's dream of creating a Paris of the North ensured that an enthusiastic welcome always greeted well-known dancers in St Petersburg.

Noverre's regime at the Opéra was followed by that of the Gardels, one of Parisian ballet's most influential families. Pierre Gardel succeeded his brother Maximilien in 1787, and steered the company through the tumult of the Revolution. He also fostered an extreme artistic conservatism, from which the Opéra would emerge only on his retirement in 1829. It is at this point, with a new and fevered aesthetic in the air, that we take up the story.

Glossary of Ballet Terms

These terms appear in italics throughout the book.

Adagio (adage). Slow passage.
Adagietto. Brief slow passage.
A la seconde. To the side.
Allegro. Quick, lively.
Arabesque. Position in which the dancer is supported on one leg with the other extended straight behind.
Attitude. Position in which the dancer is supported on one leg with the other extended behind. The raised leg is bent at the knee.
Ballerina. Principal female ballet dancer.
Ballet blanc. Lit. 'white ballet'. Unearthly sequences, usually moonlit, as in *Swan Lake*, *Giselle*, *La Bayadère*, *Les Sylphides*, etc.
Ballet d'action. A ballet shaped by the requirements of character and story.
Ballon. High-speed reactive 'bounce'.
Bourrée. Fast step, usually performed on pointe.
Bransle. Antique French court-dance.
Cabriole. Jumped step in which the dancer's extended legs are beaten together in front or behind.
Chanson dansée. Lit. 'danced song'.
Coda. Final part of formal pas de deux (duet) sequence, danced by both dancers.
Corps de ballet. Balletic chorus, presented either as a formal group (like the swans in *Swan Lake*), or as individuals.
Cracovienne. Polish dance.
Csardas. Hungarian dance.
Developpé. Step in which the raised leg unfurls to full extension.
Danseuse aerienne. Airborne, ethereal dancer.
Divertissement. Self-contained showpiece.
Enchaînement. Step-sequence.

Entrechat. Jumped step in the course of which the dancer's extended legs rapidly criss-cross or 'beat' in the air.

Entrée. Opening dance.

Épaulement. Oppositional torsion of the waist and shoulderline. If the right leg is extended in front of the body, for example, the left shoulder moves forward. If the right leg is extended behind, the left shoulder moves back. This physical interplay lends life and three-dimensionality to sequences which might otherwise appear merely academic, and is one of the means by which a dancer colours his or her performance.

Fondu. The bending (lit. melting) of the supporting leg.

Fouetté. Spinning turn in which the raised leg whips the body round. The most famous example is the sequence of thirty-two non-stop fouettés in Act 3 of *Swan Lake*.

Gaillard. Antique French court-dance.

Grand jeté. Big leap from one extended leg to the other.

Jeté. Any jump from one leg to the other.

Legato. Slow, smooth.

Mazurka. Polish dance.

Pas d'action. Ensemble dance in which the plot is advanced, usually containing the formal elements of *entrée*, *adagio*, variations and *coda*.

Pas de bourrée. Small linking-step.

Pas de chat. Sideways spring in which the legs are gathered 'cat-like' beneath the body.

Pas de deux. Lit. 'dance for two'. Duet, or formal duet sequence. The classical pas de deux is usually composed of an *entrée* and *adagio* for the two dancers, a *variation* (solo) for each dancer, and a *coda* (finale).

Pas de trois, quatre, cinq, six, dix. Dances for three, four, five, six or ten dancers. The *pas de trois* is often structured as formally as the *pas de deux*.

Petit allegro. Small fast steps.

Pirouette. Lit. 'spinning-top'. Turn or turns on one straight leg with the other raised.

Polonaise. Polish dance.

Port de bras. Carriage of the arms.

Posé. Preparatory step from one foot to the other.

Prima ballerina. Title bestowed on the leading ballerina of a company, although present-day usage rare.

Prima ballerina assoluta. Even rarer title. Galina Ulanova was Prima Ballerina Assoluta of the Bolshoi and Margot Fonteyn of The Royal Ballet.

Régisseur. Ballet manager / rehearsal director.

Sarabande. Dance of Hispanic origin.

Saut de basque. Leaping step.

Scherzo. A playful measure, usually in 3/4 time.

Sortie. Exit.

Tarantella. Italian dance.

Tendu. Stretched or held. Usually refers to the stretching of the foot.

Terre-à-terre. Designates low, ground-skimming dancing.

Tour en l'air. Jumped step, in which the male dancer performs vertical turns in the air (usually two).

Variation. Solo dance.

The Romantic Ballet

The earliest ballets that are still danced in anything like their original form are those of the 1830s and 40s. This was the era when the ballerina took centre stage, and assumed the cultish and mysterious glamour which she enjoys to this day. On stage, weightlessly flitting and skimming through the painted landscape, she became a not-quite-human figure – a fairy, a sylph, or a spirit. Someone to whom the laws of gravity deferred.

The ballerina was aided in her ethereality by three very down-to-earth nineteenth-century innovations. The first of these was gas lighting, perfect for suggesting moonlight and the supernatural, and the second was the tutu, the ballerina's gauzy tulle skirt. In combination these gave us the *ballet blanc* – the famous 'white ballet' passages of *Giselle*, *Swan Lake*, *La Bayadère* and others, all of which take place at dusk or at night. The third innovation – and it was this that summarily despatched all that went before it to the store cupboard of history – was the pointe shoe. The pointe shoe gave us ballet as we know it today.

No one knows for sure which ballerina first stiffened the toe of her shoe with glue and darning-cotton and rose on to her pointes, but Geneviève Gosselin in Paris and Avdotia Istomina in St Petersburg were both dancing on pointe before 1820. The Russian writer Pushkin writes worshipfully of Istomina's dancing feet in his verse novel *Evgeny Onegin*, and clearly subscribed to the keen interest that men of his day took in women's extremities. Toe-dancing, as it was then called, played up to this interest. In the early court ballets, the pointed foot was displayed in order to show off the ribbons and buckles on the shoe. In the pointe shoe, the foot itself became the object of admiration, and the high arch (developed by pointe work), a desirable feature of balletic line.

In early nineteenth-century Europe, the mood of the cultured classes was one of mystical introspection. The roots of this attitude lay in late eighteenth-century German Romanticism. Goethe's *The Sorrows of Young Werther* and Bürger's ballads had been echoed in tone by the works of Wordsworth and Coleridge, and had encouraged an interest in the transcendent and the sublime. The personification of this movement was the yearning poet, ideally situated in an exotic landscape, like Byron's Greece. As the years passed, so the mood darkened. By the century's third decade the popularity of books like Hoffmann's *Phantasiestücke*, paintings like Fuseli's *The Nightmare*, and compositions like Berlioz's *Symphonie Fantastique* – all of them dealing with terror and the irrational – suggested that the Romantic was evolving into the fully blown gothic.

This was the moment at which ballet joined the feast. In 1831 an opera named *Robert le Diable* was mounted at the Paris Opéra. The production featured an episode in a ruined convent in which, at midnight, the spectres of nuns who had broken their vows were summoned from their graves to dance beneath the moon and to seduce the opera's hero to the music of a demonic choir. The scene, brilliantly and atmospherically evoked beneath the new gas lights, caused a sensation. The unholy ghosts were played by the dancers of the ballet, and their leader, a pale, slender twenty-seven-year-old named Marie Taglioni (whose father Filippo had choreographed the scene), became the talk of Paris.

Taglioni had been admired by Paris audiences since her first appearence at the Opéra in 1827. Her dancing was subtle and apparently effortless, with none of the overt sex-appeal with which her contemporaries laced their performances. Her pointe work, by the same token, was an integral element of her dancing, rather than mere acrobatic trickery. Taglioni was not especially beautiful – her portraits show prim, rather sharp features – but she was exquisitely graceful, and brought a spirituality to her performances which ravished those who watched them. 'Her debut will open a new epoch,' wrote *Le*

Figaro's critic. 'It is Romanticism applied to the dance.'

Now, it seemed, Taglioni's dancing had touched a darker chord. In the ghostly seductress rising from her ruined cloister in *Robert le Diable*, Parisians had recognised a thrillingly perverse object of desire, and the ultimate femme fatale. Word of her ambiguous appeal spread ('What lack of restraint, yet how chaste,' wrote the poet Théophile Gautier, one of her most fervent admirers), and within the year, in *La Sylphide*, Taglioni was dancing another other-worldly role, that of the beautiful but unattainable spirit-girl who lures a young Scottish laird away from his bride on his wedding day.

La Sylphide proved a perfect marriage of style and content (the medieval Scottish setting had been made fashionable by the novels of Walter Scott). As the ethereal sylph, Taglioni was the archetype of the Romantic ballerina-heroine whose luminous charms, once glimpsed, lead the hero to forswear the mundane world – and with it, any chance of earthly happiness. In the Romantic ballet the heroine's luminosity sometimes indicates a delicate virtue, sometimes a dangerous insubstantiality. She symbolised the unattainable object of desire whom poets eulogised and opium-smokers chased through their dreams. Unattainable, that is, this side of death, but then the nineteenth-century Romantics were at least half in love with the notion of death. In *Giselle* (as in *La Bayadère*, choreographed thirty-six years later) the ballerina-heroine only becomes truly desirable to her lover – and truly interesting to her choreographer – when she is dead, transfigured, and dressed in white tulle.

Generally considered the quintessential Romantic ballet, *Giselle* was inspired by a passage in Heinrich Heine's *De l'Allemagne*. In this account of German folklore Heine wrote of the wilis, the vengeful girl-spirits who haunted the dark woodlands of the north and forced men to dance themselves to death. At the ballet's first performance in 1841, the title role of Giselle fell to twenty-two-year-old Carlotta Grisi, the Opéra's new sensation and the lover of the choreographer Jules Perrot. 'Carlotta danced with a perfection, lightness, boldness and a chaste and refined seductiveness which put her in the first rank,' wrote Gautier after the premiere, casually switching to Grisi the devotion that he had previously reserved for Taglioni.

Giselle, like *La Sylphide* ten years earlier, was an immediate popular success. Its choreography was divided between Jean Coralli, the chief ballet-master at the Opéra, who devised the ensemble work, and Perrot, who created the dances for Giselle. Perrot had previously been a popular dancer at the Opéra, where he had partnered Taglioni. He had left after a contractual dispute in 1833, and despite the success of *Giselle*, the Parisian dance establishment now refused to readmit him. He received no credit for his work on *Giselle*, and it was not long before Grisi left him for her handsome young partner, Lucien Petipa.

The five most important ballerinas of the Romantic era were Marie Taglioni, Fanny Elssler, Fanny Cerrito, Carlotta Grisi and Lucile Grahn. Fanny Elssler was an Austrian who joined the Paris Opéra in 1834, and became a pupil of Auguste Vestris (son of Gaetano, 'le Dieu de la Danse'). Her appeal was frankly sensual, she could not have been more different from the maidenly Taglioni, and ballet historians consider her a *demi-caractère* dancer rather than a 'pure' Romantic ballerina. Nevertheless the Opéra saw the business advantage in setting up a rivalry between the two, and for three years boulevard society was divided into rival camps.

In 1837 this rivalry drove Taglioni from Paris. She travelled to St Petersburg, where for five years she became the star ballerina (and where, it is said, a group of devoted balletomanes cooked and ate one of her pointe-shoes). In Paris, meanwhile, as if to underline her victory, Elssler danced *La Sylphide*, Taglioni's signature role.

In 1839, twenty-year-old Lucile Grahn joined the Paris Opéra from the Royal Danish Ballet, where she had been the company's ballerina. A great beauty, whom Hans Christian Andersen called 'a rosebud born of the northern snows', she was swiftly established as Elssler's new rival. In 1840 Elssler in her turn departed Paris for a two-year tour of the United States, where she earned a fortune, and incurred a thumping fine from the Opéra for breach of contract. Elssler's departure ceded the ballet stage to Lucile Grahn, and left the way clear for Carlotta Grisi's historic triumph in *Giselle*.

Fanny Cerrito, an Italian whose dancing was characterised by a brilliant fluency, made her debut in 1832 in Naples, and thereafter blazed a triumphant trail across the ballet stages of Europe. She was considered tempestuous, and her marriage to her stage partner, the choreographer Arthur Saint-Léon, broke up when Cerrito became the mistress of a marquis.

In 1845 an astute businessman named Benjamin Lumley, manager of Her Majesty's Theatre in London, had the idea of presenting Taglioni, Cerrito, Grisi and Grahn on stage together. With considerable tact, Jules Perrot created a suite of plotless dances which showed off each performer to her best advantage. The piece was named *Pas de Quatre*. Perrot's ballet suite encapsulated the Romantic era, and is the ultimate expression of the ballerina cult which it engendered. By 1844, Gautier was already complaining that 'white was almost the only colour in use' on the Paris ballet stage, and after Lumley's triumph at Her Majesty's Theatre (attended by Her Majesty herself, and Prince Albert) the *ballet blanc* began to fade into the enchanted mists which had always threatened to envelop it.

For all its rapid advances as an art-form, ballet in the first half of the nineteenth century was dominated by a handful of individuals. We know them through the engravings and lithographs of the day, but these give little impression of their energy. Dancers and choreographers occupied a colourful but lethally insecure demi-monde, from which only the most brilliant were able to raise themselves. This handful made their own rules, knowing even as they accepted the adulation of the public and flaunted their amours that their professional span was brief, and that if they were not to end their lives in poverty (as Taglioni did, her savings gone) they had to be tirelessly resourceful. For all its international reach, the ballet world was still a small one, and the paths of its inhabitants crossed constantly. The most important behind-the-scenes figure of the day was Auguste Vestris. After a long dancing career (and a brief period of imprisonment for debt), Vestris joined the staff of the Opéra as a coach, where his influence was without parallel. Taglioni, Elssler and Grahn were his pupils, as were the choreographers Didelot, Perrot, Bournonville and Petipa.

Charles-Louis Didelot was the oldest of these pupils. He travelled to Russia in 1801, and over the next thirty years reorganised the teaching system at the Imperial ballet school, created more than fifty ballets, and set in place the foundations of the great St Petersburg style. Jules Perrot, as we have seen, was the creator of *Giselle* and *Pas de Quatre*. August Bournonville joined the Paris Opéra in 1826. Returning to Copenhagen three years later, he became the director and chief choreographer of the Royal Danish Ballet, and over the next half-century built the company into one of the finest in the world. His first and greatest ballet was *La Sylphide*, made in 1836. The ballet had originally been choreographed by Filippo Taglioni, five years earlier, but it is Bournonville's highly characteristic text which comes down to us today. His first Sylphide, and his muse, was Lucile Grahn.

Bournonville went on to create the series of works which, to this day, forms the basis of the Royal Danish Ballet's repertoire. *La Sylphide* was followed by *The Festival in Albano* (1839), *Napoli* (1842), *Conservatoire* (1849), *A Folk Tale* (1854), *La Ventana* (1854), *Flower Festival at Genzano* (1858), and *Far From Denmark* (1860). The Bournonville ballets are characterised by their charm, wit and sweet nature. They reject the gothic morbidity that was Romanticism's dark side, and embrace the supernatural only in its fairy-tale aspect. Choreographically they appear deceptively simple, but in fact they demand brilliant footwork, spring-heeled *ballon*, subtle *épaulement* and an airily generous leap. Few companies outside Scandinavia have ever mastered the style, although many have tried.

By the 1860s, the Romantic era was over. The great ballerinas had left the stage, expressiveness had given way to vulgar exhibitionism, and European ballet was in steep decline. Arthur Saint-Léon, however – by now long divorced from the faithless Fanny Cerrito – was enjoying a late flowering of his talents. Having succeeded Jules Perrot as ballet-master in St Petersburg in 1859, he made sporadic return visits to Paris, where in 1870 he choreographed *Coppélia*, the last of the great nineteenth-century ballets.

It would be left to Marius Petipa, the last and most influential of the pupils of Auguste Vestris, to move the story forward.

La Sylphide

Two acts. Choreography by Filippo Taglioni, music by Jean Schneitzhoeffer, designs by Pierre Ciceri and Eugène Lamy.
First performed at the Théâtre de l'Académie Royale de Musique, 1832.

In 1831 Marie Taglioni came to the attention of the Parisian public in *Robert le Diable*. The following year, anxious to capitalise on his daughter's success, Filippo Taglioni created *La Sylphide*, a reworking of a Milanese piece named *La Silfide*. The ballet was a sensation, and as intended, made Taglioni a star. Five years after its premiere August Bournonville rechoreographed the piece in Copenhagen for himself and Lucile Grahn to music by Hermann Løvenskjold. It is Bournonville's version which comes down to us today.

~ Plot

ACT 1

The setting is the 1830s – contemporary with the ballet's creation. In a Scottish farmhouse, James is sleeping in front of the fire. It is his wedding day; he is to be married to Effie, but at his feet is the figment of his dreams, the beautiful winged Sylphide. The Sylphide dances and James wakes. He chases her but she vanishes like smoke up the chimney. James's friend Gurn (who loves Effie) enters with the bride-to-be and her friends. The sorceress Madge appears from a dark corner, and the girls ask her to read their palms. She tells Effie that she will be happily married, but to Gurn, not James. Angry, James expels her.

When James is once more alone, the Sylphide reappears. She seems heartbroken, and explains that she loves him, but because her love is unrequited, she must die. Overcome, James tells her that he loves her in return. Gurn sees James kissing the Sylphide and tells Effie. As Gurn and Effie enter, the Sylphide hides under Effie's tartan shawl in the chair. Gurn lifts the shawl, but the Sylphide has vanished.

The wedding celebrations commence, and Effie, piqued at James's absent-mindedness, suggests that he dance with her. James does so, but the Sylphide appears. Visible only to the distracted bridegroom, she joins in the dance. The ceremony begins, but the Sylphide snatches the ring from Effie's finger and escapes. James follows her, leaving a shocked Effie to be comforted by Gurn.

ACT 2

It is night. In the forest, Madge has summoned her fellow witches. In a cauldron, she has prepared an enchanted scarf. At dawn, James enters with the Sylphide. She introduces him to her fellow sylphs, but to James's frustration becomes increasingly elusive.

When Madge appears he is at a low ebb. The sorceress offers her help, and gives James the scarf. If it is placed round the Sylphide's shoulders, Madge tells him, the magical creature's wings will fall off and she will be his for ever. The Sylphide reappears and James applies the scarf. Her wings fall off, as promised, but she dies an agonising death in front of him. As he kneels, heartbroken, the other sylphs appear, and bear their sister away. In the distance, we see the wedding procession of Effie and Gurn.

∿ Notes

In its hero's infatuation with a beautiful but unattainable creature for whom he will abandon everything, *La Sylphide* is an archetypal Romantic ballet. It lays out a series of opposites: the solidity of the home against the shifting other-worldliness of the forest (the domain of the Sylphide and Madge), the dutifulness of Gurn against the Romanticism of James, the humanity of Effie against the ethereality of the Sylphide. Throughout, earth is contrasted with air. When James dances with Effie, she is clearly earthbound; when he dances with the Sylphide he appears to be trying to prevent her flying away.

Tailor-made for Taglioni, the original ballet capitalised on its star's modest bearing, expressive arms, and soft, billowy leap. Taglioni was considered a *danseuse aerienne*, and her exceptional *ballon* enabled her to give the impression of momentary stillness in flight. The same qualities are demanded of those who dance the Romantic roles today. The ideal Sylphide or Giselle must combine a steely physical control with (as Gautier said of the Neapolitan ballerina Fanny Cerrito), 'a smiling ease which knows neither labour nor weariness'. As the legs do the work beneath the gauzy tutu – beating, turning, and leaping – the upper body is poised coolly and apparently weightlessly above them.

Male dancing in Bournonville's ballets is no less brilliant. Having exported the Romantic style to Denmark, the choreographer cut it to diamond sharpness. Lightning-fast beats, a buoyant leap, and an airy carriage of the arms are amongst the characteristics of the Bournonville style, and its grace and charm is perfectly demonstrated in *La Sylphide*. The 1836 production remains in the repertoire of the Royal Danish Ballet to this day, and has been recreated all over the world.

Giselle

Two acts. Choreographed by Jean Coralli and Jules Perrot, libretto by Théophile Gautier and Vernoy de St Georges, music by Adolphe Adam.
First performed at the Théâtre National de l'Opéra, Paris, 1841.

> 'My dear Heinrich Heine; when reviewing your fine book *Über Deutschland* a few weeks ago, I came across a charming passage . . . where you speak of elves in white dresses, whose hems are always damp; of nixies who display their little satin feet on the ceiling of the nuptial chamber; of snow-coloured Wilis who waltz pitilessly, and of those delicious apparitions you have encountered in the Harz mountains and on the banks of the Ilse, in a mist softened by German moonlight; and I involuntarily said to myself: 'Wouldn't this make a pretty ballet.'
>
> Théophile Gautier, 1841

At the first performance of *Giselle* at the Opéra in 1841, the title role was danced by twenty-two-year-old Carlotta Grisi, the lover of the choreographer Jules Perrot. Its choreography was divided between Jean Coralli, the Opéra's chief ballet-master, who devised the ensemble work, and Perrot himself (very much the greater artist), who created the dances for Giselle. The ballet caused a sensation. Within five years of its first night in Paris it had been produced in London, St Petersburg, Vienna, Berlin, Milan and Boston. By then, Grisi had left Perrot, who received no credit for his work.

~ Plot

ACT 1
The story is set in the Rhineland where a young man named Loys has been wooing Giselle, a village girl. 'Loys', however, is not the simple countryman that he is pretending to be, but

the aristocratic Count Albrecht. Giselle suspects nothing, but her mother Berthe is suspicious of the young man. She would prefer that her daughter marry Hilarion, a local forester. She recounts the legend of the Wilis – the spirits of young girls who have been jilted, and die unmarried. During the hours of darkness, the legend tells, the Wilis kill any man who dares approach their unhallowed burial ground in the forest. Ignoring Berthe, Giselle and Albrecht join in the celebration of the grape harvest.

Albrecht's squire warns him that a hunting party is approaching. Hilarion, who is as suspicious as Berthe, witnesses the meeting, and decides to break into Loys' cottage and find out his true identity. The hunting party arrives, led by the Duke of Courland. Amongst the retinue is Albrecht's bride-to-be, Bathilde. Charmed by Giselle's dancing, and learning that she, too, is to be married, Bathilde gives Giselle a necklace. Then, tired from the hunt, Bathilde asks if she may rest in Berthe's cottage. The Duke departs, and a hunting horn is left outside the cottage so that when Bathilde is rested, she can recall the ducal party.

Hilarion has discovered Albrecht's sword. Comparing it with the hunting horn, he discovers that both bear the same coat of arms. Interrupting the harvest celebrations, he accuses Albrecht of deceit. The truth becomes apparent when Bathilde exits Berthe's cottage, recognises Albrecht, and greets him as her fiancé. For Giselle, the shock is so great that she loses her mind. Seizing Albrecht's sword, she kills herself.

ACT 2

Hilarion keeps solitary vigil by Giselle's grave in the forest. At midnight the Wilis materialise, summoned by Myrtha, their queen. Seeing them, the terrified Hilarion runs deeper into the forest. Albrecht enters. He lays lilies on Giselle's grave and catching sight of her spectral form, follows her. The Wilis, meanwhile, have surrounded Hilarion, and force him to dance himself to death. Myrtha now orders Giselle to entice Albrecht, through the beauty of her dancing, to the same fate.

Giselle attempts to resist Myrtha's power, and to help Albrecht, but she is driven to dance, as he is. Nevertheless she does all that she can to protect him until, close to death, he is saved by the first light of dawn. The Wilis fade away and Giselle, released from their enchantment by love, returns to her grave, from which she will no longer stir. Albrecht is left to grieve alone.

∼ Notes

With its hauntingly mysterious atmosphere, and with its poignant statement of the power of love over death, *Giselle* represents the quintessence of the Romantic era. It lasts because of its formal perfection and symmetry, but also because – more than any other ballet, perhaps – it touches our hearts.

Act 1, with its harvest-time colours and its earthbound, temporal concerns, is expressed through essentially *terre-à-terre* choreography. Gravity is the keynote, not only in the country dances, but also in the groaning carts of produce and the heavy robes of the Courland retinue. Giselle is frail; her mother warns her not to dance for the sake of her health (an edict some have taken as a suggestion that she is pregnant). The message, like that of the autumn gathering of the grapes, is one of gentle inexorability. Like the physical world around them, human beings enjoy a brief flowering, they age, and they die.

Act 2, by contrast, is mysterious, lunar, and fearful. In the place of the gravitational pull of Act 1, the choreography suggests weightlessness and insubstantiality. When Albrecht dances with Giselle, he seems to be bearing her earthwards out of the night air. Only Hilarion is earthbound; he cannot sustain the flight – the metaphysical skills – necessary to survive in this terrible place. With Giselle's help, Albrecht can survive. But Giselle is divided, and herein lies the tension of the second act. She loves Albrecht, but she is powerless to resist Myrtha. In contrast to Act 1, she now *must* dance. And her dance must lure Albrecht away from the safety of the cross on her grave – echoes of the old vampire tales – to his death.

It is often said that the challenge for a ballerina in *Giselle* is to portray with equal conviction the unaffected country girl and the ethereal spirit-creature. This is true enough, and the famous 'mad' scene which provides a bridge between the two must be performed with absolute conviction if it is to convince, but the greater and subtler challenge is that of Act 2, when Giselle is torn between love and the demands of her 'undead' identity, and has to express both simultaneously in dance. Producers tend to underplay the dread aspect of the Wilis. They may be a beautiful, fairy-winged *corps de ballet* but they are also a vengeful sisterhood, reanimated by hate. At the first performances of the ballet in Paris, people fainted when they saw their blanched and bloodless forms. The libretto does not explicitly state that they are all suicides, but Giselle certainly is, and it is for this reason that she is buried beyond the reach of grace in the unhallowed ground which Myrtha nightly claims as her own. Through the power of her love, however, and through her refusal to pursue vengeance against Albrecht, Giselle finds redemption. And through Giselle's redemption, Albrecht finds his own.

The *Giselle* that we see today is attributed to Perrot and Coralli, but owes much to Marius Petipa's 1884 production for the Imperial Ballet in St Petersburg. One of the most sparkling of the Petipa-amended passages is the Peasant *pas de deux*, a self-contained display piece with music by Friedrich Burgmüller which was added to the ballet's first act in the original 1841 production. The main score was by Adolphe Adam, who was a friend of Jules Perrot and Carlotta Grisi. It is not especially sophisticated but it is theatrically effective and was one of the first to employ leitmotif. The themes for the principal characters and ideas are stated overtly at the beginning of the ballet and then referentially as the story progresses – for example in the 'mad' scene, where Giselle and Albrecht's love theme is re-presented but in fractured and incomplete form.

Today, *Giselle* is danced by companies all over the world, and in many different settings. The Dance Theatre of Harlem set their 1984 production on a Louisiana plantation, with Act 2 in the watery bayous. Mats Ek's 1987 production paints Giselle as the village simpleton, and the Wilis as her fellow inmates in a lunatic asylum. Sylvie Guillem's 2001 La Scala production places the action on a bleak, Goya-esque Hispanic prairie. The traditional Germanic setting, however, remains the most popular, and the ballet (like *Swan Lake*), remains a great ballerina rite of passage. Amongst the ranks of those who have triumphantly made the role their own are Olga Spessivtseva, Galina Ulanova, Gelsey Kirkland and Alina Cojocaru.

∾ View from the Wings

For classical ballerinas, Giselle is amongst the most coveted of roles: a technical and dramatic challenge and a chance to measure yourself against the great dancers of the past. The role of Giselle requires a brilliant tech-nique allied to an aptitude for the so-called Romantic style. While in classical ballets like *Sleeping Beauty* the ballerina must dance with a refined grandeur, all elegance and poise, in Romantic ballets like *Giselle* and *La Sylphide* she must appear ethereal, other-worldly, ghost-like, as if she has emerged only temporarily from the dry-ice mists which soften the box lines of the stage. Movements must be lightly traced in the air rather than boldly etched on the space. Jumps are carried on the breeze. The arms are soft and even slightly limp, as if early morning dew were dripping gently from the fingertips. At the same time, though, the choreography demands a steely strength and underneath her gossamer skirts and willowy sleeves, the ballerina's engine – her technique – is working overtime.

Like many nineteenth-century ballets, *Giselle* has not one, but two principal roles for the women, one repre-senting good and the other, evil. My role in life – at least in the ballet world – seems always to have been to dance the bad girl and Giselle was no exception. Not for me the eponymous heroine. I was Myrtha, Queen of the Wilis.

For Myrtha, the challenge is to maintain all the essentials of the Romantic style whilst dancing choreography which must surely have been created with a man in mind. It starts gently enough, with a series of smooth, skimming bourrées across and around the stage, but these only serve to create such fearsome cramp in your feet and calves that by the time the hard work starts – a succession of bounding solos which build to a breathless climax of *sauts de basques* around the stage – you can't feel anything below the knees. It's twenty minutes, no more, with plenty of resting time in the wings, but even so, Myrtha never ceased to be a role I would absolutely dread.

Napoli

Three acts. Choreography by August Bournonville, music by Edvard Helsted, Holger Paulli and others, designs by C. F. Christensen.
First performed at the Theatre Royal, Copenhagen, 1842.

If his reworking of Taglioni's *La Sylphide* is Bournonville's best-known ballet, *Napoli* is his greatest original work. He created it, aged thirty-six, after a visit to Italy. By then he had already been the director of the Royal Danish Ballet for a dozen years.

∼ Plot

ACT I
In the port of Santa Lucia, Naples, Teresina is waiting for Gennaro, the fisherman whom she loves. Watching her are two other suitors whom her mother Veronika favours – Giacomo who sells macaroni, and Peppo who sells lemonade. The fishermen return, and Veronika reluctantly gives Teresina permission to marry Gennaro. Fra Ambrosio carries out the rite. The couple sail in the bay, but a storm gets up and Teresina is lost. Gennaro, distraught, returns to port before setting out to search for her, carrying an image of the

Madonna for protection which Fra Ambrosio has given him.

ACT 2

In the Blue Grotto on the island of Capri, the lifeless Teresina is brought to the abode of the sea-god Golfo. Intrigued, the god restores her to life and transforms her into a naiad, and she forgets her past life. When the fisherman arrives in his boat, Golfo attempts to divert him, but Gennaro recognises Teresina. The image of the Madonna undoes Golfo's spell, and the couple are allowed to leave.

ACT 3

Gennaro, Teresina and Veronika give thanks to the Madonna at a shrine. Giacomo and Peppo try to convince the local populace that Teresina's rescue was effected by witchcraft, and the lovers are shunned. Fra Ambrosio is sent for, and tells the crowd that Teresina owes her rescue to the intercession of the Virgin Mary. The crowd believe him, and the couple's wedding is celebrated with joyful dances.

~ Notes

Although a full-length version of *Napoli* remains in the repertoire of the Royal Danish Ballet, most companies perform only the final act, with its colourful *tarantella* and happy whirl of *divertissements*. On these occasions, arrangers sometimes add the *pas de deux* from another Bournonville ballet – *Flower Festival at Genzano*. Either way, the ballet shows the Danish choreographer's style at its airy, charming best. Bournonville believed that the arts should edify, and (except in *La Sylphide*) avoided Romanticism's darker, more gothic aspects. His choreography, by the same token, is conversational and naturalistic. There are no anticipatory halts in the music as the dancer formally prepares for his or her solo, nor are the big jumps and lifts 'showcased' in the Russian manner. Instead, everything is danced out in a swift, logical and unbroken flow. For those not brought up in the Bournonville style (and even the Danish hold on the style is slipping), the necessary fluency can be hard to achieve, and applying meaningful light and shade to the steps even harder. Performed to full effect, however, *Napoli* and the other Bournonville ballets are unmatched in their fragrant charm.

∼ View from the Wings

During my years with The Royal Ballet, we danced very little of the Bournonville repertoire, but the early 1980s saw revivals at the Royal Opera House of both *Napoli* and *Conservatoire*. In fact, I had already danced a solo in *Napoli* at the Wimbledon Theatre as part of The Royal Ballet School's annual performances in 1980. It was good to have a chance to tackle it again on joining the company. The Bournonville repertoire is characterised by quick, fleet and intricate footwork, with the ability to bounce like a rubber ball an absolute essential. It's no good having a strong jump, as I did. Dancing Bournonville requires a light, speedy jump: the ability to rebound at speed, to take off again the very moment you land. Bournonville probably didn't know this, but he was actually choreographing for dancers with a high proportion of fast twitch muscle fibres – the dance equivalent of a sprinter rather than a marathon runner. The other unusual characteristic of the Bournonville repertoire, for non-Danish-trained dancers, is the apparently restricted use of *port de bras*. Many of the tricky jumps and turns are executed with the arms held low and immobile, *bras bas*, by the sides of the body. Anyone who has ever tried to jump high – either on a sports field or simply to reach something from a top shelf – knows how much help the arms can give in gaining momentum and height. Until you get used to it, keeping your arms still whilst attempting to dance Bournonville is a bit like dancing in a straitjacket. When danced by an expert – Johan Kobborg at The Royal Ballet, for instance – it looks effortless.

Pas de Quatre

Divertissement. Choreography by Jules Perrot, music by Cesare Pugni.
First performed at His Majesty's Theatre, London, 1845.

When Benjamin Lumley (the manager of His Majesty's Theatre in the Haymarket) succeeded in uniting Marie Taglioni, Carlotta Grisi, Fanny Cerrito and Lucile Grahn on his stage, it was regarded as a tremendous entrepreneurial coup. Lumley may have considered inviting Fanny Elssler too, but a state of mute warfare had existed between Taglioni and Elssler since the Austrian had had the temerity to dance *La Sylphide* at the Opéra seven years earlier, and the project would certainly have foundered if she had been involved. As it was, the idea found cautious acceptance, and it was to Jules Perrot (the former lover of Carlotta Grisi), that Lumley entrusted the tricky business of choreographing a suitable *divertissement*. All went well until a decision had to be made about the order of the dances (the later in the piece, conventionally, the greater the prestige). The deadlock threatened to sink the whole ballet until Perrot had the idea of suggesting that the dancers proceed by age – youngest first!

∾ Outline

The dancers are discovered grouped respectfully around Taglioni. Grahn performs a short *variation*, Cerrito and Grisi dance a brief duet, and Taglioni traverses the stage in a series of *grands jetés*. The four dancers then proceed to their main variations. Grahn is light and bright, Grisi romantically commanding, Cerrito crystalline and spectacular, Taglioni gracefully authoritative. The sense of muted competition increases until all four are dancing together, but then, as if in courteous acceptance of their equality, the four return to their original grouping.

∼ Notes

Pas de Quatre was performed only four times with its original cast. Perrot did not notate his choreography, so his steps are impossible to reproduce exactly. In 1941 Anton Dolin staged the piece for American Ballet Theatre, basing his composition on the accounts of critics who attended the first performances. The staging was later adopted by the Kirov Ballet. Today the piece is regularly revived as an exhibition piece, and is often referenced by contemporary choreographers like Matthew Bourne, whose wittily post-modern *Spitfire* (1988), featured four male underwear models.

Conservatoire
Konservatoriet

One scene. Choreography by August Bournonville, music by Holger Paulli.
First performed at the Theatre Royal, Copenhagen, 1849.

As originally staged (under the title *The Conservatory*, or *A Proposal of Marriage by Advertisement*) the ballet concerned the adventures of two young dancers, who come to Paris to study at the Opéra and, as it turns out, to involve themselves in a complicated web of romantic intrigue. Unfortunately much of this original work (including the second act, which contained a cancan) is now lost, but in 1941 an abbreviated revival was mounted in Copenhagen. The choreography of this single scene has been preserved intact for more than 150 years, and is Bournonville's personal reminiscence of his student days in Paris (1824–30) under the celebrated Auguste Vestris.

∼ Outline

In a Parisian ballet studio of the 1820s, the piece shows a dance class for virtuosi. The scene is one of dusty grandeur, with a chandelier and gilt-framed mirrors. To the music of a violinist, a ballet-master with a cane sets *enchaînements* of increasing complexity. Prominent amongst the dancers are a male soloist and the original ballet's protagonists, Elisa and Victorine.

∼ Notes

Conservatoire is a charming and elegant piece, but it is also of particular choreographic interest, in that it demonstrates the Parisian teaching style which Bournonville learnt from Vestris and took back to Denmark with him. One of Bournonville's pupils, Christian Johannsen, would later implant the same style in Russia as Petipa's senior teacher at the Imperial Ballet school in St Petersburg (where his pupils included Anna Pavlova and Tamara Karsavina). *Conservatoire* is now in the repertoire of several companies, including the Paris Opéra Ballet (1976), The Royal Ballet (1982) and the Bolshoi Ballet (1989). In 1995 the Royal Danish Ballet mounted a reconstructed two-act version.

Coppélia
La Fille aux Yeux d'Email

Three acts. Choreography by Arthur Saint-Léon, music by Léo Delibes, libretto by Saint-Léon and Charles Nuitter from *Der Sandmann* by Ernst Hoffmann.
First performed at the Théâtre National de l'Opéra, Paris, 1870.

Coppélia, created after an extended period as ballet-master in St Petersburg, was Saint-Léon's last and greatest work. Creativity had staled under the Second Empire, and the piece marked Paris's last gasp as a significant centre of nineteenth-century ballet. At the premiere in May 1870 the role of Swanilda was created by the seventeen-year-old Giuseppina Bozzacchi. Within half a year Bozzacchi would be dead of smallpox, Saint-Léon would have died of a heart attack, and France would be at war with Prussia. In balletic terms Paris would not be reawakened until the arrival of Serge Lifar some sixty years later.

∿ Plot

ACT 1

The action is set in a small Middle European town. This is home to Doctor Coppélius, a mysterious figure suspected by the townspeople of dabbling in alchemy, and to a young engaged couple named Franz and Swanilda. Coppélius has created a life-size doll which sits on his balcony, apparently reading. The townspeople are suspicious but fascinated. They think the doll might be his daughter, and have called her Coppélia. One morning Swanilda sees Coppélia reading on her balcony and greets her. There is no response, and when Swanilda sees Franz wave and blow a kiss to the doll she is upset. When Coppélia (animated by her creator) waves back, Swanilda's upset turns to anger. She quarrels with Franz, and breaks off their engagement. Night falls, Coppélius leaves his house and is set upon by a bunch of young men who make fun of him. In the mêlée he drops his key. Swanilda finds it, and accompanied by her friends, unlocks and enters Coppélius's house, determined to discover his secrets. At the same time, wanting to discover the identity of Coppélia, Franz takes a ladder to the balcony.

ACT 2

In Coppélius's sinister workshop the girls are greeted by life-size automata, which they set in motion, causing havoc. Swanilda, meanwhile, discovers that Coppélia is merely a doll like the rest. Coppélius enters. The friends scatter and Swanilda hides in Coppélia's alcove. Franz enters by the balcony, and encounters Coppélius, who offers him wine and drugs him. Through magic, the Doctor hopes to transfer Franz's soul to the doll. Brought from her alcove, Coppélia seems to respond. In reality, of course it is Swanilda, and soon she is disobeying her supposed creator. Franz wakes up, and the young couple escape. Coppélius, meanwhile, finding his unclothed doll, realises that he has been duped.

Act 3

Along with the other young couples of the town, Franz and Swanilda celebrate their wedding. There are dances for various allegorical figures, amongst them Aurora (Dawn) and Prayer. The couples are given gifts of gold, and Coppélius is recompensed for the damage to his workshop.

∾ Notes

Choreographically speaking there are many fine things in *Coppélia* – the character dances, the movements of the automata, the extended Dance of the Hours in Act 3 – but few of them are directly traceable to Saint-Léon. Despite being the inventor of a system of notation, he failed to notate the ballets he created himself. In 1884 Petipa staged his own version, and it is this, with some modifications, which we see performed today. Its heroine is sympathetic and strong; Swanilda is no moonstruck Giselle, but a lusty, resourceful young woman who knows her own worth. Her dancing must echo her nature: she needs an assertive line, a fine sense of attack and fast, stage-skimming *petit allegro*. Franz, by contrast, must struggle to make his mark if he is to come across as more than a handsome dimwit (it's him, after all, who falls for the doll, is gulled by Coppélius, and then has to be rescued by his fiancée). He is assisted in this by Petipa's arrangements for Act 3, which include a spectacular solo.

For all the sunny atmosphere created by Petipa's choreography and Delibes' wonderful score, however, certain elements of the ballet can strike a discordant note. Doctor Coppélius is the town's 'outsider'; he is old, and his ways are different to those of the other townspeople, so he is regarded as fair game for any amount of ridicule. We learn in Act 2 that his purpose is malign (his attempt to transfer Franz's spirit to Coppélia is a reference to rumours that occultists had been engaged in creating golems, or quasi-human homunculi) but there is still something very disquieting in the sight of young Teutonic townsmen bullying an elderly, skull-capped Doctor.

Today the ballet exists in several stagings, of which the most important are the 1954 Royal Ballet version, the 1974 New York City Ballet production by Balanchine, and Pierre Lacotte's Saint-Léon reconstruction for the Paris Opéra Ballet (1973).

View from the Wings

Given The Royal Ballet's status as a classical company, it's surprising that *Coppélia*, a standard amongst the classics, remained absent from the repertoire during my twenty years at Covent Garden. I did, however, enjoy exploring many of its variations throughout my years at school. It's also a great vehicle for studying mime, that specific gestural and body language which nineteenth-century choreographers used to tell bits of the story which couldn't be put into dance: ballet's equivalent, if you like, of the recitative in opera. For the ballerina dancing Swanilda, it's a bit of a romp – a chance to be that girl at school that everyone wanted to be: leader of the pack, clever, naughty, yet so loveable that despite her antics no one could possibly remain cross with her for long.

Petipa and the Imperial Ballet

In the mid-1840s, two brothers named Petipa were principal dancers at the Paris Opéra. The older was Lucien, who in 1841 had created the role of Albrecht in *Giselle* (and stolen the twenty-two-year-old Carlotta Grisi away from Jules Perrot), and the younger was Marius – a fine dancer, but overshadowed by his glamorous brother. In 1847, a note arrived for Marius from St Petersburg: 'Monsieur Petipa, His Excellency Monsieur Gedeonov, director of the Imperial theatres, offers you the post of premier danseur. Your salary will be 10,000 francs a year, with one semi-benefit performance.'

St Petersburg had been an important ballet centre since the days of Catherine the Great. An enthusiastic francophile, Catherine built the Hermitage museum, corresponded with Voltaire, and was a generous patron of the ballet. Her son, Paul I, invited the choreographer Didelot to the city, and by the time Nicholas I assumed the throne in 1825, ballet was all the rage. All the great ballerinas of the Romantic period appeared in the city – from 1837 to 1842 Taglioni was in near-permanent residence – and all of the great choreographers worked there. Petipa's superiors at the Imperial Ballet would include Perrot (ballet-master 1851-8) and Saint-Léon (1859-69). To these artists, the St Petersburg ballet offered a well-cushioned refuge from the waspishness and competition of Paris. Conditions were excellent, audiences were discerning, and new productions were amply provided for out of the Imperial purse.

At the Maryinsky Theatre, the ballet's sumptuously appointed home, the demand was for escapist spectacles on the grand scale. These were calculated to reflect the majesty of the Tsar, and in so doing, to reinforce the status quo. For despite the panoply with which it surrounded itself, the Romanov dynasty's hold on power was uncertain. Catherine the Great had become Empress by having her husband

murdered, and Paul I was assassinated within five years of succeeding her. From 1881, following the death of Tsar Alexander
II at the hands of a terrorist bomber, the country lived under
strict martial law. Wealth enabled a privileged few to maintain
lavish lifestyles, but a vast discontent rumbled beneath the surface.

This was the world – tense, glittering, insecure – which
Marius Petipa found on his arrival in St Petersburg. In London
and Paris, ballet audiences were now predominantly middle-
class, but there had been no such evolution in Russia. At the
Imperial theatres, all of the best seats were reserved for the
court and for members of fashionable clubs, and less than a
third were available to the public. A powerful cabal of reac-
tionary balletomanes, meanwhile, exerted a stifling control
over casting and repertoire.

Petipa noted all of this, and set about establishing himself.
In 1854 he married one of his pupils, the attractive Maria
Surovshikova, and refined his choreographic talents by watching
and assisting Perrot and Saint-Léon. His first major success
came in 1862. *Pharaoh's Daughter*, created when he was still
assistant ballet-master, was inspired by the excavations in Egypt,
and skilfully deployed a huge *corps de ballet* (overall the cast was
four hundred strong). This was the kind of grand spectacle that
the court enjoyed, and it helped to secure Petipa's future.

In 1869 he became principal ballet-master. He choreographed *Don Quixote* the same year and *La Bayadère* in 1877.
Little else from this period survives in its entirety and Petipa
seems to have been content to spend most of it producing
formulaic showpieces for popular ballerinas. When August
Bournonville visited St Petersburg from Copenhagen he was
saddened to see how the principles of the *ballet d'action* were
being neglected. He was swiftly led to the understanding,
however, that Petipa – by now a divorcee with a daughter in
the ballet company – was answering the demands of his pay-
masters.

And in truth, Petipa's interest in the plot-led *ballet d'action*
was limited. His supreme talent, as the best passages of *Don*

Quixote and *La Bayadère* illustrate, was for the decorative sequence – the brilliant variation, the crystalline *divertissement*, the mesmerising dream or vision scene – during which narrative time stands still. While this represented a departure from the principles of Vestris and Noverre, Petipa would refine balletic structure and geometry to the point where it has never been surpassed. Perhaps most importantly in formal terms, he established the classical *pas de deux*, or 'dance for two'. This consists of the *entrée* or *adagio*, in which the ballerina and her consort conduct a measured duet; the *variations* (solo dances) for the male and then the female dancer; and the *coda*, in which the pair are finally and climactically united. While the *pas de deux* invariably acts as a dramatic peak in the overall structure of a ballet, it is also musically and choreographically self-contained, allowing it to be lifted out of its larger context and performed independently. Petipa's *grand pas de deux* from *Don Quixote*, for example – a staple of galas the world over – is much more frequently performed than the entire three-act ballet.

In the 1880s an influx of Italian ballerinas, led by the sensational Virginia Zucchi, caused a sudden surge in ballet's popularity in St Petersburg. Zucchi enjoyed particular success in a series of French ballets which Petipa had reworked and updated for the Maryinsky, amongst them *La Fille Mal Gardée*, *Esmeralda*, *Paquita* and *Coppélia*. Observing ballet's new ultra-fashionability, the new director of the Imperial theatres, a clever ex-diplomat named Ivan Vsevolojsky, determined to capitalise on it. Abolishing the post of official composer of ballet music (previously held by competent but unprofound music-makers like Cesare Pugni and Ludwig Minkus), Vsevolojsky extended a commission to the celebrated Pyotr Ilyich Tchaikovsky. Petipa had already mapped out a ballet based on a French fairy story, *The Sleeping Beauty*, and was able to present Tchaikovsky with a detailed scheme, to which the composer responded with a voluptuous symphonic score. Vsevolojsky designed the costumes personally, and drawing an adroit parallel between the Tsar's court and that of Louis XIV, commissioned sumptuous sets based on the palace at Versailles.

The ballet, which had its premiere at the Maryinsky in 1890, was a triumph – musically, visually, choreographically and expressively. A new standard had been set, and *The Sleeping Beauty* was followed in 1892 by *The Nutcracker* and in 1895 by *Swan Lake*. This extraordinarily rich and productive partnership came to an end with the death of Tchaikovsky in 1893, but Petipa would continue to create important ballets (*Raymonda*, 1898, *The Seasons*, 1900) until his retirement in 1903.

It was an extraordinary career. In the fifty-six years of his employment in St Petersburg, Petipa never learnt proper Russian and his greatest triumphs were achieved when he was over seventy years old. His contribution to the art of dance, however, cannot be overstated. Under his direction the Imperial Ballet acquired an absolute pre-eminence, and in his work – marrying as it does the refinement and brilliance of the French and Italian schools to the grandeur of Tsarist Russia – balletic classicism finds its purest and most absolute expression.

Paquita
Pas de Trois and Grand Pas. Choreography by Marius Petipa, music by Ludwig Minkus (1881).

The original *Paquita* was a two-act ballet choreographed by Joseph Mazilier. Its premiere was at the Paris Opéra in 1846, and the principal roles were taken by Carlotta Grisi and Lucien Petipa (in 2001 Pierre Lacotte mounted a reconstruction of this production for the Paris Opéra Ballet). The plot, set in the Napoleonic wars, told of the romance between a French officer and a Spanish gypsy. The following year, as his debut production, Marius Petipa mounted the ballet in St Petersburg (not a place, one would have thought, where Napoleon's officer corps would be especially popular), and thirty-five years later he asked Minkus to write music for a *pas de deux* and *grand pas* that he wished to add to the piece. Today, these are the only passages that are regularly danced.

᧥ Outline

The *Paquita divertissement* is very much a movable feast, with individual dances added or subtracted as required around the unchanging core of Petipa's *adage*, *pas de deux* and *coda*. As danced by the Kirov Ballet in St Petersburg, the piece opens with a march for children (usually cut outside Russia). This is followed by the entry of the *corps de ballet* and the two principal dancers, who dance the *adage* (a slow duet). The *pas de deux* follows (this is a self-contained section, the three *pas de deux* dancers are not seen again). A selection of solos then ensues – usually taken from a body of Russian works including *Sylvia*, *Le Pavillon d'Armide*, *Don Quixote*, *Le Roi Candaule* and *The Humpbacked Horse* – and the principal pair then dance their *coda* (finale).

᧥ Notes

Despite the rather prosaic description above, *Paquita* is one of the most exciting and stylish showpieces in the classical repertoire. Many companies attempt it, but few achieve the panache of the Kirov, who are brought up with its glittering challenges.

Don Quixote

**Three acts. Choreography by Marius Petipa 1869,
revised Petipa 1871, further revised Alexander Gorsky
1900. Music by Ludwig Minkus.
First performed at the Bolshoi Theatre, Moscow, 1869.**

As its many revisions suggest, the evolution of *Don Quixote* was a complex one. 1869 was the year that Petipa finally became artistic director (as we would now say) of the Maryinsky Ballet, and the ballet, and particularly its vision scene, may reasonably be read as a statement of future intent. The Petipa–Gorsky choreography was the basis of the Kirov Ballet production (Lopukhov, 1923), which Nureyev brought to the West when he defected in 1961. Despite the many hands through which the ballet has passed, its most important passages – those created by Petipa – remain intact.

 Plot

ACT 1

Don Quixote dreams that he is a knight of old. He tells himself that he must undertake a quest and protect the lady of his dreams – the fair Dulcinea. Enlisting his oafish servant Sancho Panza as his squire, he sets out in search of adventure. In Barcelona, meanwhile, a penniless barber (Basilio) is flirting with an innkeeper's daughter (Kitri). Kitri loves Basilio, but her father wishes her to marry the wealthy Gamache. Don Quixote and Sancho Panza arrive, and the ageing Don becomes convinced that Kitri is his Dulcinea. In the hustle and bustle the young couple slip away to get married. They are seen, however, and followed by the innkeeper Lorenzo, Gamache, and Don Quixote, all of whom have their separate reasons for the pursuit.

ACT 2

Kitri and Basilio take shelter beneath a windmill, but find themselves surrounded by a performing troupe of gypsies. The penniless couple persuade the gypsies to turn their attentions to Lorenzo and Gamache, who are duly robbed. Don Quixote and Sancho Panza arrive and the Don, mistaking the windmills for monsters, attacks them. Still pursued by Kitri's father and Gamache, the young lovers escape once again. Don Quixote, meanwhile, dazed from his unhappy battle with the windmills, dreams that he is in a heavenly garden, where the Queen of the Dryads commends him for his chivalry and presents him with his Dulcinea.

ACT 3

Back in Barcelona, surrounded by their friends, the couple face their pursuers. Determined to outwit the innkeeper and

Gamache, Basilio pretends to stab himself out of broken-hearted despair. Kitri begs Don Quixote for help, and true to his knightly vows, the Don forces Lorenzo to bless the couple's union. Gamache, furious, fights a duel with Don Quixote, but loses. Basilio, miraculously cured, springs to his feet, and the happy couple celebrate their engagement. Don Quixote and Sancho Panza, meanwhile, continue on their travels in search of further adventures.

∼ Notes

The plot, extracted from Book 2 of Cervantes' picaresque novel, is paper thin, the knockabout clowning of the Don, Lorenzo, Gamache and company is distinctly creaky, and there is a notable absence of dramatic tension throughout. The whole ballet is really just a linking device for some glorious passages of classical dance. And these it delivers. The best are those which we know to have been choreographed by Petipa, which include the dances for Kitri and her friends in Act 1, and the entire vision scene in Act 2. The most popular piece is the spectacular (if textually rather formulaic) *grand pas de deux* in Act 3, when the lovers celebrate their wedding-to-be. This (along with the Act 2 *pas de deux* from *Le Corsaire*), is probably the most frequently performed gala piece in the world. The real choreographic gem, however, is the vision scene, and in particular the variation danced by the Queen of the Dryads. With its 'Italian' *fouettés* and huge, billowy leaps *à la seconde*, this is a real star-maker of a role, particularly in Russia.

Nureyev produced the ballet for several companies after his defection, notably the Vienna State Opera Ballet (1966) and the Australian Ballet (1970 – this version was revived for The Royal Ballet in 2001). Mikhail Baryshnikov (another Kirov defector) mounted the piece for American Ballet Theatre in 1978. George Balanchine mounted his own version for New York City Ballet in 1965.

∿ View from the Wings

In the mid-1990s, The Royal Ballet took *Don Quixote* into the repertoire. As a ballet, it's best known for the showpiece *pas de deux* of the final act, but the first and second acts contain some pretty tough dancing, too. Act 1 in particular, with its non-stop jumping, leaves you with such limp legs that you wonder how you'll ever sustain the controlled variation in Act 2, never mind the famous fireworks of Act 3. *Don Quixote* is not a ballet I ever expected to dance. Its required flamboyance and technical wizardry hadn't, hitherto, been much associated with The Royal Ballet, but with dancers like Irek Mukhamedov, Tetsuya Kumakawa, Darcey Bussell and Miyako Yoshida making up the principal roster when it entered the repertoire in 1993, the company was able to field no fewer than six casts. I was delighted – and a bit surprised – to be amongst them. It was, from start to finish, a joy. The ballet has little to do with the Cervantes novel and, to be honest, it's a bit of a silly story. But it contains the type of dancing a girl dreams about: huge phrases of movement which tap your every technical resource and ride the crest of the rather second-rate – but extremely danceable – score like a galleon on the high seas. Despite a generous smattering of castanets, toreadors and tortoiseshell combs, it's about as Spanish as kiss-me-quick hats and flamenco-doll toilet-roll covers. Still, it offers a great chance for Kitri to claim the stage with its myriad challenges: the ubiquitous set of thirty-two *fouettés*, unsupported balances centre stage and a one-handed overhead lift which I fear I never quite mastered. But I did give some of my most satisfying performances in *Don Quixote*, most notably in Japan when I was (yet again) replacing an injured dancer at the shortest possible notice.

It isn't only Kitri who has some exacting variations to contend with. Throughout, there are supporting roles which demand extreme technical accomplishment yet conceal their difficulties from the untrained eye. The Queen of the Dryads, for instance, in the second act, has a long sustained solo which draws a seamless thread from start to finish and concludes with the notorious 'Italian' *fouettés* – a variant of the more traditional *fouettés* which still demands sixteen consecutive relevés on one leg: on and off pointe sixteen times without the other leg touching the floor. That hurts.

La Bayadère
The Temple Dancer
Four acts. Original choreography by Marius Petipa 1877 (revised by Petipa 1884, further revised 1900), music by Ludwig Minkus.
First performed at the Maryinsky Theatre, St Petersburg, 1877.

Although Petipa was fifty-nine when he created *La Bayadère*, his best-known ballets still lay ahead of him. *La Bayadère* was a vast, and vastly expensive, production (Act 2 was conceived for two hundred dancers and a stage elephant) with which Petipa tinkered for decades. His final version of the ballet was staged when he was eighty-two, and nearing retirement. In 1947 this four-act version was in its turn edited, very much to its advantage, by the Soviet dancer–choreographer Vakhtang Chaboukiani. It is the resultant three-act text which Rudolf Nureyev, and later Natalia Makarova, brought to the West.

∼ Plot

ACT 1
The ballet is set in ancient India. Solor, a noble young warrior, is in love with Nikiya, a temple-dancer or bayadère. The High Brahmin of the temple is also in love with Nikiya, and tells her so. She rejects his advances, and returns to her duties at the

temple. Later, after the celebration of a fire-ceremony, she keeps a rendezvous with Solor in the forest. The couple swear eternal love over the sacred fire, but they are seen by the High Brahmin. In a fury of jealousy he calls on the gods to help him destroy Solor.

Warriors are gathering in the Rajah's palace, where Solor is to be rewarded for his bravery. The reward in question is the hand of the Rajah's daughter Gamzatti in marriage. Solor begins to protest, but is silenced by the princess's beauty and by the prospect of his own advancement. The High Brahmin arrives as Solor is dallying with his new wife-to-be, and taking the Rajah aside, tells him about Solor's love for the bayadère. In so doing he intends to cause Solor's death, but to his horror the Rajah orders that Nikiya be executed. Gamzatti has overheard this conversation and sends for Nikiya. A confrontation between the two women ensues, in the course of which Nikiya draws a knife and rushes at the princess. She is disarmed by a servant, and escapes. Gamzatti is unharmed.

Nikiya returns to dance at a ceremony to celebrate Solor and Gamzatti's betrothal. The bayadère expresses her grief and is given a basket of flowers, ostensibly a gift from Solor. It has been sent by Gamzatti, however, and contains a deadly snake, which bites her. The High Brahmin offers Nikiya an antidote, but knowing that Solor is to marry Gamzatti, the bayadère allows the poison to take its course, and dies.

Act 2
Hoping to deaden the remorse that he feels at Nikiya's death, Solor smokes opium in his tent. As the drug takes hold, he hallucinates, dreaming that he has descended to the Kingdom of the Shades, where an infinity of Nikiyas processes before him. As the vision fades, Solor's fellow warriors arrive to prepare him for his wedding.

Act 3
The ceremony begins. A bronze idol performs a whirling dance, Solor and Gamzatti enter, and the bayadères perform a

purification rite. During the nuptial dances which follow, Solor is haunted by the spectre of Nikiya, which he alone can see. Without explanation a basket of flowers appears, and a terrified and conscience-stricken Gamzatti orders her father to complete the ceremony without further delay. Solor, however, refuses to speak the marriage vows. The gods, angered by the murder of the bayadère, bring the temple crashing down on all of those present. In death, Solor and Nikiya are eternally reunited.

∿ Notes

La Bayadère is the ballet with everything. It has a strong plot from beginning to end, beautiful settings (jungle temples and palaces, misty Himalayan vistas), two highly dramatic ballerina roles, extended passages of virtuoso dancing for all three principals, beautifully intricate soloist and *corps de ballet* work, and last but not least, an earthquake. The music (composed to fit Petipa's choreography, rather than the other way round) is untroublingly pretty for most of the ballet's three acts. When in doubt Minkus favours Viennese café-style waltzes – a bizarre-sounding juxtaposition, but this is the India of the nineteenth-century Romantic imagination, and the result is curiously effective. When sweeping lyricism is required, as in the Kingdom of the Shades, the composer does not fail us. The scene, in which the white-clad *corps de ballet* wind their way down a ramp and around the moonlit stage, endlessly and mesmerisingly repeating the same step-sequence (*posé arabesque*, *fondu*), is one of the most hauntingly beautiful in all classical ballet.

La Bayadère's comparatively unknown status outside the dance world relates, I suspect, to its French name, as well as to the fact that the ballet has only been seen outside Russia in the last forty years. One of its most attractive characteristics is the amount of dramatic leeway that Petipa has left his interpreters. Solor can either be played as a decent man placed in an impossible position (in that the Rajah cannot be disobeyed), or as a cynical adventurer on the make. Nikiya's knife-attack on Gamzatti can be interpreted as a desperate gesture, half-meant at worst, or as a real attempt to eliminate her rival. Gamzatti can be played as an initially sympathetic young woman who wishes to sort things out with Nikiya face-to-face and then finds events spiralling out of control (the snake could have been hidden in the basket on her father's orders), or as an imperious, cold-hearted murderess.

In 2002 an ex-dancer named Sergei Vikharev reconstructed Petipa's four-act 1900 version of *La Bayadère* for the Kirov Ballet, having performed similar reconstructions of *The Sleeping Beauty* (1999), *Petrushka* (2000), and *Coppélia* (2001). The result is extraordinary. It enables us to travel back a century in time to Tsarist St Petersburg, and to see the piece on the stunningly lavish scale that Petipa himself intended. While academically fascinating, however, this version is also (to twenty-first-century eyes, at least) vastly over-extended. In excising repetitive choreographic material and tautening the narrative Chabukiani and the other Soviet revisers knew exactly what they were doing. The best versions of the ballet are the 1947 Kirov production, and those by Rudolf Nureyev (Royal Ballet, Kingdom of the Shades only, 1963; Paris Opéra Ballet, 1992) and Natalia Makarova (American Ballet Theatre, 1980).

◆ View from the Wings

La Bayadère is another nineteenth-century ballet which splits its principal dancing between two women: the sweetly spiritual Nikiya and the worldly, grasping Gamzatti. Nikiya gets the gently lyrical choreography, a vision of unattainable womanhood expressed in sinuous, snaky solos. Gamzatti gets the firecracker stuff: spins, jumps and multiple turns which dazzle and seduce the man on whom both women have set their sights. I danced *La Bayadère* dozens of times after it entered The Royal Ballet's repertoire in 1989, my relatively secure technique and strong physical presence leading me, once again, to

the bad girl role of Gamzatti. Tired, by this point in my
career, of being pigeon-holed and keen to reveal
Gamzatti as something more than just a scheming, evil
bitch, I delved deep into her character to explore the
roots of her ruthless greed. As a result, my Gamzatti was
not so much evil as woefully spoilt: a princess unable to
imagine a world in which she didn't get her own way, and
so consumed by her passion for Solor that she would go
to any lengths whatsoever – including murder – to secure
him for herself.

The Sleeping Beauty
La Belle au Bois Dormant
**Three acts. Choreography by Marius Petipa, music by
Pyotr Ilyich Tchaikovsky, libretto by Petipa and Ivan
Vsevolojsky, designs by Vsevolojsky and others.
First performed at the Maryinsky Theatre,
St Petersburg, 1890.**

The Sleeping Beauty was the ballet in which Petipa and
Tchaikovsky's genius found its most formally perfect expression,
and is regarded as the pinnacle of nineteenth-century Russian
classicism. With its huge cast and its sets reflecting the golden
age of Versailles, it was probably the most expensive ballet
ever mounted by the Imperial theatres. Ivan Vsevolojsky's
choice of decor permitted exceptional levels of grandeur, but
the Director of the Imperial theatres was politically as well as
aesthetically motivated. The ballet was created in the shadow
of the assassination of Tsar Alexander II in 1881, and martial
law was still in place in 1890. By recreating the domain over
which the Sun King had presided two centuries earlier,
Vsevolojsky sought to reassure his audience of the virtues of
absolute monarchy. By choosing Perrault's tale, with its pre-
occupations of blood and bloodlines, he underlined the
essential nature of dynastic succession. The Tsar, however,
greeted the production with polite uninterest, describing it to
Tchaikovsky as 'nice'. Less than two decades later the

Romanov dynasty, with its blood-inheritance of porphyria and haemophilia, would fall.

 ## Plot

PROLOGUE

It is the christening of Princess Aurora at the Court of King Florestan. Among the guests of the King and Queen are six fairies, who endow the baby princess with their particular gifts. Candide (sometimes called Sincerity) presents beauty and openness, Fleur de Farine (Wheatflower) grace, Bread-crumb generosity, Violente (Temperament) passion, Canary eloquence, and the Lilac Fairy wisdom. The ceremony and its harmony are shattered by the arrival of Carabosse, an evil fairy whom the master of ceremonies has neglected to invite. Carabosse curses the child. One day, she warns, Aurora will prick her finger on a spindle and die. The Lilac Fairy mitigates the curse. Aurora will not die, she announces, she will sleep for a hundred years until awoken by a prince's kiss.

ACT 1

It is Princess Aurora's twentieth birthday. All over the kingdom spindles have been forbidden, and when a trio of crones is discovered spinning they are arrested. Given the day's propitiousness, however, the king intervenes and pardons them. The ensemble joins in a celebratory waltz (the Garland Dance), and then Aurora enters and dances with her four princely suitors (the Rose Adagio). Shortly afterwards she catches sight of a woman with a spindle, which she seizes. The spindle pricks Aurora's finger, she collapses into sleep, and is borne away. Gradually the whole court falls asleep and a forest grows around the palace, hiding it from the outside world.

ACT 2

Hunting in this forest a century later, Prince Desiré is visited by the Lilac Fairy, who grants him a vision of Aurora with her attendant naiads (the Vision Scene). The prince dances with Aurora, and vows to marry her. He implores the Lilac Fairy to lead him to the princess, and she leads him to the castle. There, he awakes Aurora with a kiss, and the court wakens around her.

ACT 3

The court and various fairy-tale characters (Princess Florine and the Blue Bird, White Cat and Puss-in-Boots, Red Riding-Hood and the Wolf, Cinderella and Prince Fortune) celebrate the wedding of the prince and princess. Aurora and Prince Desiré dance a *grand pas de deux*, and the entire ensemble joins in a final dance (the Apotheosis).

～ Notes

When Vsevolojsky commissioned the score for *The Sleeping Beauty* from Tchaikovsky, he was determined to initiate a more productive dialogue between composer and choreographer than had previously been the case (the usual pattern at the Maryinsky Ballet was that choreographers ordered scores by the yard from official hacks like Minkus or Drigo, specifying only length and time signature). Petipa's instructions to Tchaikovsky were extraordinarily detailed. He had laid out the entire scheme of the ballet in advance, specifying not only the style of individual phrases but even their orchestral scoring. This precision served not to limit Tchaikovsky (as one might have expected), but to inspire him, and the result was a masterpiece of symphonic form.

In *The Sleeping Beauty* both music and choreography have multiple layers of meaning. The Louis XIV Prologue and Act 1 setting allowed Petipa to make reference to early French baroque ballet, and then, with Aurora's hundred-year sleep, to leap forward a century to the Romantic style of Marie Taglioni. Within this time arc he placed, like gems, a series of exquisite dances in the then contemporary style (a distillation of the best of the French and Italian schools), so that *The*

Sleeping Beauty becomes – amongst many other things – an extended meditation on ballet's own history. From the fairies' variations in the Prologue onwards, choreographic themes are stated, reprised and cross-referenced with extraordinary variety and brilliance. The ballet has two overarching subjects: the struggle between good and evil (represented musically by the conflicting themes of the Lilac Fairy and Carabosse), and the maturing of a young woman – Aurora.

This process begins when the princess is still in her cradle. Each of the gifts brought by the fairies in the Prologue is expressed choreographically, and as the ballet progresses we can see the incorporation of these gifts into Aurora's own dancing, and thus her personality. Candide, for example, presents beauty and openness, and it is from Candide's variation that Aurora takes the *arabesque* that is to become her signature. We soon see this signature displayed – in the Rose Adagio. Having presented her with roses, the four suitors promenade Aurora in *attitude*, a position symbolic of promise for the future. They then release her to balance on pointe alone. She balances – her first adult statement of independence – and at the music's climax, in a visible progress from promise to fulfilment, extends her *attitude* into high *arabesque*. This has all of the beauty and the openness promised by Candide – there is no 'pretending' an *arabesque* on pointe – and the unfurling of the leg between the two positions echoes the unfurling from bud to flower of the rose which is her symbol. This too is now beautiful and 'open'.

In Aurora's progress towards womanhood (her name means 'the dawn') we can also read the progress of the solar day. The roseate-hued Garland dance, with its semicircular choreographic and floral motifs, represents the sunrise. The Rose Adagio is noon, with the suitors representing the four points of the compass which, at midday, are equally bathed in the sun's rays. Dawn, at the court of the Roi Soleil, has become Day, *attitude* has become *arabesque*, rosebud has become rose.

The sun is also the symbol of Apollo, god of the arts.

When sleep (ignorance, philistinism, brutality) descends on the court and the forest grows around the castle, the Apollonian light of the sun cannot penetrate. The destruction of Carabosse's enchantment sees the return of the light, and the reinstatement of Apollonian harmony. In the final scene of Act 3 – the apotheosis – the god descends to bless the bridal couple, and we understand that the ballet is a metaphor for all the arts, and by extension, for civilisation itself. So at an almost covert level, Petipa, Tchaikovsky and Vsevolojsky's ballet was a signal to the initiated that, no matter how long the darkness (and in 1890s St Petersburg, the banking storm clouds would have been unmistakable) the light of dawn would eventually be seen.

When Aurora appears in the Vision scene in Act 2 she is elusive and mysterious. Her choreography continues to incorporate the attitudes, *arabesque* and other fairy-gifted motifs of Act 1, but in more oblique and complex ways. She is a woman rather than an adolescent, and in her solitude and her sleep-darkness she knows the world's sadness. She and Desiré dance together, but almost tangentially; it is as if they occupy different dimensions which the Lilac Fairy has only briefly managed to unite. But it is enough. He sees her. He loves her. He fights his way through the dark forest to reach her.

Act 3, set in a palatial sunlit exterior, begins with a series of duets by fairy-tale characters and progresses to the *grand pas de deux* for Aurora and Desiré. This is the ballet's climax, and in it all the preceding musical, choreographic and conceptual strands are drawn together. There are visible and audible echoes of the Rose Adagio, and of all that has gone before, but these have now been subsumed into the fully realised persona of Aurora herself. The choreography of the *grand pas de deux* makes it clear that she approaches marriage as a royal equal, not as a subordinate, and in her final variation, in a moving reprise of the fairies' variations in the Prologue, she demonstrates her mastery of all the 'gift' motifs. It has been argued that the Prince in *The Sleeping Beauty* is little more than a handsome cipher but in truth, this is not his story. He is a player in an allegory, and all that we need to know about him – his courtesy, his chivalry – is contained in the steps which Petipa has given him.

The Sleeping Beauty is the piece from which, in a sense, all classical ballet radiates. A study of its choreography is a choreographic education in itself, as Balanchine, Ashton, MacMillan and many others have attested. It was the Maryinsky *Sleeping Beauty* that led Diaghilev to fall in love with ballet. And with its spectacular (and spectacularly difficult) dance passages – the Rose Adagio remains one of the great ballerina challenges; the Bluebird variation, with its repeated fluttering leaps, is one of the most dazzling and exhausting in the male repertoire – it is easy to enjoy the ballet as pure dance. But as we have seen, it is very much more than that.

In 1918, after the October Revolution, Nicholas Sergeyev (the Maryinsky Theatre's former Director-General), departed Russia with the notation of many of the company's most important classical ballets. From these texts he helped Diaghilev to mount his 1921 Alhambra (London) production of *The Sleeping Princess*, and in 1946 performed the same service for Ninette de Valois when The Royal Ballet moved into the Royal Opera House. As the ultimate expression of the Maryinsky classicism on which The Royal Ballet's style was based, *The Sleeping Beauty* became for many years the company's flagship production, with Fonteyn as the definitive Aurora.

In the Soviet Union, the original staging was revised in 1922 by Fyodor Lopukhov and in 1952 by Konstantin Sergeyev. With designs by Simon Virsiladze, the latter production served the Kirov Ballet faithfully for almost half a century. In 1999 Sergei Vikharev reconstructed the original Petipa–Vsevolojsky production for the company. Very beautiful and lavish, this is of considerable ballet-historical interest, but lacks the heart and the narrative pulse of the Sergeyev production. Ironically, the closest version to the Sergeyev production is now in the care of The Royal Ballet, courtesy of Natalia Makarova (2003). This production replaced Anthony Dowell's textually superior version (1994). Other recent productions include Peter Martins' version for New York City Ballet (1991). A number of modern productions have taken the ballet for their starting point. Maurice Béjart's *Ni Fleurs ni Couronnes* (1968) and *Rose Variations* (1973) are both Petipa-inspired, and Mats Ek's *Sleeping Beauty* (1996) has Aurora as an intravenous drug-user.

∿ View from the Wings

Every little girl who has ever wanted to be a ballerina has wanted to dance *Sleeping Beauty*. The ultimate fairy tale and perhaps the ultimate ballerina role, *Sleeping Beauty* is a ballet I lusted after for years. When I finally got my chance, it was with ten days' notice as I worked my way back to fitness after a six-month lay-off. No matter. I wasn't about to say no. *Beauty* is one of those ballets characterised in many fans' minds by a single moment: in this case, the Rose Adagio. The Rose Adagio is, give or take a thirty-second entrance, the first dancing the ballerina does, and it takes place ten minutes into the evening's second act. Imagine how weird it is to adjust your pre-performance ritual to take into account the fact that you won't be required on stage until a full forty-five minutes after curtain up. Imagine sitting in the dressing room, selecting shoes, applying make-up and warming up while a range of soloists and the entire *corps de ballet* are getting on with the show. By the time the second act begins, you're a bag of nerves. The introductory arpeggios of the Rose Adagio are to me, even now, as the sound of bells to Pavlov's dogs. Except whereas the dogs reacted with an increase in saliva, I react with an increase in adrenalin. It is, quite simply, the most terrifying dance in the ballet repertoire, and all because of two short sequences at its beginning and its end. The sequences in question require nothing more from the ballerina than a step into *attitude*, centre stage, posed on one leg with the other raised behind. In turn, each of four suitors takes her right hand and then releases it as she momentarily balances, alone, right arm joining the left above her head in fifth position. When the sequence returns at the end of the *adagio*, a 'promenade' with each prince is incorporated – she remains statue-like in her *attitude* as each partner walks around her, rotating her through 360 degrees before she takes the balance. Sounds simple, and in the studio, it is. I can balance for hours. Put me on stage and it's a different story. A combination of dazzling lights, jangled nerves and the absence of the studio's four comforting walls make balance an impossibility.

Incidentally, my history with *Sleeping Beauty* was a chequered one. Several times I replaced other dancers, sometimes at ridiculously short notice. Once, just once, I had a scheduled performance of my own. Due to an unscheduled case of salmonella, I only went and missed it.

The Nutcracker
Casse-Noisette

Two acts. Choreography by Lev Ivanov, music by Pyotr Ilyich Tchaikovsky, libretto by Marius Petipa, designs by Ivan Vsevolojsky and others.
First performed at the Maryinsky Theatre, St Petersburg, 1892.

In the wake of the popular success of *The Sleeping Beauty*, Ivan Vsevolojsky commissioned Tchaikovsky to compose the score for a second ballet, based on a Hoffmann tale entitled 'Nutcracker and Mouse King'. Petipa had written the libretto and was to choreograph the ballet, but in the event he fell ill, and responsibility for the piece was passed to Petipa's assistant, the charming, alcoholic and intermittently brilliant Ivanov (who three years later later would choreograph the famous white acts of *Swan Lake*). The ballet was not well received. Petipa's libretto was considered unreasonably bizarre, the decor in poor taste, and the ballet childish.

∿ Plot

There are many versions of *The Nutcracker*. The following contains the story elements common to most of them:

ACT 1

The Stahlbaums, to the excitement of their teenage daughter Clara (Marie in the US, Masha in Russia) are giving a Christmas party for their friends and their friends' children. Amongst the guests is Drosselmeyer, a magician and maker of toys and automata. He delights the children by making and bringing to life several figures – a soldier, a Harlequin, Columbine – and with his imaginative presents. Clara's brother is given a gun, Clara gets a wooden Nutcracker doll. With the festivities over, the guests leave, and the children go to bed. Later that night, Clara creeps downstairs. The owl on the grandfather clock flaps its wings as the clock strikes midnight, and the Christmas tree grows to many times its original size. A battalion of giant mice enters, terrifying Clara. Led by the Nutcracker, the toy soldiers do battle with the mice. At a critical moment Clara intervenes, throwing her slipper at the Mouse King. The mice are defeated, and as a result of Clara's selfless and courageous act, the Nutcracker becomes a prince. He leads her to the Kingdom of Snow, and they dance amongst the Snowflakes.

ACT 2

Clara and the Nutcracker are transported by sleigh to the Land of Sweets, where they meet the Sugar-Plum Fairy. The Nutcracker describes the battle against the mice, and Clara's vital role in the victory, and the Sugar-Plum Fairy arranges an entertainment for them. A number of colourful, candy-themed *divertissements* ensue, usually including a Spanish, Arabian, Chinese and Russian dance and the Waltz of the Flowers. Afterwards the Sugar-Plum Fairy dances a *grand pas de deux* with her Prince, and Clara is returned home, waking beneath the Christmas tree with her Nutcracker beside her.

∾ Notes

Over the years *The Nutcracker* has become a Christmas favourite, and it is many children's first ballet. Tchaikovsky's music is both magical and accessible and the ballet contains many lovely moments, particularly Ivanov's inspired Snowflake dance. Structurally, however, the piece is problematical. Act 1 works well, in that it tells a good and imaginative story with Clara at its centre. We understand immediately that we have entered her dream – a dream tinged with the vague romantic longings of adolescence, in which the Nutcracker Prince is her courtly (and erotically unthreatening) spirit guide. The world outside the Stahlbaum house – a midnight blizzard – is shown to be not fearful but beautiful, and the stage is set, Freudian props and all, for Clara's metaphorical transformation from childhood to womanhood.

But the ballet reneges on its promise. In Act 2 Clara is quickly sidelined, and she and the Prince reduced to the role of passive spectators. This is the point at which children lose interest – quite reasonably, given that they've made an emotional investment in Clara. All dramatic tension evaporates, and while the *divertissements* which follow are entertaining enough, the act as a whole is static and overlong. The Sugar-Plum Fairy and her consort have attractive choreography, but it is applied to the ballet like decorative gilding, and its grandeur serves only to efface our memory of Clara and her Prince.

Over the years producers of the ballet have addressed these shortcomings with varying degrees of success. One of the most intelligent and imaginative of the twentieth-century *Nutcrackers* was Rudolf Nureyev's 1967 version for the Royal Swedish Ballet (and later for The Royal Ballet). Amongst other changes, Nureyev gives Clara the Sugar-Plum choreography and her own Prince to dance with in Act 2, thus illustrating her coming-of-age, and substitutes a darkly Freudian passage for the Kingdom of the Sweets. Peter Wright's 1999 production for The Royal Ballet, by contrast, places Drosselmeyer at the centre of the piece. Through the use of back-story, we learn that the Nutcracker Prince is the magician's enchanted nephew. Clara becomes the means by which the enchantment is lifted, rather than the tale's protagonist.

Flawed or not, *The Nutcracker* is probably the most frequently performed ballet in the world. Vassily Vainonen revised the Ivanov production for the Kirov in 1934, the same year that Nicholas Sergeyev mounted the first full-length version in the West (for Sadler's Wells Ballet). The first US version was by William Christensen for the San Francisco Ballet in 1944, and this was followed in 1954 by Balanchine's New York City Ballet production. In recent years contemporary choreographers have turned their attention to the piece. Popular iconoclastic versions have included Mark Morris's *The Hard Nut* (1991) and Matthew Bourne's *Nutcracker* (1992).

∿ View from the Wings

My earliest memory of *The Nutcracker* involves a once-plush red banquette and an appalling bout of gastro-enteritis. I was thirteen, a third-year pupil at White Lodge, the junior branch of The Royal Ballet School, and I had been chosen, along with several of my classmates, to play the part of a rat in The Royal Ballet's Christmas production. I was beside myself with excitement. It seemed like the culmination of all my childhood dreams, and if my career had ended there and then I would still have achieved more than I ever hoped for. Unfortunately, while my friends were rehearsing onstage alongside the company's stars – Lynn Seymour, Merle Park and Antoinette Sibley – I was lying prone in the dressing room, feeling horribly sick. The bug was short-lived. I recovered in time for the first night and spent the rest of my Christmas 'holiday' happily commuting between the school dormitory and the Covent Garden stage.

You cannot imagine what a thrill it was for us to be involved. Never mind that we were clad, head to toe, in dusty grey costumes, our faces hidden behind fur and whiskers. Never mind that our dressing room was a windowless cellar, tucked away behind the staff canteen. This was the Royal Opera House and for the first time ever, I was dancing with The Royal Ballet. Best of all, the cannon which exploded loudly and scattered the rats at the end of our battle with the toy soldiers fired real chocolates in bright foil wrappers. Our job was to pick up as many as we could find and leave the stage clear for the snowflake waltz which followed immediately afterwards. Not only was I in *The Nutcracker*, there were chocolates, too. I thought I was in heaven.

Five years later, I joined the company. Christmas came around and with it, a new production of *The Nutcracker*. I was promoted from cellar-dwelling rat to 'party reveller' and *corps de ballet* snowflake. The role of Clara, usually danced by a member of the company, was, in this version, taken by a third-year 'White Lodger' called Sarah Wildor. Talented beyond her years, I immediately fell in love with this porcelain-perfect, pocket-sized ballerina. The star quality which led her to her debut, twenty years later, in the ballet's Sugar-Plum role was, even then, blindingly obvious.

Ever since then, throughout my career, I had Christmas laid on for me, courtesy of *The Nutcracker*: the grandest of all house parties, where no one groaned about playing parlour games and stropped into the other room, muttering that they'd rather watch *The Simpsons* instead. Beautifully wrapped gifts with floppy satin bows, and freshly scrubbed boys dressed in knickerbockers and waistcoats – not a shell suit in sight – who didn't complain when their parcel turned out to contain a tin soldier rather than Playstation 2. Little girls, in satin shoes and Laura Ashley frocks, ooh-ed and aah-ed over baby dolls rather than disturbing plastic effigies of Britney Spears.

A mysterious relative, Herr Drosselmeyer, arrived every year to magic a perfect Norwegian Fir to gargantuan proportions but, even so, I never once found a single pine needle on the floor. Then, with a wave of his hand, he conjured up an icing-sugar sleigh to transport us through a whirling snowstorm to a Kingdom of Sweets.

Of course, all this is seen through rose-tinted retrospectacles. At the time, I complained like mad that dancers had the same cross to bear as vicars: a so-called holiday season that was more like the busiest time of the year. This perfect Christmas meant ballet class and a double show on Boxing Day, followed, usually, by matinées and evenings for the rest of the week. It meant holding back on the mince pies and refusing the second glass of wine. It meant early to bed and early to rise, especially if you had to catch the first train back from somewhere up north. As every dancer knows, it's hard to tuck into Christmas when you'll be squeezing into tutu and tights twenty-four hours later. The role of the Sugar-Plum Fairy includes a demanding *pas de deux* and a long solo with all the trimmings: brilliant footwork, virtuoso circles around the stage and an embellished version of the *pas de chat* which goes under the bizarre name of gargouillade. To cap it all, Ivanov throws in the obligatory series of *fouettés*. You don't want to try that little lot on a hangover.

But despite the demands, at least the seasonal trappings at the theatre made it feel like Christmas, even if the reverse side of the tree exposed the fraud: Christmas had been constructed out of plywood. Nowadays, post-retirement from The Royal Ballet, I'm suffering cold turkey and Christmas just doesn't seem like Christmas any more. Still, I only have to turn on the television for *The Nutcracker* and it all comes flooding back. For two magical hours, I imagine myself back in the *corps de ballet*: exhausted, overworked and only moderately paid, but an integral part of the perfect Christmas.

Swan Lake
Le Lac des Cygnes
Four acts. Choreography by Marius Petipa and Lev
Ivanov, music by Pyotr Ilyich Tchaikovsky.
Petipa–Ivanov version first performed at the Maryinsky
Theatre, St Petersburg, 1895.

In 1875, fifteen years before the first staging of *The Sleeping
Beauty*, Tchaikovsky was commissioned to write a score for
the Bolshoi Theatre in Moscow. The choreographer of this
earliest version of *Swan Lake* was the Bolshoi's ballet-master,
an Austrian hack named Julius Reisinger. Failing to appreciate
Tchaikovsky's symphonic creation, Reisinger cut it freely. The
ballet's first night was a benefit performance for an over-
the-hill ballerina named Pelagia Karpakova, and the score
was further mutilated when Karpakova insisted on replacing several sections of the music with display-pieces from
other ballets in her repertoire. The production limped on
until 1883 (in all, thirty-three performances were given) by
which time a third of Tchaikovsky's music had been cut or
replaced. When Tchaikovsky died of cholera a decade later,
it seemed unlikely that either the score or the ballet would
ever be resurrected.

The composer's death, however, stimulated a re-examina-
tion of his work, and the following year the defunct ballet's
second act was included in a Tchaikovsky memorial evening at
the Maryinsky Theatre in St Petersburg. Reisinger's unin-
spired choreography had been jettisoned, and the act
reworked from scratch by Lev Ivanov, Petipa's self-effacing
deputy. Tchaikovsky's sublime score and Ivanov's luminous
choreography won an enthusiastic response, and a full-length
production was commissioned by the management of the
Imperial theatres. Petipa undertook the re-choreography of
Acts 1 and 3, and Ivanov added a new Act 4 to his Act 2.

Postponed on account of the death of the Tsar, the new
Swan Lake opened in 1895, with the Italian guest star Pierina

Legnani dancing Odette–Odile. In the choreography for Act 3 (the Black Swan act) Petipa included the famous sequence of thirty-two *fouettés*. This feat, which no Russian ballerina of the day could equal, was Legnani's speciality. Word of her brilliance spread, and as the ballet's popularity grew, its deeper qualities became evident.

∾ Plot

ACT 1
It is Prince Siegfried's coming-of-age, and his friends and the local villagers have gathered in the grounds of the castle to celebrate the occasion. The light-hearted atmosphere is disturbed by the arrival of the Queen Mother, who reminds her son that he now has adult responsibilities. The following night, at a formal ball, he must choose a bride, so that the royal line may be continued. As night falls the prince's friends depart, and he expresses his yearning for true love. A flight of swans passes overhead, and to distract himself from his melancholy thoughts Siegfried decides to pursue them.

ACT 2
At the lakeside he happens upon one of the swans, and sees her transformed into a beautiful woman – the Princess Odette. She and her companions, the prince learns, are the victims of an enchanter, the evil Von Rothbart, who watches over them in the guise of an owl. By night they are allowed to assume their human form, by day they must become swans. The enchantment can only be broken by a vow of eternal love. Siegfried is captivated by Odette. Certain that this is the being of whom he has dreamed for so long, he expresses his love for her. Odette, who loves him in return, warns him that if he pledges himself to her, and then betrays her, she will remain a swan for ever. Siegfried makes the vow. Dawn approaches, and Odette and her companions depart to resume the form of swans.

ACT 3

The following night the royal family and their guests are assembled in the castle ballroom. Foreign princesses have been invited in the hope that Siegfried will choose one to be his bride. But the prince, his thoughts full of Odette, is distracted. Suddenly, two uninvited guests are ushered in. They are Von Rothbart, now in human form, and his black-clad daughter Odile, who has assumed the likeness of Odette. Transfixed, Siegfried dances with her. A vision of the real Odette appears, imploring him to remember his vow, but Von Rothbart's magic prevents the prince from seeing it. To the delight of the assembled company, he asks for Odile's hand in marriage. Von Rothbart makes him swear fidelity, and as he does so – too late – he sees the vision of Odette. Triumphant, Von Rothbart and his daughter depart. The prince, despairing, rushes out in search of his vanished love.

ACT 4

At the lakeside, surrounded by her swan-maidens, Odette is desolate. She no longer wishes to live. Siegfried appears, and braving the tempest that Von Rothbart causes to rage over the lake, begs for her forgiveness. She gives it, but tells him that Von Rothbart's spell cannot be reversed. In this world at least, they can never be united. They decide to end their lives, and cast themselves into the stormy waters of the lake. This assertion of true love destroys Von Rothbart, and Siegfried and Odette are united for ever in a world beyond death.

(In the twentieth-century productions which survive at the Kirov and Bolshoi, the ballet ends with a struggle between Von Rothbart and Siegfried, which the prince wins when he tears off one of the magician's wings. Through this victory Von Rothbart's power is broken, and Siegfried and Odette sail into a new dawn together. The reason for this bathetic plot reversal was that the original nineteenth-century story, which incorporates ideas of the immortality of the spirit, was considered 'religious' in nature, and so 'anti-Soviet'.)

⌒ Notes

Swan Lake is the moon to *The Sleeping Beauty*'s sun. Beautiful, fatalistic and nightbound, set in a gothic fantasy of the Rhineland, it is the most mysterious of the classical ballets. At the same time its quintessentially Romantic love story, borne on that sublime Tchaikovsky score, speaks straight to the heart. From its first night at the Maryinsky it has never left the Kirov repertoire, and today is danced in countless versions all over the world. Like all the great ballets, *Swan Lake* could not be more clearly or transcendently expressed in any other form than classical dance. Dance and music are one, dance and story are one, dance and character are one.

For a ballerina the dual role of Odette–Odile is probably the greatest challenge in the classical canon; only Giselle makes comparable dramatic demands. The contrast between the gentle, vulnerable Odette and the glittering, seductive Odile could not be greater. Odette's character, and the tragic fate which awaits her, are inscribed in the great Act 2 *pas de deux*. In this most tender and beautiful of duets, Ivanov abandoned the conventional *pas de deux* form established by Petipa in favour of an extended lyrical *adagio*. The choreography demands a high, pure line and *legato* dancing (soft, melting, luminous) of the highest order. Odette's character is defined by the lyrical carriage of her arms, by turns yearningly extended and self-protectively in-folded, by the softness of her backbends, and by the subtle tension between her downcast gaze and the skyward line of her *arabesque*.

Odile, meanwhile, is Odette's dark shadow, in whom malignity and self-assertion are thrillingly entwined. Her dancing is sharp-edged and staccato, her steely *port de bras* a vicious parody of Odette's feathery lyricism, and her gaze is challengingly direct. The famous thirty-two *fouettés*, icy and relentless, are her statement of power – sexual, magical and personal – over the prince and those around her. For their duration the court and the audience are hypnotised, and female agency reigns supreme (a scene of comparable power in another medium is Sharon Stone's famous leg-crossing scene in the film *Basic Instinct*). To successfully embody these two extremes of character in a single performance requires exceptional dramatic and technical reserves. Great ballerinas are few, and great Odette–Odiles far fewer. Amongst the role's finest interpreters have been Anna Pavlova, Olga Spessivtseva, Natalia Makarova and, more recently, Yuliana Lopatkina.

Swan Lake has been reworked countless times. John Neumeier's *Illusions – Like Swan Lake* (1976, for Hamburg Ballet), is based on the life of the paranoid, deluded Ludwig II of Bavaria. Mats Ek's version (1987, for Cullberg Ballet) featuring both male and female swans, presents the prince as the Oedipal child of a domineering single mother. Matthew Bourne's West End and Broadway version of the ballet (1995, for Adventures in Motion Pictures) has the unloved, brow-beaten prince encounter a beautiful, powerful male version of Odette, and later a heartless, leather-clad male Odile. These differing versions of the story prompt the question of what exactly lies at the heart of *Swan Lake*. In the post-Freudian interpretations of Ek, Bourne and others, the black and white swan-figures are presented as twin aspects of the same object of desire, and gender distinctions assume shades of grey. If we are to find fulfilment in another, we learn, we must embrace both black swan and white. These readings make forceful emotional sense, but there is more to *Swan Lake* than the politics of desire wrapped up in a fairy tale. The ballet's construction is multi-dimensional and its nature essentially mystical.

To decode its deep meaning we have to examine the origins of the *Swan Lake* story. The ballet is usually said to be based on a tale named 'The Stolen Veil' by the eighteenth-century German folklorist Johann Karl August Musäus, which concerns shape-shifting swan-maidens. To late nineteenth-century Russian audiences, the image of such creatures was a familiar one. Swan-maidens feature in two Rimsky-Korsakov operas: *Sadko* and *Tsar Saltan*. In Wagner's *Lohengrin* the hero's ship is escorted by a swan who is later transformed into an angel. In the classical world, the swan was associated with Venus, who was believed to ride it between the worlds of earth and spirit. The association of the swan with transcendence is repeated in culture after culture, and it is not hard to see how the pure, beautiful vision of a swan in flight so universally came to symbolise the soul's ascent.

Apply this symbolism to *Swan Lake*, and the ballet's metaphysical underpinnings are revealed. Siegfried's longings are not for earthly love, but for transcendence – the journey of the soul. Odette is the embodiment of this dream, and the lake by which she lives is the world of spirit to which the prince longs to return. Her element, however, is one in which he cannot live. To become one with Odette is to become one with Odile, and Odile is a symbol of death. The tragedy at the heart of the *Swan Lake* story, and the subtext of the great Act 2 *pas de deux*, is that Odette already knows what Siegfried has to discover for himself: that the transcendence for which he yearns is unachievable this side of the grave. These mystical underpinnings give resonance to an already beautiful and tragic love story. Within all of us, however expressed, is the longing for rapture, for perfect love. It is to this longing which *Swan Lake* speaks.

∾ View from the Wings

Perhaps the ballet I least expected to dance during my career, *Swan Lake* proved, in the end, to be one of the ballets from which I derived the most satisfaction and joy. Like *Sleeping Beauty*, *Swan Lake* has a place at the top of ballet's most wanted list – you can't really say you've attained ballerina status until you have a *Swan Lake* or two under your tutu. I danced it several times over several years and never failed to find something new to explore within the role: aspects of the character, a new technical approach, a different kind of musicality.

Swan Lake is notable amongst the nineteenth-century classics for combining its seemingly obligatory pair of lead females into the body of a single dancer. For me, that led to a rare treat: accustomed, in most ballets, to playing the bad girl, in *Swan Lake* I got to dance the good girl, too. It was the search for the contrasts – and the connections – between the two roles that made *Swan Lake* such a fascinating, and never-ending, challenge.

The key to it all lies in the choreography. From her very first entrance in Act 2, Odette's dancing has all the yearning, all the sadness, and all the optimism of a heart-felt sigh. Her steps ebb and flow on the back of Tchaikovsky's melodies: each rise on to pointe is followed by a resigned sinking, symbolising her enduring hope that one day her Prince will come along to rescue her from her fate – and her boding despair that perhaps he might not. Her arms move like wings, soft and seamless; her body is pliant, her head brushes her shoulder like a swan nuzzling its feathers. The steps she dances make visible her inner state, her restless longing, her quiet despair.

Odile, in contrast, is all show, her steps designed to hide the evil secrets of her soul even as they dazzle and entrap the guileless prince. She pulls out every trick in the ballet book: brilliant spins, ice-cold balances, razor-sharp footwork, speedy circles around the stage and then, just at the point of total exhaustion, the infamous thirty-two *fouettés*. Thirty-two repeated spins centre-stage, up and down on the left leg with the right whipping in and out on each turn. Ballet's Beecher's Brook, the ultimate hurdle. As ever, it's not really the *fouettés* themselves that are the problem. Most dancers in a professional ballet company, these days, can whip off thirty-two *fouettés*, just as any competition-level runner can manage a four-minute mile. No, it's the point in the ballet at which they crop up: right on top of a solo which seems to punish the left calf in a style of which the Marquis de Sade would be proud. It starts with a series of three turns in *attitude* (on the left leg), interspersed with nine rises (on the left leg), throws in three sweeping *renversé relevés* (on the left leg) and concludes with a circle around the stage of thirty tight, fast turns, all pushing off and landing on the left leg. By this point in the ballet, whenever I danced *Swan Lake*, my left calf was awash with lactic acid, every nerve end screaming at me to stop. I would take my bow after the solo as if I'd just delivered the Gettysburg address, milking every last clap in order to steal precious seconds of recovery time. But no matter how much I managed to milk the applause, the opening chords of the following *coda*, with its faintly ludicrous 'bang on the drum' intro, still sounded like a death knell. The first forty seconds or so of the *coda* belong to the prince, and as he leapt around the stage and down the diagonal, I would will the world to slow down, let me catch my breath, get some life back into my calf. But the music was relentless and so, smiling through gritted teeth, I'd walk on to the centre of the stage and launch myself into the turns.

Amazingly, I don't think I ever totally messed up. Once or twice I came close. The idea is to spin on the spot but from time to time I'd travel so far forward that I'd finish dangerously close to the footlights. Sometimes – although this wasn't one of my specialities – the ballerina manages to travel sideways, a disconcerting experience for the 'courtiers' dressing the stage who find themselves leaning precariously in a sympathetic effort of will designed to get her back on the centre. Frequently the double spin which finishes the sequence was more of a one-and-a-half. But no matter: the sense of relief, of sheer delight at the end of the *fouettés* was fantastic.

Raymonda
Three acts. Choreography by Marius Petipa, music by Alexander Glazunov.
First performed at the Maryinsky Theatre, St Petersburg, 1898.
Like *Le Corsaire*, *Raymonda* has an inordinately daft plot, but

the ballet is redeemed by the beauty of Glazunov's score and the sparkling inventiveness of Petipa's choreography. The Soviet era saw two major revisions of the ballet (Vainonen 1938, Sergeyev 1948), Balanchine produced a shortened version for the Ballet Russe de Monte Carlo in 1946, and Nureyev revisited the piece several times following his 1961 defection, mounting both full-length and abbreviated versions.

∾ Plot

ACT 1

Raymonda, a noblewoman, is to be married to Jean de Brienne, a knight, as soon as the latter returns from the crusades. To her considerable surprise, she is visited by Abderakhman, a Saracen knight, who has heard tell of her great beauty and has travelled from the Orient to woo her. Raymonda does not welcome these attentions but custom and her aunt Sybilla demand that she show hospitality. Sleeping, Raymonda dreams of her husband-to-be, but to her distress his image is displaced by that of Abderakhman.

ACT 2

The Saracen continues to importune Raymonda, and she continues to resist him. Finally he attempts to abduct her, but is foiled by the supernatural intervention of the White Lady (an ancestral statue which comes to life), and by the return of Jean de Brienne and the King of Hungary, under whose banner Jean has been campaigning. Jean and Abderakhman fight a duel, and the Saracen is slain.

ACT 3

Amidst much pageantry, the wedding of Jean and Raymonda is celebrated. In honour of the visiting king, the dances framing the *grand pas de deux* have a Hungarian character. They include a *csardas*, a *pas de quatre* for male dancers, and a *pas de dix* (the Grand Pas Hongrois).

∾ Notes

In the course of his many revisitations to *Raymonda*, Nureyev attempted to inject some sense into the plot, most significantly by expanding Raymonda's Act 1 dream. In this version (for Zurich Ballet, 1972), Abderakhman is Jean de Brienne's knightly rival, and the duel occurs in the course of the crusade. Only when Jean has vanquished the Saracen (and, as subtext, Raymonda's fantasies concerning her fiancé's rival have been laid to rest) can the marriage happily take place. In this psychologically precise reworking, we see further evidence of the theatrical ingenuity that Nureyev displayed in his 1967 staging of *The Nutcracker*. In 1969 he mounted an extended version of Act 3 for The Royal Ballet, and it is in this abbreviated, plotless form that the ballet is most often seen today.

∾ View from the Wings

Raymonda always felt to me like the ballet equivalent of a box of chocolates. In The Royal Ballet's version, staged by Nureyev, the women wore cream tutus with crinkly gold decoration, and each had a solo which revealed a different centre: some creamy and smooth, some brisk and hard as a nut, some fruity, some liquor sweet. As the couples worked their way into the ranked lines of the final flourish, I was always reminded of neatly wrapped, tightly packed chocolates nestling in their box.

Le Corsaire

Three acts. Choreography by Marius Petipa, music by Adolphe Adam, Cesare Pugni, Léo Delibes, Ricardo Drigo, Prince Oldenbourg.
Revised Petipa version first performed at the Maryinsky Theatre, St Petersburg, 1899.

Le Corsaire has had a complex evolution, and by the time that Petipa turned his attention to the story differing versions of the ballet had been produced in London (François Albert,

1837), Paris (Joseph Mazilier, 1856), and St Petersburg (Jules Perrot, 1858). Petipa himself produced two versions for the Imperial Ballet: the first as a vehicle for his wife Maria in 1868, and the second, a final editing of the piece, in 1899. It is the latter version on which subsequent productions have been based.

∾ Plot

ACT I
Following a shipwreck, three adventurers (Conrad, Ali and Birbanto) are washed up onto a Greek beach. They are befriended by Medora and her female friends, who conceal them when a Turkish patrol approaches. Medora and her friend Gulnara, however, are captured by the patrol and handed over to a slave trader, the evil Lankadem. In the marketplace, Gulnara is sold to the wealthy Seid Pasha, and Medora is about to suffer the same fate when a mystery bidder appears. It is Conrad in disguise. Revealing themselves, he and his men release Medora and the other captives, seize Lankadem, and escape.

ACT 2
Conrad and his party are lying up in a cave on a Greek island. They celebrate the freeing of Medora and her friends. Medora dances a spectacular *pas de deux* with Conrad and Ali; her women friends, meanwhile, express their wish to be returned to their villages. Conrad agrees, but Birbanto and the other men want to keep the women. Noting this disagreement, the captive Lankadem approaches Birbanto. In exchange for his freedom he offers Birbanto a sleeping potion. Birbanto pours this over a bouquet of flowers which he persuades Medora to give to Conrad. Accepting the flowers, Conrad passes out, and Lakadem absconds with the unwilling Medora.

ACT 3

Seid Pasha has made Gulnara the queen of his harem, but he is bored with his other women. So when Lankadem appears at the palace with Medora, the Pasha is delighted. He pays the slave-master, and an exquisite entertainment (Le Jardin Animé) unfolds. As the entertainment ends a party of pilgrims appears, and are invited to join the evening prayers. The pilgrims, as Medora and the audience soon realise, are Conrad and his men, come to rescue her a second time. The operation is successful, and the Pasha is bamboozled once again. Conrad and Medora are reunited, and they and their friends set sail in search of new adventures.

∾ Notes

Even by the standards of the nineteenth-century ballet theatre, *Le Corsaire* is a profoundly silly story. In an attempt to endow the piece with high-art credentials, producers often cite its connection to Lord Byron's poem 'The Corsair' (on which Mazilier based his 1856 production), but in truth it is best enjoyed as a series of choreographic gems loosely linked by old-fashioned pantomime. Conrad, Lankadem and Gulnara are all given an opportunity to dazzle in Act 1, and Act 2 contains the highly spectacular *pas de deux* for Conrad, Ali and Medora, danced to music by Drigo. In the 1930s this section was extracted from the ballet (by the Soviet choreographer Chaboukiani) and, by eliminating Conrad, reduced to a *pas de deux*. In this reduced form, and containing some of the most thrilling balletic pyrotechnics ever devised, it has become probably the most popular competition and gala-piece in the ballet repertoire. At the end of Act 2 there is also a beautiful *adagio* duet for Medora and Conrad, in which the ballerina has the opportunity to display ribbon-smooth *legato* dancing as a complement to the fireworks and *fouettés* of the earlier *pas de deux*. Act 3 contains the ravishing Jardin Animé (the living garden of beautiful women assembled for the Pasha's delectation). This section, created by Petipa in 1868 to music by Delibes, comprises a *pas de deux* of filigree delicacy and an elegant suite of dances for the *corps de ballet*. With all of this choreographic *richesse*, and performed as the Russians perform it (i.e. with suitably melodramatic overstatement), the ballet remains a fabulous entertainment. Full-length versions, all slightly different, are in the repertoires of the Bolshoi Ballet, the Kirov Ballet and American Ballet Theatre.

∿ View from the Wings

I was lucky enough to dance the *pas de deux* from *Le Corsaire* on a summer tour of Canada and North America in the late 1980s. Like all 'gala' numbers, it's far easier taken out of context than danced as part of the three-act ballet from which it originates. Although it has all the apparent hallmarks of a virtuoso showpiece, in fact it's relatively easy. The opening duet is simple and short, and the ballerina can choose from no less than three variations: one, which I've never danced, is bright and brisk while the other two are taken from different ballets which I danced many times – Gamzatti's first act variation from *La Bayadère* or the Queen of the Dryad's solo from Act 2 of *Don Quixote*. As the *coda* is little more than the obligatory thirty-two *fouettés* and one quick series of diagonal turns, *Le Corsaire* is a far preferable option for one-off galas on unfamiliar stages to the Black Swan or *Don Quixote pas de deux*.

Diaghilev: The Early Years

By the turn of the twentieth century, ballet was all but dead in Europe. It survived in the schools of Paris and Milan, and in the entr'actes and *divertissements* of the opera, but as a serious art-form it existed only in Russia. There, funded by the Imperial purse, it was flourishing. Petipa and his chief teacher Christian Johannsen had built on the foundations laid by Didelot, Perrot and Saint Léon, and by the century's end the Maryinsky ballet school was producing dancers of unsurpassed skill and refinement. This golden generation of performers included, amongst others, Anna Pavlova and Vaslav Nijinsky.

In 1905, protests in the streets of St Petersburg were accompanied by a dancers' revolt. A group including Anna Pavlova, Tamara Karsavina and Mikhail Fokine – all of them destined for greatness – was determined to have a greater say in the Maryinsky's artistic policy, which they considered constricting. The revolt failed, and Sergei Legat, one of the ringleaders – his morale already depleted by an unhappy affair with Petipa's daughter Maria – cut his own throat. The spirit of change was in the air, however, and this soon found its expression in the activities of a small circle of St Petersburg artists, musicians and thinkers. The circle's leader was a would-be impresario named Sergei Diaghilev, a man of extraordinary sensibility and originality of thought.

In 1909, having tested the water with overseas exhibitions of Russian art and seasons of Russian opera, Diaghilev took a company of Moscow and St Petersburg dancers to the rather dowdy Châtelet Theatre in Paris. Amongst them were Nijinsky, Pavlova and Karsavina, the designers Alexandre Benois and Léon Bakst, and a young choreographer named Mikhail Fokine. The season, which lasted a month (the length of the dancers' summer break from their parent companies) was a vast success. Diaghilev had the theatre redecorated at his own expense, and the fashionable audiences that he invited were awestruck by the virtuosity of Nijinsky, captivated by the ballerinas, and alternately thrilled and enchanted by Fokine's choreography.

Almost all of the works shown at the Châtelet season were new. At the Maryinsky, many of the great ballets were now merely backdrops against which star ballerinas like Mathilde Kchessinska (the Tsar's mistress, and later a Grand Duchess) showed off the latest technical tricks. Fokine, by contrast, insisted on a return to expressiveness, and gave his male and female dancers equal status. His best-known ballets from that first Paris season are the warrior dances from the opera *Prince Igor* and *Les Sylphides*, a misty evocation of the Romantic era with designs by Benois.

When Diaghilev returned to Paris the following year, this time to the Opéra, the programme was once again almost entirely made up of Fokine's ballets. *Schéhérazade* was a perfumed orientalist fantasy, and *Le Carnaval* invoked the world of Harlequin, Columbine and the commedia dell'arte. Nijinsky starred in both ballets, and his cult status grew. The season's most significant work, however, was Fokine's *The Firebird*, based on a Russian folk tale, for it introduced a young man who would become the twentieth century's most important ballet composer – Igor Stravinsky.

After the success of these two seasons, which had taken place during the dancers' summer break, Diaghilev decided to form a permanent company. Nijinsky, Karsavina and Fokine all agreed to join him, as did Enrico Cecchetti, a legendary Maryinsky ballet-master whose teaching system is still employed in ballet schools today. The first year of the new company's existence saw the creation of two more major works by Fokine, *Le Spectre de la Rose* and *Petrushka*. The latter, although it contains almost no actual dancing, was considered by those who saw it to be a perfect synthesis of choreography (Fokine), performance (Nijinsky), music (Stravinsky), and design (Benois), and demonstrates Diaghilev's genius for discovering and inspiring highly gifted individuals.

Many said that Diaghilev's judgement had deserted him when he persuaded Nijinsky, by then his lover, to become a choreographer. Feeling himself sidelined, Fokine resigned, and when after more than a hundred rehearsals *L'Après-midi d'un Faune* finally appeared, it seemed both shocking (it culminates in an orgasmic pelvic thrust) and choreographically bizarre. It was admired, however, by the broader-minded, amongst them the sculptor Rodin. Much greater controversy greeted Nijinsky's *The Rite of Spring*. Based on an imaginary Slavic sacrifice ritual, its heavy and seemingly anti-balletic movements combined with a clamorous Stravinsky score which many denied was music at all. A riot broke out on the first night, with spectators shouting and fighting, and the ballet was quietly dropped. An astute publicist, Diaghilev was not wholly displeased.

Later that year the company sailed for South America, leaving Diaghilev in Europe (it had once been foretold that he would die on water, and he avoided sea travel whenever possible). In Buenos Aires, shortly after the company's arrival, Nijinsky married a young, well-born Hungarian dancer who had made a point of cultivating him on the voyage. Diaghilev took this as a personal betrayal. He replaced Nijinsky with a young Moscow dancer named Léonide Massine, and re-employed Fokine, but in 1914 war broke out. The Diaghilev ballet survived, but its most brilliant period was over. Fokine, although not yet forty, would never rediscover the dazzling inventiveness of his youth. Nijinsky returned briefly to the company but it became increasingly clear that he was the victim of mental illness, and in the summer of 1917, aged just twenty-seven, he danced for the last time. With the October Revolution, Russia entered an artistic purdah from which she would not emerge for three quarters of a century. For Diaghilev and his company, there was no longer any possibility of return.

The Dying Swan
Le Cygne
Divertissement. Choreography by Mikhail Fokine, music by Camille Saint-Saëns.
First performed at the Noblemen's Hall, St Petersburg, 1907.

In December 1907 Anna Pavlova asked Fokine to create a short concert-piece for her. She had recently become the Maryinsky's prima ballerina; he had enjoyed his first major choreographic success with *Le Pavillon d'Armide* a month earlier. Fokine knew the Saint-Saëns music well and composed *The Dying Swan* in a few minutes. Properly speaking, *The Dying Swan* is a product not of the Diaghilev era but of the post-Petipa Maryinsky years. The piece found fame, however, as Pavlova's signature ballet on her many international tours. When she died, a memorial performance was given in which the music was played before an empty stage, while a moving spotlight recreated her performance.

∼ Outline

The ballet (which has no direct connection to *Swan Lake*), depicts the final moments in the life of a swan, and lasts about two minutes. The stricken swan slowly circles the stage. She attempts a brief last flight but sinks defeated to the ground. Her wings fold and she dies.

∼ Notes

Historically, *The Dying Swan* is important because it illustrates several of Fokine's most strongly held beliefs: that dances should be created in a manner expressive of their subject rather than as classical display-pieces, that storytelling should be incorporated into dance (rather than separated out into mime), and that the whole body should be involved in the expressive process. These ideas sound conventional enough today but at the time, in the intensely conservative confines of the Imperial Ballet, they were revolutionary (Fokine and Pavlova had been leading lights of the 'dancers' revolt' of 1905, and in 1909 both would be recruited by Diaghilev).

From its interpreters, the piece demands absolute musicality and control. Apparently simple, in that it appears to contain no great technical challenges, *The Dying Swan* is actually one of the most exposing pieces of sustained *legato* dancing in the classical canon, and the list of those who have triumphed in the role is a short one. Expressively performed, however, as we may imagine that Pavlova performed it, the piece has an exquisite poignancy. The dying struggles of the swan, and her yearning to take wing one last time, reflect not only the ephemeral nature of the ballerina's art, but of life and beauty itself.

∼ View from the Wings

The Dying Swan is a ballet which, quite literally, I only ever saw from the wings. It was at one of those concerts-with-dancing at the Albert Hall in London, where a repertoire of popular orchestral classics is interspersed with excerpts from ballets-you-have-loved. I was dancing the *pas de deux* from *Sleeping Beauty* except, in the event, no one seemed to have told the orchestra that there would be moving bodies involved and we were left with a strip of floor as a stage, narrowly squeezed between the conductor and the footlights. So we got off lightly, dancing only the *pas de deux* and cutting the solos and *coda* which normally accompany it.

It would have been a distinctly unmemorable evening, were it not for the fact that I was sharing the bill with the legendary Soviet ballerina, Maya Plisetskaya. In fact it was better than that. I was sharing a dressing room with her, too. I was able to watch, at the closest of quarters, as she effected the extraordinary transition from pension-able female (she was about sixty-seven at the time) to swan. Her carefully constructed tutu, its shimmering translucent sleeves making her softly pliant arms even more swan-like. Slipper-soft pointe shoes and palest of tights, the dark make-up emphasising her expressive eyes. And then the performance: *bourrées* so fast that they blurred and the bent, broken lines of her body as the swan breathed its last. And, as she finished, the thunderous applause. She was still dancing the role in 1996, at the age of seventy-one. If she's still at it when you read this, I suggest you try and catch her.

Les Sylphides
Chopiniana
One act. Choreography by Mikhail Fokine, music by Frédéric Chopin, designs by Alexandre Benois.
First performed at the Théâtre du Châtelet, Paris, 1909
Les Sylphides began life in 1907 as *Chopiniana*, a ballet suite choreographed by Fokine for the Maryinsky Ballet. It consisted of a series of dramatic dances arranged to piano pieces by Chopin. One of these, a *pas de deux*, featured a ballerina in a long tulle skirt in the style of the Romantic era of the 1830s and 40s, and was intended as a homage to Marie Taglioni. The *pas de deux* was particularly successful, and the following year Fokine returned to the piece and reworked the whole suite as a homage to the Romantic ballet. The revised work proved popular with St Petersburg audiences, and in the spring of 1909 Fokine offered it to Diaghilev for the first Ballets Russes season in Paris. Diaghilev accepted, but insisted on further changes, including the renaming of the piece, and the resultant version is the one we see in the West today. In Russia the title *Chopiniana* is retained.

∾ Outline
The ballet is plotless. The overture plays (in the West the Prelude op. 28, no. 7, in Russia often the Polonaise op. 40, no. 1), and the curtain rises on a moonlit forest glade. A ballerina,

two female soloists and a female ensemble, all in long tulle skirts, are grouped in a symmetrical tableau. The Poet is centre-stage. The dancing begins (to the Nocturne op. 32, no. 2) and a series of variations ensues. The first soloist dances (Waltz op. 70, no. 1), followed by the ballerina (*Mazurka* op. 33, no. 2), the Poet (*Mazurka* op. 67, no. 3), and the second soloist (to the repeated Prelude op. 28, no. 7). The Poet and the ballerina then dance a *pas de deux* (Waltz op. 64, no. 2) and then all dance together (Waltz op. 18), returning at the close to the original tableau.

∿ Notes

The image of the moonlit glade and of the winged sylphs in their gauzy tulle dresses is one of ballet's defining images. At the time of its creation, however, *Chopiniana* was unusual in that Fokine's intention was not to tell a story but to create a mood. Or rather to recreate a mood – that of the high Romantic era of seventy years earlier.

Ballet had travelled a long way since the days of Marie Taglioni. By the early years of the twentieth century the Romantic style, with its delicate *épaulement*, soft *port de bras* and airy jumps, was a thing of the distant past, celebrated in lithographs and engravings but long since overwritten by the classicism of Petipa and his contemporaries. In recalling Taglioni's heyday, Fokine was offering the Maryinsky audiences a charming period piece, but he was also delivering a mute reproach to a ballet establishment which seemed to prize only bravura displays of technique. In Paris (where the cast included Nijinsky, Pavlova and Karsavina) the piece had a different resonance, chiming with the nostalgia of an elite who saw the old cultural order disappearing about them.

Conceptually, despite its apparent retrospective gaze, *Chopiniana* was extraordinarily innovative, in that it distilled the essence of a narrative genre while itself remaining plotless. By 1908 Fokine had arrived at a truth that would not find general currency for another half-century: that the subject of dance could be dance itself. In his crystalline and academic reworking of an archaic form, Fokine is closer to choreographers like Balanchine and van Manen than to any of his contemporaries. For all its misty enchantment and its fragrant style, there is not an iota of sentimentality in *Les Sylphides*. There is Romanticism, but a Romanticism whose choreographic underpinnings unfold with spare, unblinking logic. This tension between delicately mannered surface and inexorable deep structure is why *Les Sylphides* has survived. The Romantic imagination is invoked, and we are profoundly engaged, but at the same time part of us stands coolly to one side.

Naturally, the ballet must be danced with supreme conviction if it is to communicate itself. The ensemble of winged sylphs must seal themselves hermetically within the misty enchantment of the piece, feeling and breathing the music as one. The faintest touch of knowingness, let alone camp or irony, and the mood evaporates. The ballerina must display what the composer Berlioz (a fervent admirer of Taglioni) called 'a sweet melancholy joy, a chaste passion', and her billowy lightness must be complemented by the elegant phrasing and refined technique of the Poet. His line must be strong – his *arabesque* inscribing itself like a pen-stroke against the enfolding dusk – and his stillness eloquent. The Kirov Ballet are without doubt the finest exponents of the piece, which they performed throughout the Soviet era. Their present production (still named *Chopiniana*) dates from 1931, and often forms a part of evenings dedicated to the work of Fokine.

The Firebird

One act. Choreography by Mikhail Fokine, music by Igor Stravinsky, designs by Alexander Golovine and Léon Bakst.
First performed at the Théâtre National de l'Opéra, Paris, 1910.

In the spring of 1910 Diaghilev began to prepare for his second Paris season. He commissioned three new ballets from Fokine

– *Le Carnaval*, *Schéhérazade* and *The Firebird* – and (despite the doubts of his circle) invited a little-known composer named Igor Stravinsky to compose the score for *The Firebird*, a Russian folktale. Stravinsky responded with a score of great colour and brilliance, which prompted Fokine to create some of his most unusual work. The dancers found Stravinsky's rhythms hard to count, and rehearsals continued up to the opening night, when the lead roles were taken by Tamara Karsavina (the Firebird), Fokine himself (Ivan Tsarevich) and his wife, Vera Fokina (the Tsarevna). Diaghilev saw nothing of this performance, because he was operating the Opéra's lighting switchboard.

∿ Plot

The curtain rises on the enchanted garden where the magician Kostcheï holds a dozen princesses captive. The princesses and a tree of golden apples are protected by a high fence. The Firebird enters, intent on stealing one of the golden apples, but she is seized by Ivan Tsarevich, who has been following her. Their struggle, and her eventual subduing, is expressed as a *pas de deux*, and Ivan refuses to release her until she gives him one of her feathers. Armed with this talisman he is assured of her help should he ever need it.

In the gathering dark one of the princesses, the beautiful Tsarevna, tells Ivan of her plight. They dance, and part at dawn. Ivan, however, fails to heed her warning not to follow her, and enters Kostcheï's castle. A crowd of grotesque creatures rush out, followed by Kostcheï himself. The grotesques grovel before Kostcheï, who approaches Ivan, intending to turn him to stone. Remembering the feather, Ivan waves it in Kostcheï's face. The Firebird appears, and forces the grotesques to dance until they are exhausted. She then reveals to Ivan that Kostcheï's soul is contained in a great egg. Ivan takes the egg and dashes it to the ground. The magician dies, and Ivan marries the Tsarevna.

∾ Notes

The Firebird is a curious ballet, and at times can seem more like an assembly of symbolic actions than a story. At first sight the most intense relationship appears to be between Ivan Tsarevich and the Firebird, with his 'capture' of this exotic female creature reminiscent of Siegfried's 'capture' of Odette in *Swan Lake*. The *pas de deux* that Ivan and the Firebird dance underscores this impression. It has clear erotic elements – she is at least as much woman as bird – and the unresolved nature of their relationship leads us to expect some denouement in which they are united. But the ballet is sending out mixed messages. The Firebird flies off and the Tsarevna appears – a dynastically appropriate partner for a Tsarevich – and Ivan dutifully and immediately falls for her. The production does little to suggest that this is a passionate union, however. The Tsarevna in her loose Russian shift is an abject figure in comparison to the glittering, figure-revealing Firebird, no *pas de deux* is danced, and the final wedding scene has a decidedly constitutional look to it. As a footnote, the sexual triangle of the ballet was paralleled in real life by its original cast; Karsavina had been Fokine's lover before his marriage to Vera Fokina.

In many ways *The Firebird* is a mirror opposite of *Swan Lake*, in which Siegfried resists a dynastic marriage in favour of a passionate union with the enchanted swan. Both feature the metaphor (so appropriate to the ballet context) of young women imprisoned by an enchanter but allowed a measure of freedom by night. In choosing the story, it is probable that Diaghilev's main concern was to find a suitably colourful 'old Russian' subject for his Paris audience. One of the principal successes of the previous year had been the Polovtsian Dances from *Prince Igor*, and Slavic folklore was an obvious seam to mine. Today, the ballet remains appealingly enigmatic, and the Stravinsky score, with its faint echoes of Rimsky-Korsakov, Glazunov and Scriabin, is as fresh as the night of its first performance. There have been many subsequent productions of the ballet, including Maurice Béjart's all-male piece set amongst a revolutionary cell (1964), and John Taras's Caribbean version for the Dance Theatre of Harlem (1982).

∽ View from the Wings

A mass of riotous colour and swirling bodies, the Infernal Dance which brings the entire company into *Firebird* could feel, occasionally, like being caught up in the spin cycle of a washing machine. Garments everywhere, whirling fabric, blurred colours . . . yet so tightly choreographed and rehearsed that when the spinning reached its climax and we fell to the floor we were, on most occasions, all in exactly the right place.

Firebird is an unusual piece for the company. It has no 'dancing' role for the principal male and while the Firebird itself is a hugely taxing role, it's a relatively easy ballet for the rest of the enormous cast. It certainly takes energy and commitment, but coming, as it usually does, at the end of a triple-bill performance, it's a welcome relief for the women to take off their pointe shoes and settle into little 'flatties' of comfortable leather. The twelve princesses have a hard time of it, though, in their dance with the apples. I don't think I ever saw – or took part in – a performance in which not one of the apples hit the floor.

Schéhérazade
One act. Choreography by Mikhail Fokine, music by Nicolai Rimsky-Korsakov, designs by Léon Bakst, libretto by Alexandre Benois.
First performed at the Théâtre National de l'Opéra, Paris, 1910.
It was Diaghilev himself who proposed a ballet to Rimsky-Korsakov's symphonic poem *Schéhérazade*, composed around themes from *The Thousand and One Nights*. Diaghilev knew

from the success of *Cléopâtre* in 1909 that oriental themes were popular with Paris audiences, and he talked the composer's widow into letting him use the music (conveniently, Rimsky-Korsakov himself had died two years earlier; his letters make it clear that he would never have allowed his music to be used for ballet had he been alive). A story was decided on, and at a preliminary meeting to discuss the piece, Sergei Grigoriev (the *régisseur* of the Ballets Russes) recalls the painter Léon Bakst jumping excitedly onto a chair and showing how the Shah's retainers should cut everyone to pieces, 'everyone: his wives and above all their Negro lovers!'

∿ Plot

Sultan Shakhriar is entertaining his younger brother, Shah Jeman, in his harem. He is angered by Shah Jeman's suggestion that all his wives are unfaithful. His gaze lingers on his favourite wife, Zobeïde. He agrees, however, on a test. The two men will go hunting, and allow events to take their course. As soon as they have left, the women bribe the Chief Eunuch to throw open the harem door. The male slaves enter, and with them the Golden Slave – the lover of Zobeïde. A sensual revel ensues, at the height of which the Sultan returns to find his favourite with the Golden Slave. The orgy now becomes an orgy of slaughter. To begin with the Sultan cannot bring himself to order Zobeïde's death, but his brother persuades him to harden his heart. Seizing a dagger, Zobeïde kills herself.

∿ Notes

The fashionable orientalism of the late nineteenth and early twentieth centuries, prompted by influences as diverse as the publication of Richard Burton's unexpurgated translation of *The Thousand and One Nights* in 1888, the exhibiting of paintings like Lecomte de Nouy's *The White Slave* (1888), and the opening up of travel routes to the Middle East, was firmly established in Paris by the time that the Ballets Russes first presented *Schéhérazade*. Much of the genre's art and literature is ambiguous. While prompted by a genuine interest in the culture and way of life it represented, it lost no opportunity of dwelling on scenes of cruelty, torture, female slavery and lasciviousness, and indeed became an acceptable way for the privileged classes to enjoy these themes at their leisure.

All of them are represented in *Schéhérazade*, and although the ballet's sexual content might seem tame today, in 1910 it caused the hoped-for *succès de scandale*. The dancers' costumes, furthermore, were as revealing as the mores of the day permitted. *Schéhérazade* exploited to the full the design genius of Léon Bakst, and the set designs created for the ballet became the most famous of their age, launching a Europe-wide fashion for all things exotically Eastern (the overall colour scheme was peacock-green and enamel blue, inspiring Cartier to set emeralds and sapphires together for the first time). In combination with Rimsky-Korsakov's narcotic score and Fokine's dramatic choreography (created in short order after the rhythmic complexities of *The Firebird*), the piece was judged to have achieved the perfect balance of artistic ingredients. It has been revived by several companies, most significantly by the Kirov Ballet in 1994.

Le Spectre de la Rose

One act. Choreography by Mikhail Fokine, music by Carl Maria von Weber, designs by Léon Bakst.
First performed at the Théâtre de Monte Carlo, 1911.
The idea for the ballet came from the writer and critic Jean-Louis Vaudoyer, who suggested that a ballet inspired by Théophile Gautier's poem 'Le Spectre de la Rose' might be set to Weber's *l'Invitation à la Valse*. The piece was choreographed by Fokine in a couple of rehearsals in St Petersburg, and formed part of the repertoire that Diaghilev took to Europe in the spring of 1911. This was the first year that the Ballets Russes operated as a permanent touring company (the 1909 and 1910 Paris seasons

had taken place during the Imperial Ballet's summer break, using dancers from the Maryinsky and Bolshoi companies).

~ Outline

Je suis le spectre de la rose
Que tu portais hier au bal.

So read the lines of Gautier's poem. In the ballet, set in the 1830s, a young girl in a white gown returns home from her first ball. She sinks into an armchair, and taking the rose from her décolletage, she inhales its scent. It is summer, and the french windows are open. The girl's eyes close, and she lets the rose drop to the ground. She sleeps. The spirit of the rose then leaps through the open window, circles the room, and lifting the sleeping girl from the armchair, dances with her. Eventually he lays her back in the armchair, and with a final leap, exits as he had entered. The girl awakes, and discovers the fallen rose.

~ Notes

Le Spectre de la Rose was unusual for two reasons. Firstly, its intimacy. When one considers the scale of most ballets of the day, Bakst's boudoir design (Romantic wallpaper, birdcage, draped bed, Biedermeyer dressing-table) must have given a curiously miniaturist impression. And secondly, Nijinsky's famous *grand jeté* from the window. He had extraordinary elevation, and as many witnesses attested, was able to sustain the illusion of hovering in the air for a moment at the height of his leap. In *Le Spectre de la Rose*, amazingly, he managed to do this at the end of an extended passage of partnering and solo dance – one of the longest in the classical repertoire. The role of the girl was danced by Karsavina, famed to this day for her beauty. There have been many revivals (and new versions created by John Neumeier and Angelin Preljocaj), but none in which the Spectre has achieved quite the inhuman quality described by those who saw Nijinsky in the role.

Petrushka

One act. Choreography by Mikhail Fokine, music by Igor Stravinsky, designs by Alexandre Benois.
First performed at the Théâtre du Châtelet, Paris, 1911.

In the autumn of 1910 Stravinsky started work on a piano concerto which he and Diaghilev agreed could be developed into a ballet about traditional Russian fairground characters. The project is typical of Diaghilev in that it combined the calculatedly commercial (the picturesque 'old Russian' setting, the exoticism and mystery of the fairground) with the deliberately challenging (a ballet in which the principal dancer cannot dance, a score so apparently discordant that the orchestra burst out laughing when they saw it). Success for a touring company, the impresario knew, lay in sophisticated novelty. If the Ballets Russes were to retain their cachet, they had to reinvent themselves every season.

Initially, all went well with *Petrushka*, and Benois, estranged from Diaghilev in the wake of a quarrel about the authorship of the libretto for *Schéhérazade*, was persuaded to create the designs and libretto. Fokine, however, had his doubts about the music, and Stravinsky disagreed with Fokine's choreographic arrangements. On the first night, after a disastrous dress rehearsal and a row with Diaghilev, Benois walked out. Despite these tensions, the critics considered the ballet a masterpiece.

∼ Plot

It is the week of the St Petersburg Butter fair. The period is 1830, snow is on the ground, and a busy crowd is enjoying the many entertainments. Amongst these is a Russian Punch-and-Judy show, presented by a sinister magician. The three puppet-characters are the Moor, the Ballerina, and the doleful, pathetic Petrushka. From the ensuing pantomime we learn that Petrushka loves the Ballerina, but that she despises him and favours the Moor. Backstage scenes confirm this. Petrushka's declarations of passion scare the Ballerina away, but she accepts the crude overtures of the Moor. The pair are interrupted by Petrushka, whom the Moor drives away with his scimitar. Petrushka appears in front of the puppet-theatre, pursued by the Moor, where he is cut down and falls lifeless to the ground. The Magician demonstrates that he is nothing but a straw puppet, and the crowd disperses into the frozen night. But suddenly Petrushka reappears, waving his arms in a final self-assertive statement from the top of the miniature theatre.

∼ Notes

The ballet stands or falls by the quality of pathos brought to the character of Petrushka. We must believe that the painted features and the inert, sawdust body conceal a beating heart – and at the end, perhaps, even a soul – but at the same time Petrushka must never cease to be a puppet. The puppet-show in *Petrushka* is the direct descendant of the commedia dell'arte, and its power is derived from its ambiguity. Nijinsky triumphed in the role, with Karsavina as the stupid, pretty Ballerina, and it is generally agreed that the original cast has never been bettered. In retrospect, there were perhaps elements of Nijinsky's brilliant, tragic performance which prefigured the mental illness which would claim him within a very few years. There have been many revivals of the ballet, and several choreographers including Béjart (1977) and Neumeier (1982) have created entirely new versions.

L'Après-midi d'un Faune
Afternoon of a Faun

One act. Choreography by Vaslav Nijinsky, music by Claude Debussy, designs by Léon Bakst.
First performed at the Théâtre du Châtelet, Paris, 1912.
In 1911, with Diaghilev's encouragement, Nijinsky started work on his first ballet. This was a highly ambitious project,

involving an entirely new movement style and a radical separation of music and choreography. Rehearsals proceeded in
secret. Diaghilev was uncertain that the experiment would
bear fruit and was anxious to conceal the project from Fokine,
who considered himself the resident choreographer of the
Ballets Russes. In the end, so unusual and counter-intuitive
were the movements Nijinsky demanded of his dancers, that
it took more than a hundred rehearsals to bring *L'Après-midi
d'un Faune* to the stage. The reaction was in the main
favourable, but after *Le Figaro* denounced the piece, the police
attended a performance to determine if Nijinsky's movements
were, as stated, 'filthy and bestial in their eroticism'. The
Parisian intelligentsia, led by the sculptor Rodin, were over-
whelmingly on the side of the Ballets Russes, and some said
the objections by *Le Figaro* and others were an attempt to
destabilise the Franco-Russian alliance. The 'anti-Faunists'
were silenced, and the ballet was a *succès de scandale*.

∿ Outline

A faun is reclining on a rocky ledge in an Arcadian glade. Six
nymphs enter, followed by a seventh who lets fall three veils.
The six nymphs mime the bathing of the seventh in a stream,
watched by the Faun, then take away two of the three veils.
The Faun surprises one of the nymphs, who exits, and then
performs a stylised duet with the seventh nymph, who escapes
him. Her companions return for the third veil but the Faun
takes it. In turn, the nymphs try and shame him into returning
it, but he will not. Instead, regarding the veil ecstatically, he
takes it up to his ledge, lowers himself onto it, and delivers
himself of an orgasmic shudder.

∿ Notes

Nijinsky's choreography is the product of an extraordinary
experiment, in which the dancers were required to assume
decorative bas-relief positions as if in a Greek frieze brought
to life. All the steps and dances from *L'Après-midi d'un Faune*

were performed in profile with angled limbs and turned-in feet – a stylisation which has the effect of partly dehumanising its characters, and reducing them to decorative, compositional elements. This angularity presented the strongest possible contrast to Debussy's fluid impressionistic score, composed twenty years earlier (helped by his sister Bronislava, Nijinsky had started choreographing the piece without music; it was Diaghilev who suggested overlaying Debussy's orchestral *Prélude*).

The idea of music and choreography coexisting in this way was a new one; it raised the question, which choreographers like Merce Cunningham would address half a century later, of music juxtaposed with dance but remaining entirely unrelated to it, or of music and dance unrolling in active opposition to each other. In the case of *L'Après-midi d'un Faune*, the drowsily sensual music combines with the starkly formal choreography to lend the piece an unexpected and mesmerising power. There have been a number of revivals. In 1953 Jerome Robbins produced *Afternoon of a Faun* (set to the same Debussy piece) for the New York City Ballet. The production shows the narcissistic flirtation of two dancers in a ballet studio.

The Rite of Spring
Le Sacre du Printemps

One act. Choreography by Vaslav Nijinsky, music by Igor Stravinsky, designs by Nicholas Roerich.
First performed at the Théâtre des Champs-Elysées, Paris, 1913.

In 1912, despite the low-key reception accorded to Nijinsky's *L'Après-midi d'un Faune*, Diaghilev entrusted the twenty-three-year-old dancer with two more commissions for the following year's Paris season – *Jeux* (Games) and *The Rite of Spring*. Stravinsky had been considering the subject of pagan Russian ritual since 1910, and encouraged by the Russian painter Roerich, had produced a powerful but rhythmically complex score. Rehearsals, in which Nijinsky was lavishly assisted by both Diaghilev and Stravinsky, proceeded with agonising slowness from the autumn of 1912 until the premiere in May 1913. The dancers hated the 'undanceable' score and Nijinsky's anti-balletic moves and so, on the first night, did much of the audience. The reaction was riotous, blows were exchanged, and it was only with difficulty that the conductor, Pierre Monteux, completed the performance at all. Conceding that he had misjudged the public's appetite for 'advanced' productions, Diaghilev soon shelved the piece. Reworked by Massine (in a production paid for by Coco Chanel), a further half-dozen performances were politely received in London and elsewhere, but the ballet was then dropped.

 ## Plot

PART 1
In the ancient Slavic Steppes, a tribe foregathers in anticipation of spring. A Shaman moves amongst them, and the young men and women perform a rhythmic, stamping dance. To a warning note in the music the men and women separate. They confront one another, then enact an abduction ritual, a circular dance, and a ritual of rivalry. The Shaman interrupts, and the men fall to the ground and worship the earth. All rise to perform the frenzied Dance of the Earth. Entr'acte.

PART 2
Nightfall, and the young women must choose a sacrificial victim. They perform a mystical circular dance, and leave the Chosen One alone at the centre of the stage. Abject and motionless, she stands as the men and women pound around her, entranced by her power, by the power of Nature, and by the spirit of the Ancestors. The Chosen One then starts to dance, in unison with the music and the earth itself. She falters, exhausted, and finds new strength. Finally she falls dead. The tribe lift her as an offering.

∿ Notes

Nijinsky's original choreography for *The Rite of Spring* is lost, but a concerted attempt at reconstruction was undertaken in 1970 by dance historians Millicent Hodson and Kenneth Archer. The process, employing oral, written and visual evidence, took fifteen years. The resultant version (which Hodson and Archer acknowledge to be incomplete), was staged by the Joffrey Ballet in 1987, and by the Kirov Ballet in 2003. The principal historical source was Marie Rambert, who acted as Nijinsky's assistant. In her autobiography, Rambert describes in detail the heavy movement and deliberately anti-balletic posture that he demanded, and which, in conjunction with Stravinsky's music, so outraged the Parisians. She also states quite unequivocally – and Rambert's artistic judgement was famously rigorous and unforgiving – that the work was a masterpiece. Watching Nijinsky demonstrate the role of the Chosen One to Maria Piltz, who danced the role in Paris, Rambert writes that his 'ecstatic performance' was 'the greatest tragic dance I have ever seen'. So one can only wonder. Certainly the Hodson/Archer production conveys something of the original's grim power. Roerich's sets display skull-and-feather totems, and shamanic figures in the pelts of stags. The men are blank-eyed and disconnected as they pound out Stravinsky's baleful rhythms. The Chosen One, meanwhile, stands literally paralysed with terror as she waits for the sacrificial dance to begin.

There have been more than 120 versions of *The Rite of Spring* since Nijinsky's, and in the 1960s and 70s an assault on Stravinsky's score was almost de rigueur for any young choreographer wishing to prove him or herself. Maurice Béjart's 1959 production memorably reworked the piece as an orgasmic fertility ritual, with sex taking the place of sacrifice. Kenneth MacMillan (1962), John Neumeier (1972), Hans van Manen (1974), Pina Bausch (1975), Michael Clark (1992), Stanton Welch (1998), and Angelin Preljocaj (2000) are amongst the many other artists who have visited this iconic work, and in different ways stamped their identities on it.

∼ View from the Wings

The Rite of Spring has been something of a rite of passage for me: I've danced it three times and each has been at a seminal moment in my career. In 1987, when I first danced Kenneth MacMillan's powerful version for The Royal Ballet, I had just recovered from an illness which had taken me out for several months. Performing the sacrificial virgin on the Covent Garden stage, while the great conductor Bernard Haitink led the orchestra in the pit, I felt not so much that I was dancing myself to death but that I was dancing myself back to life. Thirteen years later, I was surprised and thrilled to be asked to dance in a different version: Millicent Hodson's reconstruction of Nijinsky's *Rite of Spring* at the Teatro dell'Opera in Rome. It felt odd to be invited to tackle this most demanding of roles at the twilight of my career, yet it never crossed my mind that it was an invitation I might refuse. Still, stamina was my main concern: The Chosen One dances herself to death in a variation lasting almost five minutes. I was thirteen years younger when I danced MacMillan's version yet even so, I remember the feeling of total, legless exhaustion at the end. I nurtured a vague hope that ballerinas of 1913 couldn't have been as fit as today's dancers and that whatever Nijinsky had choreographed, it couldn't be nearly as hard. I was soon to discover that while sprinters run faster and jumpers jump higher, dancing yourself to death doesn't change much over the years.

Rehearsals had already started when I arrived in Rome so I had to work fast, not only taking in the choreography, but reprogramming my posture to suit Nijinsky's style. In each piece he created, Nijinsky abandoned the traditional foot positions of classical ballet,

replacing them with a different, hallmark stance. In
L'Après-midi d'un Faune, the dancers move in bas-relief,
as if in an Egyptian frieze. In *Jeux*, the feet are parallel,
heels flat, the pointe shoe less ballet footwear than tennis
pump. In *Sacre*, the toes meet to form the point of an
arrow, the normal 'ten to two' position of the ballerina
inverted to twenty past eight. I had constantly and con-
sciously to remind myself, on every landing of every
jump, to adjust my toes inwards. And there are 123 of
them: a sequence of twenty-five high bounces, alternat-
ing with deep lunges, which returns halfway through the
dance, arms slicing the air in sharp diagonals. And then,
when you think you can't go on, it comes back, in a complicated variation dubbed 'the test'. If you survive the
test, you know you'll make it to the end, but by now
you're starting to lose control over your legs. You think
they're doing the steps, but the chain of command
between brain and feet has somehow been severed and
you have to trust that although you can't feel anything
below the hips, except the numbing effect of lactic acid,
the message is still getting through. Ten darting turns,
right and then left, before the final effort: a dozen more
bounces, flailing arms, before you drop to the floor. The
drop is real.

Dancing *Sacre* on stage, in Nicholas Roerich's costume
and pigtailed wig, I felt as if I had been transported back
to the Théâtre du Châtelet in 1913. Ballet-masters ran
up and down the wings, screaming counts, trying to keep
the Italian *corps de ballet* in time. Stravinsky's pounding
accents drove the dancing onwards, winding up the
tension to the point where the Chosen One's first leap
from her frozen pose came as a release. And I felt truly
Chosen: both honoured and terrified and, by the ultimate
note, unable to go on. The final drop was real.

To a twenty-first-century ballerina, schooled in Graham,
MacMillan and Forsythe, the work feels not exactly
modern, but markedly different from anything else I've

danced in either classical ballet or abstract contemporary dance. To Hodson, Nijinsky's style is a lost technique, somewhere between the classical ballet of Petipa and *Ausdruckstanz* and the expressionistic moderns of the 1920s. As a critic wrote at the time: this is not just a new work, it's a new way.

My final performances of *Rite*, in Rome in September 2002, will perhaps turn out to have been the most significant of all – the final performances of my career. But then I'm not sure dancers ever give up dancing, so who knows?

Parade

One act. Choreography by Léonide Massine, libretto by Jean Cocteau, music by Erik Satie, designs by Pablo Picasso.

First performed at the Théâtre du Châtelet, Paris, 1917.

The winter of 1916–17 was a low point in the fortunes of the Ballets Russes. Europe was at war, and a US tour had proved a failure due to the bizarre behaviour of Nijinsky, who was soon to be diagnosed as mentally ill. Picasso and Cocteau were at the time part of the avant-garde set which gathered around Diaghilev. They had started work on a circus ballet the year before (the theme was a popular one in avant-garde circles, as the paintings of Picasso, Daumier, Seurat and others attest), and Satie had composed the score. Diaghilev, meanwhile, was determined to mould twenty-two-year-old Massine into a choreographer, and entrusted him with the piece. From February to March the collaborators worked together in Rome. The ballet premiered in June.

∼ Plot

The setting is a Parisian street circus. A French and an American manager are attempting to lure passers-by into the show by parading some of the talent. The French Manager introduces the Chinese Conjuror (the role danced by Massine), who performs tricks, and then the American Manager introduces the Little American Girl – actually a child impersonator – who performs a dance and enacts snatches of melodrama, including the Sinking of the *Titanic*. When an audience fails to materialise a Horse appears and dances, followed by a pair of acrobats. All the acts are reprised but still no one comes in. As the curtain falls, the entire routine is beginning again.

∽ Notes

Parade displays Diaghilev's genius for generating artistic collaboration. Satie's impressionistic score, which features a typewriter, a ship's siren and revolver shots, is an atmospheric masterpiece in miniature. Picasso's extraordinary designs, which in the case of the Managers' carpentered costumes towered to eleven feet in height, were the first Cubist works for the theatre. And Massine's choreography is engagingly witty, particularly the sequence for the Little American Girl. In a programme note by Guillaume Apollinaire describing *Parade*, the word 'surrealism' appeared in print for the first time, and the Paris audience hailed the ballet as the perfect synthesis of music, design and dance. Despite these plaudits and the piece's novelty, *Parade* was rarely performed in Diaghilev's day, and in 1926 the impresario tried (unsuccessfully) to sell the Picasso drop-cloth to raise money for new ballets. In recent years the piece has been successfully staged by several companies.

Diaghilev: The Twenties

The Russian Revolution saw the final severing of Diaghilev's links with Russia, and his enthusiastic embrace of the European avant-garde. As the director of the Ballets Russes (the company's full title was Les Ballets Russes de Serge Diaghilev) he would devote the rest of his life to a continuous search for the new – new stars, new collaborators, new ideas. This was due in part to his own intellectual curiosity – as *The Rite of Spring* had shown, he was more interested in challenging his audiences than placating them – and in part to the need to maintain an exciting edge in the eyes of the public. Touring companies, he well understood, survive only by constantly reinventing themselves.

Nijinsky was replaced in the company and in Diaghilev's affections by the dancer–choreographer Léonide Massine, who produced in rapid succession *Parade*, *La Boutique Fantasque*, *Le Tricorne* and *Pulcinella*. The ballets were all a single act in length (the form which Diaghilev preferred, because it allowed for variable programming and short audience attention spans) and their designs, by Derain and Picasso, demonstrated the impresario's brilliance at setting up collaborations from which all benefited. The ballet acquired the fashionable modernist sheen which Diaghilev valued; the artists (whose number would eventually include Braque, Matisse, Utrillo, Rouault, Ernst, Miró and De Chirico) saw their work placed before an enthusiastic new audience.

In 1921, following a falling-out with Massine and the latter's departure, Diaghilev mounted an extravagent full-length version of Petipa's classic *The Sleeping Beauty* at the Alhambra Theatre in London. He called the production *The Sleeping Princess*, and it ran for more than a hundred performances, but its scale and running costs were vast and it eventually lost money. The exercise was prompted partly by the absence of a company choreographer, partly by nostalgia ('This is the last relic of the great days of St Petersburg,' he told friends), and partly by the departure from Russia of Nicholas Sergeyev, the former Director General of the Maryinsky Theatre. To the incalculable advantage of ballet in the West, Sergeyev had brought with him the notated choreography of more than twenty of the Maryinsky classics, including *Giselle*, *Coppélia*, *The Sleeping Beauty*, *The Nutcracker* and *Swan Lake*, and was able to help stage the production accurately.

After the financial failure of *The Sleeping Princess*, Diaghilev returned to France. In 1922, thanks to his aristocratic connections, the Ballets Russes acquired a home for six months of each year at the Monte Carlo Casino, to which were attached rehearsal rooms and a theatre. Despite the fact that it brought Diaghilev close to bankruptcy (not for the first or the last time), the Alhambra season was far from a total debacle. It saw the emergence of a significant choreographer in Bronislava Nijinska, sister of the legendary Vaslav, who staged several of the dances for *The Sleeping Princess* and went on to choreograph for the company. Her most important ballets were the powerful and ritualistic *Les Noces* (1923) and the coolly sophisticated *Les Biches* (1924), both of which are now recognised as masterpieces. Nijinska worked with Diaghilev until 1925, when she resigned following a disagreement.

The season also produced a number of fine ballerinas, of whom the greatest was the ethereally beautiful and technically impeccable Olga Spessivtseva. The ballet-master Cecchetti considered Spessivtseva the equal of Anna Pavlova, comparing them to two halves of an apple – to which Diaghilev famously replied that Spessivtseva was the half that had seen the sun. We cannot achieve a meaningful comparison today, but Spessivtseva (whose defining role was Giselle) was without question one of the greatest ballerinas of all time. She danced regularly for Diaghilev, and in 1927 created the title role in *La Chatte*, choreographed by his new chief choreographer – a twenty-three-year-old émigré Russian named Georgi Balanchivadze.

Anna Pavlova danced with Diaghilev's company between 1909 and 1911, but thereafter, unwilling to submit herself to his experimental repertoire, bought a house in London and put together her own company. For the rest of her life (she died in 1931) she toured tirelessly, taking her repertoire of solos and cut-down classics to the capital cities of Europe, Asia and the Americas, and also to the provinces, to the corners of the world where ballet had never been seen before. By all accounts a dancer of transfixing poignancy and glamour, she inspired a whole new generation of dancers and choreographers (amongst them Frederick Ashton, who saw her perform in Peru when he was thirteen).

After *The Sleeping Princess*, Diaghilev returned to the lean, contemporary one-act pieces that had always served him so well. The last of the great Ballets Russes choreographers was Georgi Balanchivadze – or George Balanchine, as he renamed himself. In 1928 he produced *Apollo* and in 1929 the company's final creation, *The Prodigal Son*. Later that year Diaghilev succumbed to a sudden attack of diabetes while on holiday in Venice. As had been foretold, he died on water. By 1931 Pavlova had gone too, exhaustion speeding her end, but ballet in the West had been given new life. All of Europe had been lit by the glamour of the Ballets Russes, and Pavlova had kindled the flame further afield. Diaghilev's company was disbanded after his death, and the ensuing diaspora of Russian teachers and dancers established balletic outposts all over the world.

During the 1930s and 40s the Ballets Russes were re-formed under other names and other directors. There were palmy summers in Monte Carlo, and there was a succession of star dancers, but few of the ballets created during those days are still performed. The era was most notable for the activity of former members of the company, who took the knowledge and experience that they had acquired with the Ballets Russes and created enterprises of their own. Serge Lifar joined the Opéra and almost single-handedly revived French ballet, which was in a near-terminal state; Marie Rambert and an ambitious young dancer–choreographer named Ninette de Valois travelled to London and founded, respectively, Ballet

Rambert and the Vic-Wells Ballet (which would become The Royal Ballet), and George Balanchine took ship for the USA.

Les Noces

One act. Choreography by Bronislava Nijinska, song-text and music by Igor Stravinsky, designs by Natalia Goncharova.
First performed at the Théâtre de la Gaîté-Lyrique, Paris, 1923.

Stravinsky started to compose *Les Noces* in 1912, but with Europe fractured by the First World War and the circumstances of the Ballets Russes changing month by month, it was 1923 before it was finally staged. In the eleven years of its genesis, the piece was assigned first to Nijinsky, and then to Massine; Nijinska was only given full responsibility for its choreography in 1923. By then the Russian Revolution had taken place, and the political subtext of Stravinsky's song-suite had changed.

~ Outline

Les Noces shows the preparations and ritual surrounding a peasant wedding. In the first scene, The Blessing of the Bride, the bride's hair, previously worn in a single plait, is braided by her female friends into two long rope-like plaits. Mimes of lament and consolation are performed. In The Blessing of the Bridegroom the men perform stamping, crouching folk-dances, and in The Bride's Departure the bride's friends – both male and female now – simultaneously console her and encourage her. In an anguished tableau, the bride's mother bids her daughter farewell. The Wedding Feast is attended by the whole village. The couple and their parents sit on a raised bench upstage, the guests are massed in gender-divided ranks before them, dancing out complex and repetitive sequences. The mothers throw open the door to the marriage chamber, and the couple step inside.

◟ Notes

For all the associations of weddings with optimism and happiness, *Les Noces* is a grim piece, as we are aware as soon as the curtain rises on Goncharova's austere, reductionist set. The music is orchestrated for four pianos, percussion, and a chorus who perform an extraordinary Joycean (the comparison was Stravinsky's) montage of vocal material. Thoughts, banalities, folk-sayings, wedding-songs, clichés, religious invocations, and drunken interjections are woven together to symbolise the many strands of expectation acting on the young couple – particularly the bride – and before which they are powerless. The couple must marry, children must be provided and the labour needs of the community must be met.

The context of the piece is notionally nineteenth-century Russia, but Nijinska's ballet is not really time-tied, and can equally easily be read as applying to post-Revolutionary Russia (the Bolsheviks paid little more than lip service to the emancipation of peasant women, and for many of the rural poor life was no better than under the Tsars), or as a metaphor for the oppression of women in general. The braiding of the bride's hair from its single plait into two is symbolic of the uniting of two families, but this 'parting' is also symbolic of sexual violence and the loss of virginity, as the lamentation accompanying the scene explicitly bears out. In the Wedding Feast scene, dance and music fuse with implacable force, with the regimented phalanxes of male and female guests pounding out the single message: that the tribe and the collective will are all. The bride knows that she can no more escape marriage, procreation and drudgery than she can death. She is as pliant and passive as the Chosen One in *The Rite of Spring*. Unlike the voiceless Chosen One, however, the bride is able to communicate her feelings – through the stream of consciousness of Stravinsky's lyrics.

That the ballet is political – not to say proto-feminist – in nature in no way diminishes its high theatricality. The piece is deeply fatalistic, as *The Rite of Spring* is deeply fatalistic, but it is also one of the most powerful, thrilling and uplifting works in the ballet canon. It has been much revived – mostly recently in a symbolic reappropriation of Nijinska's work by the Kirov Ballet. Maurice Béjart (1962), Jerome Robbins (1965) and Jiri Kylian (1982) have all created original versions.

~ View from the Wings

It's an extraordinary experience dancing in *Les Noces*. There are plenty of other large-scale *corps de ballet* pieces in which you could lose yourself amongst the sheer number of dancers on stage, but *Noces* has something different. It feels almost mechanical, as if the individual dancers are cogs and wheels in a massive movement machine. The corps doesn't appear until the fourth movement and so as the third section drew to a close, we would all shuffle around blind on a darkened stage, getting into lines behind the curtain. Reaching for hands to check spacing, whispering nervously as we searched for someone who seemed to be missing, a frantic last-minute think through the complicated counts and then we were ready, stretched out across the stage in massed ranks, men and women clad alike in rough brown work wear. Stravinsky's score added to the sense of anticipation, a low, barely audible rumbling with intermittent chimes ringing out like a single church bell summoning us to our toil. Often on stage, one feels as if one is playing a role: the work required to convey a story or idea is not the same as the idea or story itself. But in *Noces*, the two become inseparable. To portray Russian peasants in a ballet which seems to presage the Soviet Union's forced collectivisation and rapid industrialisation, when the subjugation of the needs of the individual to the needs of the state became paramount, the *corps de ballet* has to become as those workers: massed ranks operating en masse, man recreated as machine. Ideas and philosophies which are alien to a dancer raised in 1980s Britain, with its Thatcherite emphasis on individuality and the self.

Les Biches
The House Party

One act. Choreography by Bronislava Nijinska, music by Francis Poulenc, designs by Marie Laurencin.
First performed at the Théâtre de Monte Carlo, 1924.

With the Ballets Russes spending a significant part of each year in Monte Carlo, Diaghilev was determined to make the principality into a centre of artistic and cultural life. In 1924 five new ballets had their premiere there. *Les Biches* – a very French piece, given its composer and designer – was a *succès de chic*. Its title is untranslatable but intimate and sensual in tone, and means something like 'the spoilt darlings'.

ᔡ Outline

Set in a Riviera drawing room during the 1920s, the eight-section ballet shows a series of exchanges at a chic house party, where an urbane hostess with a long cigarette holder presides over a predominantly female ensemble. Into this hothouse venture three musclebound male athletes. Much louche flirtation ensues, with an ambiguous blue-jacketed female character (the Page Boy) and a sapphic duo (the Gray Girls) lending the frivolity an oblique eroticism. Poulenc's score has a faint jazzy undertone; the Page Boy dances a stylised *adagietto* and the Gray Girls an ambiguous *chanson dansée*.

ᔡ Notes

The piece, which strongly influenced Frederick Ashton (who worked with Nijinska's company in Paris as a young man), has a period, not-quite-innocent charm. Poulenc said of *Les Biches* that you may read the worst, or you may see nothing at all. In 1964 Ashton revived the work for The Royal Ballet. He had not done so earlier, he told the musical director John Lanchbery, because Ninette de Valois was jealous of Nijinska.

∿ View from the Wings

> In complete contrast to *Les Noces*, *Les Biches* offered us
> corps de ballet girls a wonderful chance to have fun, gig-
> gle and flirt, its oh-so-refined postures and positions con-
> cealing a simmering undercurrent of sexual intrigue and
> just-repressed desires, in true 1920s style.

Apollo
originally Apollon Musagète

**One act. Choreography by George Balanchine, music by
Igor Stravinsky, original designs by André Bauchant.
First performed at the Théâtre Sarah Bernhardt, Paris,
1928.**

Stravinsky and Balanchine first met in Monte Carlo in 1925.
The composer was forty-five, the fledgling choreographer
twenty-one. Introduced by Diaghilev, they worked together
on a ballet suite named *Le Chant du Rossignol*. Stravinsky saw
that Balanchine not only had an instinctive understanding of
his music and its often complex architecture, but was able to
produce dance material which complemented it perfectly.
The two agreed on fundamental matters of composition; both
were committed to formal rigour, austerity and clarity. Both,
furthermore, disliked Diaghilev's increasing high-handedness,
and had begun to feel like outsiders in the openly homosexual
atmosphere which the impresario encouraged in the Ballets
Russes. In the spring of 1928, Diaghilev assigned the choreography of *Apollon Musagète* (as a completed score by Stravinsky was titled) to Balanchine. The ballet opened later that year.

∿ Outline (original ballet)

The ballet shows the youth of Apollo, god of the arts and the
sun. An orchestral prologue identifies the theme which is to
be identified with him, and the curtain rises on a night scene,
on the Aegean island of Delos, where the god is born to his

mother Leto (his father is Zeus). He is quickly independent, but fearful and unknowing. Two maidens bring him a lute, and encourage him to pluck it – the first step in his hurtling voyage of self-discovery. There is a blackout, and Apollo is rediscovered playing the lute, whirling his arms around in a circular sun motif. He dances alone, and then with the lute.

Three Muses enter. They are Calliope the Muse of Poetry and Rhythm, Polyhymnia the Muse of Mime, and Terpsichore the Muse of Dance (which combines rhythm and mime, making Terpsichore the greatest of the three). Apollo dances briefly with them in turn; they interlink, separate and dance alone. He then presents each with her appropriate symbol. To Calliope, a writing-tablet, to Polyhymnia a mask, to Terpsichore a lyre. The Muses are childishly pleased with their gifts.

Calliope dances, to an Alexandrine rhythm (the rhythm of French poetry). She writes on her hand, and shows it to Apollo. She seems unconfident, and the god is not impressed. Polyhymnia dances, but quickly puts aside her mask; in its place, she puts a finger to her lips, but finally speaks and in her turn displeases Apollo. Terpsichore then dances with her lyre, and the god judges her dance to be perfect.

Apollo dances, demonstrating that all of the qualities which he demands of the Muses are contained within his person. He performs a lyrical *pas de deux* with Terpsichore, and as a playful reward, gives her a swimming lesson on his back. The god and the three Muses then perform a *coda* which concludes with Apollo driving them across the stage in a chariot race.

In an orchestral crescendo, Zeus summons his son to Olympus. Apollo blesses the Muses, and drawing them across the stage, leads them up the rock on which he was born. As the four figures reach out their arms to the sun, Leto bids her son farewell.

∼ Outline (revised version)

Over the course of his career Balanchine constantly returned to this ballet, altering steps and design elements. In 1978–9 he cut the opening scene showing Apollo's birth, eliminated the set, and played out the ballet on a bare stage against an Aegean blue cyclorama. In the final scene, in place of the ascent of the rock, he arranged the three Muses and Apollo in an *arabesque* formation, so that their extended limbs formed the rays of the sun. The original version is still performed today, but the revised version is more often seen.

∾ Notes

Balanchine considered *Apollon Musagète* to be 'the turning point in my life'. Stravinsky encouraged him to 'eliminate . . . limit . . . clarify . . . reduce', and with the example of his shimmering neo-classical arrangement for strings (very much a product of reduction, the original score included parts for piano and a harp), showed him how to do so. The ballet is a revealing expression of a creative partnership: Stravinsky's score has the limpid serenity of middle life, while Balanchine's choreography is equally clearly the work of an impetuous talent straining at the boundaries of existing form. The changes of mood are lightning-fast. Balanchine swoops in a breath from the lyrical to the quirky – the 'swimming-lesson' – reminding us that this Apollo was born on a Jazz Age Olympus. At the same time Balanchine's work is never less than utterly respectful of Stravinsky's music. The dances are not applied to the score, they are extracted from it. The ballet's surface themes are wry, witty and referential in all sorts of ways, but they never overtake Balanchine's commitment to the glass-clear rendering of music in physical form. The essential interplay is not between Apollo and the Muses but between Balanchine and Stravinsky. For all its cerebrality, however, the piece is nothing if not theatrical, and to see the ballet with no foreknowledge of its themes or musical structure is still to be ravished by its azure, dawn-of-time intensity. *Apollo* remains one of New York City Ballet's signature works, but is danced by companies all over the world.

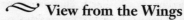 **View from the Wings**

A cool, minimal, modern masterpiece, I find it impossible to believe that *Apollo* dates back to 1928. It's another
of those ballets in which every woman in the company
longs to be cast, each team of three Muses, once assembled, huddling closer together as rehearsals progress
until they form an impenetrable clique. In truth, this
kind of team spirit is essential in order for the ballet to
succeed. The three Muses must, despite their individual
variations and particular graces, dance as one throughout
the ensemble sections, synchronising style, technique
and musical response. They must each subjugate their
individuality – or at least save it for their solo – to the
unity of the whole. The deceptively simple choreography
requires intense concentration and a constant steadying
of nerves, from the very first entrance – high kicks, on
pointe, progressing on to the stage from three separate
corners – to the complicated timings and rhythms of the
final movement.

The Prodigal Son
Le Fils Prodigue

**Three scenes. Choreography by George Balanchine,
music by Sergei Prokofiev, designs by Georges Rouault.
First performed at the Théâtre Sarah Bernhardt, Paris,
1929.**

The Prodigal Son was the third ballet score composed by
Prokofiev for Diaghilev (the others were *Chout* and *Pas
d'Acier*). Balanchine was entrusted with the choreography – a
decision which Prokofiev felt to be wrong, as he did not
believe that the young choreographer was capable of handling
emotional subjects. In the event, despite Rouault having to
be locked into his hotel room to force him to finish the sets
and costumes, the production proved popular, and was
regarded as a welcome return to expressiveness after a

decade's fashionable experimentation. The ballet opened in May, and was Balanchine's final work for the Ballets Russes. By August Diaghilev was dead.

~ Plot

The story, with minor variations, is that of the Biblical parable. The curtain rises on a bright Middle Eastern scene. The ancestral tent is surrounded by a picket fence. The Prodigal appears, excited by his new wealth and his plans to seek adventure. His sisters and his father are apprehensive, but he ignores them. When his father tries to bless him he aggressively turns away. After further displays of indifference and arrogance he leaves with his companions.

The scene changes to a distant land. Grotesque revellers are arriving in a tent, and playing enigmatic games. The Prodigal enters, and after plying the revellers with wine, appears to gain their friendship. The Siren enters, dazzling and exotic. She dances sinuously and exhibitionistically, luring the fascinated Prodigal to her. They dance an erotically charged duet, and then his drunken companions intervene. With their help, the Siren pours more wine into the Prodigal, who staggers around and collapses. The others, led by the triumphant Siren, rob him of all he owns. The Prodigal wakes. He realises the extent of his self-deception and betrayal. The thieves sail away in a boat.

Time has passed. Exhausted and ragged, the Prodigal crawls slowly across the stage. Finally he recognises the gate to his home. His sisters find him, and joyfully accompany him towards their father, who gathers him up in forgiveness.

~ Notes

The Prodigal Son is an intense, dramatically charged piece whose chill force is in no way lessened by our knowledge of what is going to happen. The central role offers a dramatic tour de force; the protagonist must be plausible as the arrogant, disdainful young man of the first scene, as the guileless, lust-dizzied mark of the second, and as the broken and contrite figure of the third. The role of the Siren – a malign dominatrix – also offers great scope for the actor–dancer.

Choreographically, the piece is dense with potent imagery, much of it inflected with a German expressionist quality. The grotesque, hunkering attitudes of the revellers, the lubriciousness with which the Siren draws her cape between her legs, and the extraordinary sexual duet in which she variously sits on the Prodigal's shoulders, slides down his back, kneels on his feet and sits on his head all contribute to the ballet's dark potency. For the Russian-born Balanchine, for whom there would be no redemptive Prodigal's return, the theme of departure and homecoming would have had particular poignancy. Over the years the ballet has been staged by many companies, amongst them The Royal Ballet (1973, with Rudolf Nureyev), American Ballet Theatre (1980, with Mikhail Baryshnikov), and San Francisco Ballet (2000).

Balanchine: Made in America

After Diaghilev's death, Balanchine founded a small chamber-company in Paris named Les Ballets 1933. The company was financed by a rich Englishman named Edward James as a vehicle for his wife, the dancer Tilly Losch, but as its name suggested, it was not destined for a long life. During the company's first and only London season, Balanchine met another wealthy patron of the arts, the American Lincoln Kirstein, who invited him to the United States to found and direct a national ballet school. Balanchine accepted, and the School of American Ballet opened its doors in 1934. Within the year Balanchine was creating *Serenade*, his first American-made ballet, on its students. A series of short-lived companies ensued, fed by the school and directed by Balanchine, and in 1948 the last of these (Ballet Society) was offered a permanent base at City Center in New York, and became the New York City Ballet.

NYCB was a new kind of company: an ensemble styled for a single choreographer. Balanchine opposed the star system and the old-fashioned cult of the stage personality, and sought a strong, unified look for his dancers. Physicality, rather than theatricality, was to be the new watchword. The NYCB women were stately and the male dancers were Apollonian, and together they became the cool, subtly distanced instruments of their director's choreographic imagination.

Over the fifty years of his career, Balanchine would produce an extraordinarily diverse body of work, from razzle-dazzle Americana like *Stars and Stripes* to gilded classics like *The Nutcracker* to mysterious dream-pieces like *Liebeslieder Walzer*. The ballets with which he and his company are most strongly associated, however, are the plotless works like *The Four Temperaments*, *Agon* and *Concerto Barocco*. In these pieces, danced in simple leotards and tights and with minimal decor, Russian classicism is pared to its essence. There are no stories, just fragmentary suggestions of mood. Narrative outlines occasionally reveal themselves, but these quickly dissolve into formal structure. At the time of their creation, Balanchine's 'neo-classical' works (as these plotless but classically derived ballets came to be known) were controversial. Today's audiences understand that when Balanchine withholds explicit emotion in his ballets, it is because the ballets themselves are constructed from layerings of emotional tone. In post-Second World War America, however, many considered these pieces soulless and impersonal, and it was not until the mid-1960s that their choreographer was accorded the status and recognition that was his due.

For Balanchine, dance was no more and no less than music given human form. 'I leave audiences to see what they will in my ballets,' he stated. While at the Imperial School of Ballet he had also studied theory and composition at the St Petersburg Conservatory, and his sophisticated understanding of music's formal architecture lent great depth to his collaborations with composers like Stravinsky and Hindemith. The resultant ballets are at once as simple and as complex as the music from which they take their life. And just as this music rarely reveals its emotional core on first listening, so Balanchine's sleek neo-classical masterpieces demand several viewings if they are to give up their secrets.

Balanchine famously insisted that 'Le ballet est la femme' – ballet is woman – and in reaction to the Romantic egalitarianism of Fokine, reinstated the ballerina on her Olympian peak. His own ballerina muses were many, and four of them – Tamara Geva, Vera Zorina, Maria Tallchief, and Tanaquil LeClerq – became his wives. These were all, in their different ways, unusual relationships. Geva described Balanchine as a cross between a poet and a field marshal and Tallchief had their marriage annulled, claiming that it had never been consummated. Before his divorce from LeClerq (and her subsequent death from polio) Balanchine became infatuated with the last and greatest of his muses, Suzanne Farrell, for whom he created several of his most beautiful dance passages, including Diamonds in *Jewels* (1967). Balanchine's possessiveness strained his relationship with his young protégée to breaking point, and Farrell left New York City Ballet for Maurice Béjart's Ballet of the Twentieth Century in Brussels (as, in a very precise parallel, 130 years earlier, Lucile Grahn had exchanged Copenhagen and the attentions of August Bournonville for the Paris Opéra). Farrell would return, however, and Balanchine would continue to choreograph until his death in 1983, by which time he had created more than two hundred ballets and defined a new, uniquely American dance language.

Serenade

Four movements. Choreography by George Balanchine, music by Pyotr Ilyich Tchaikovsky, costumes by Jean Lurçat (later by Karinska).
First performed (by students of the School of American Ballet) at the estate of Felix M. Warburg, White Plains, New York, 1934.

Balanchine's setting of Tchaikovsky's Serenade in C major for string orchestra was his first work on American soil. It was the result of a series of evening classes taught by Balanchine at the School of American Ballet in New York, which had been started shortly before by the writer and patron Lincoln Kirstein and Balanchine himself. The piece's choreography depended on how many pupils turned up on a given evening. Seventeen girls came to the first class; the piece opens with seventeen female dancers on stage. A girl arrived late, another fell over and began to cry; both incidents were incorporated into the piece.

∾ Outline

MOVEMENT I: ALLEGRO

The curtain rises on a tableau of female dancers in blue skirts against a blue cyclorama. Their hands move and they begin to dance. One appears to assume a solo role, but her leaps and turns are followed by others until suddenly the ensemble is still, and the opening tableau is restated. A female latecomer joins the line, and a male dancer enters upstage and begins to walk towards her. The others exit.

MOVEMENT 2: WALTZ
The pair dance together. The other women reappear, and the duetting pair lead them into a group dance.

MOVEMENT 3: ANDANTE, ALLEGRO CON SPIRITO (THIS IS THE FOURTH MOVEMENT IN TCHAIKOVSKY'S ORIGINAL COMPOSITION)
Five women remain. They arrange themselves on the stage and then suddenly rise and dance. A male dancer enters and a duet ensues with one of the girls. She falls, and her companions exit, leaving her lying on the stage.

MOVEMENT 4: ELEGY
A woman leads a man to the fallen dancer. Her hands seem to direct his eyes. The man dances with both women, then faced with a choice, leaves with his original companion (sometimes known as the 'Dark Angel'). The other subsides once more to the stage, and is lifted and carried off by three men.

ᔕ Notes

Serenade is plotless, and (as Balanchine himself has told us) was choreographed in such a way that chance was allowed to play its part. The atmosphere is romantic, and the Dark Angel section has an enigmatic quality which suggests there is more to the ballet than is shown on stage, but in fact the piece is simply the product of a number of notionally Romantic elements – amongst them the long pale-blue Karinska dresses, the elegiac music, and the lunar lighting. Balanchine does not intend us to shape *Serenade*'s pure dance into a narrative: his concern is for the patterns formed by the music, and the business of recreating those patterns in dance. If story-like motifs appear they should be treated like wisps of smoke which have unexpectedly formed themselves into a recognisable shape – brief, beautiful but certain to evaporate. *Serenade* is the most widely performed of all Balanchine's ballets, and is in the repertoire of companies all over the world.

∼ View from the Wings

Over the years, I danced several roles in *Serenade*: the *corps de ballet* as well as two of the three principal female roles. Each time, we had a different expert from the Balanchine Estate to teach the choreography and ensure we danced it to the required standard. The Balanchine Estate was established after Balanchine's death to protect his choreographic legacy and you don't get permission to dance the ballets unless the Estate considers that you're up to it. Once consent is given, the steps have to be taught by a recognised authority to make sure that the work is performed accurately and in appropriate style. Sometimes, a first draft of the ballets is learnt in advance, from the Benesh Notation Score – a method of writing down dance on staves of music – and the final touches added by the visiting teacher. I remember once that the version we had learnt differed so radically from the version the expert brought along that we had to pin up lists of the changes in the wings and revise furiously before each entrance. When I moved on to the principal roles, I danced the bouncy 'Russian' girl and then the more serene 'Angel'. I never performed the *pas de deux*, though, set to the second movement of Tchaikovsky's Serenade for Strings – to my ears, the most danceable waltz of all time.

Concerto Barocco

Three movements. Choreography by George Balanchine, music by Johann Sebastian Bach, designs by Eugene Berman.
First performed (by American Ballet Caravan) at the Theatre of Hunter College, New York, 1941.

The American Ballet was a product of Balanchine and Kirstein's School of American Ballet. In 1935 (a year after the creation of *Serenade*), the company took up residence at the Metropolitan Opera House, but in 1938 it split with the Met over artistic issues, and an offshoot, Ballet Caravan, was formed. In 1941 the original company was reassembled for a South American tour by Nelson A. Rockefeller, and named American Ballet Caravan. Balanchine was its director. *Concerto Barocco*, danced to Bach's Concerto in D Minor for Two Violins, dates from this period.

∾ Outline

MOVEMENT 1: VIVACE
A corps of eight women performs the opening sequence, with the group halving and quartering into duet-pairs as the music demands. As the two violins of the music's title come in, so do the two female solo dancers, who act as the physical echo of the violins' dialogue.

MOVEMENT 2: LARGO MA NON TANTO
The two soloists leave the stage. One returns with a male partner. They perform a lyrical duet which builds towards a series of ever-higher lifts. At the movement's conclusion he slides her repeatedly across the stage, a process from which she elegantly recovers on each occasion.

MOVEMENT 3: ALLEGRO
The full complement of ten dancers respond to the music with a jubilant *ballon* sequence highlit by *entrechats* and by idiosyncratic 'scything' motions of the arms. As the piece ends, the dancers kneel.

∾ Notes
Concerto Barocco, like *Agon*, *Four Temperaments* and others, is one of Balanchine's 'black and white' ballets, performed in

practice clothes before a blue-washed cyclorama. The piece was originally performed in Eugene Berman's richly decorated costumes, but these were dropped in 1951. The absence of costume serves to purify and intensify the work, focusing the attention entirely on the interplay of music and dance. There is no plot to *Concerto Barocco*; as in the Baroque generally, structure and form are all. That said, the piece conjures whole worlds into being; Balanchine ballets are always dense with atmosphere. It lasts about twenty minutes, and is notoriously exhausting (if exhilarating) to perform. The piece is a staple of American companies and is danced all over the world.

Symphony in C
Four movements. Choreography by George Balanchine, music by Georges Bizet, designs by Léonor Fini.
First performed at the Théâtre National de l'Opéra, Paris, 1947.
Balanchine first staged this ballet for the Paris Opéra, where he was guest choreographer, under the title *Palais de Cristal*. Out of courtesy to his French hosts (Serge Lifar, having weathered accusations of collaboration during the war, was the ballet director at the Opéra), Balanchine selected a little-known piece by a French composer. The piece was assembled in a fortnight and in 1948 staged for Ballet Society in New York. Later the same year Ballet Society would become the New York City Ballet, and *Symphony in C* would enter its permanent repertoire.

∼ Outline
The ballet is one of Balanchine's most popular 'institutional' pieces, designed to show off a classical company to maximum, sparkling advantage. It is divided into four movements – *Allegro vivo*, *Adagio*, *Allegro vivace*, *Allegro vivace* – with each movement danced by a separate ensemble. Each of these ensembles comprises a principal male dancer and ballerina, two male and two female soloists, and a *corps de ballet*. At the ballet's end

the full complement of dancers is presented on stage in a final tableau.

∽ Notes

To perform *Symphony in C* successfully a company needs to be able to field four ballerinas of absolute technical assurance but of contrasting types, so that the personality of each movement is properly matched. The heart of the piece, following the sparkling *entrée*, is the *adagio* second movement. The third movement is sharper and ornamented with jumps, and the fourth builds to a high-speed ending. As *Les Sylphides* was Fokine's homage to the spirit of the Romantic ballet, so *Symphony in C* is Balanchine's homage to the spirit of the Petipa years. The piece is entirely and assertively plotless, and any attempt to 'emote' within it works counter to its mood. Successful interpretations, however, treat the piece as much more than a bravura display item. The dancers, rather than meeting the audience's gaze, seem to see beyond the confines of the stage to another place – to the glacial blue-white domain of the choreographer's imagination. Several of the major companies have the piece in their repertoires, with New York City Ballet and (since 1996) the Kirov Ballet offering definitive versions.

∽ View from the Wings

In *Symphony in C*, I was not first or second, but fourth principal girl. Each of the four movements has its leading couple and I made up the final member of the team. This involved waiting for around twenty minutes while the other movements ran their course and then dashing on, all smiles, to dance a firecracker number which was, from time to time (depending on who was conducting the orchestra), a literal race to the finish. It was like being shot out of a cannon, and a huge shock to the system. Whenever you start to exercise, there is an inevitable onset of lactic acid within the first few seconds while the heartbeat gradually gets up to the speed required to pump sufficient oxygen around the body. The only way to do *Symphony in C* without suffering from the sudden flood of lactic acid was to get to the panting stage before I went on. Once, tired of being tired, I resolved to jog in the wings throughout the two movements which preceded mine. Everyone thought I was mad, but it was the best performance of *Symphony in C* that I ever gave.

The Four Temperaments
Five parts. Choreography by George Balanchine, music by Paul Hindemith.
First performed at the Central High School of Needle Trades, New York, 1946.
In 1946 Balanchine and Kirstein founded Ballet Society, the forerunner of New York City Ballet. *The Four Temperaments* was choreographed for Ballet Society the same year, and had its premiere in a hall without a pit, so that the musicians shared the stage with the dancers. The piece was considered by some critics of the day to be cold and unemotional, and its status as a masterwork was not generally acknowledged for more than a decade.

∽ Outline
The ballet is an abstract representation of the medieval theory of the four humours, or temperaments, which were once believed to make up human personality. In ancient Greek thought each of these temperaments – the Melancholy, the Sanguine, the Phlegmatic and the Choleric – was believed to correspond to one of the elements (Earth, Air, Water and Fire respectively).

The ballet starts with a three-part introduction – each part (or 'Theme') in the form of a *pas de deux* – of Hindemith's score. The mood is pensive; several physical motifs are careful-ly developed, and by the third *pas de deux* the music's speed is gathering.

The first variation is for the Melancholic male dancer. His movements are articulate, plastic and considered, but he is Earth-bound, and so abject. He searches for escape, but is imprisoned by his fascination with his own condition. He is joined by two female partners and then by a corps of four further women. The presence of this lightweight but determined-seeming group finishes him off, and he sinks to Earth.

The second variation (Sanguine) is for a couple, in *allegro* duet form. Their steps and lifts are lit with morning bright-ness, hungry and speedy, and four more corps women accompany them. Once again, this latter group is implacable – part kick-line, part ant-colony – and performs as if in response to hard-wired instinct.

Phlegmatic, like Melancholic, is a man of considerable articulacy, but his elaborate designs come to nothing in conse-quence of his intense inward focus. In the introductory First Theme the female dancer has made much play of her feet, now Phlegmatic reworks the motif, lifting his right foot in both hands until it is in front of his face. His foot is his means of expression – the source of his movement – but he is watching it so closely that he has immobilised and all but blinded him-self. He recovers, and dances an idly witty measure in which he is accompanied by a third quartet of women.

Choleric, as her name suggests, is angry. The arms and legs of this solo ballerina cut the air and the entire cast of two dozen gathers on stage to witness the ritual of her fury. Physical and musical themes are restated and finally, tide-like, her anger ebbs, and she draws the elements of the piece together. The finale – couple after couple flying across the stage in soar-ing *grand jeté* lifts – is one of the most exhilarating in all ballet.

～ Notes

The creation of *The Four Temperaments* (a ballet now danced by companies all over the world) represented the turning-point in Balanchine's creative career. *Apollo* and *Concerto Barocco* had preceded it, but this ballet moved beyond neo-classicism to the abstract space beyond. In several respects it prefigures *Agon*. As in the later ballet, Balanchine runs a French courtly theme through *The Four Temperaments*, its gestures distorted and reduced but recognisable nevertheless. The way that Balanchine uses three-dimensional space in *The Four Temperaments* is (as in *Agon*) extraordinary; it is as if the performance area expands and contracts – breathes, perhaps – with the choreography. It is through this manipulation, rather than any kind of dramatic 'performance', that Balanchine expresses the idea of the temperaments. When occupied by the Melancholic and the Phlegmatic dancers, the performance space seems to draw in, like the contracting human spirit. With the reassertion of classical verities, however – and the classical elements of Air and Fire – the same space expands to infinity along the lines described by the ballet's geometry. These are abstract rather than literal readings of the piece, of course, and they are entirely subjective. Watching Balanchine is like peering into one of those eighteenth-century cabinets inlaid with multiple mirrors. The gaze is drawn in a thousand directions, each tiny reflection a window on the infinite. At the same time, glass and quicksilver being what they are, the gaze is confronted with itself. Watching *The Four Temperaments*, the viewer is neatly manoeuvred into a similar interrogative. Am I soaring to the infinite, or am I staring, captivated, at my foot?

Agon

One act. Choreographed by George Balanchine, music by Igor Stravinsky.
First performed at City Center, New York, 1957.
In 1948 Lincoln Kirstein approached Stravinsky with the suggestion that a third Balanchine ballet be created on the theme of Greek mythology, to accompany *Apollo* (1928) and *Orpheus* (1948). Stravinsky suggested the title, which in Greek means 'contest' or 'struggle', but finally decided to base his music on a seventeenth-century suite of French court dances. The composition – highly modernist by the standards of the

ballet music of its day – brings into play Webern and Schoenberg's twelve-note serial technique. It contains twelve parts divided into three sections, and was created for twelve dancers. Unusually, Stravinsky outlined much of the on-stage action in the score. It was his last creation for dance.

∾ Outline

The first section consists of a *pas de quatre* for four men, a double *pas de quatre* for eight women, and a triple *pas de quatre* for all twelve dancers. A man and two women then dance a *pas de deux*, and the man then dances alone to Stravinsky's interpretation of a *sarabande* (which is only vestigially related to the formal seventeenth-century step). The two women then perform Stravinsky's *gaillard*, and the three are reunited in a modernistic *coda*.

Two men and a woman perform a *bransle* simple (for two men), a *bransle* gai (for solo female), and a *bransle* double (for all three dancers). Once again, Stravinsky's compositions take little more than the rhythms of the old forms.

The *pas de deux* (conventionally structured with *adagio*, variations and *coda*) is the ballet's longest section. At its conclusion three couples enter for the passage known as Four Duos, and are eventually joined by the last four women for the finale (Four Trios).

∾ Notes

The passage above describes the technical skeleton of *Agon*, but this most complex and sophisticated of ballets (the greatest, quite possibly, of the twentieth century) is susceptible to almost limitless interpretation. As its title suggests, the piece is energised by tension. This is sometimes competitive, sometimes sexual, sometimes merely a tension of opposites, and its waxing and waning echoes, in some essential manner, the anxiety and unstillness of contemporary urban life.

Vestiges of formality and immutable order can be seen and heard in the references to the antique dance measures. The extreme degree to which these measures have been reworked, however, along with the non-classical elements in the choreography and the jazzy strands audible in the music, all serve to highlight a sense of slippage. The older order has not altogether vanished, but it has suffered a sea change. The *pas de deux* at the ballet's centre, for example, suggests an unmistakable sexual ecstasy, but it is not positioned within any particular social context; the ballet's other sections seem to stress that all manner of relationships are desirable, and that the courtesies once elaborated in the court dances of France have taken a newer, stranger form. In *Agon*, Balanchine and Stravinsky have scrupulously avoided any sense of resolution; the ballet ends as it begins, with the four men standing facing upstage away from the audience. This, like the women's en masse departure from the stage which precedes it, suggests that the ecstasy of the *pas de deux* should not be mistaken for an event which changes the 'inner order' of the individuals involved.

When watching Balanchine the essential thing is to ask oneself questions to which it is possible to provide answers. Not 'What does it mean?', in other words, but 'What seems to be being said?' What seems to be being said, for example, in the slow, intricately detailed *adagio* section of the *pas de deux* when the man supports the woman's *arabesque* by holding the calf of her leg, and then manipulates her foot upwards behind her, through the *attitude* position, until it is touching the back of her head? Is he physically and metaphorically manipulating her? Are they mutually trusting equals? Is he serving her? Is it possible that all of these things could be happening at the same time? With Balanchine, it is always instructive to ask who, in a given dance-passage, has 'agency'. Who is making things happen? What does this say about the relationship between those present?

One of the things that Balanchine is doing in this erotic but ice-cool duet is referencing the great Petipa ballets that he saw as a young man in St Petersburg. In its minimalist practice costumes and with its pared-back Stravinsky score, *Agon* seems light years away from the Imperial Ballet Theatre, but it is not. *Agon*'s strangely convoluted *adagio* is a logical extension of supported *adagio* passages in ballets like *The Sleeping Beauty*. As in those ballets, we are reminded that courtly behaviour and court dances are often coded in such a way as to render questions of agency subtly ambiguous.

To examine Balanchine's personal life further complicates issues such as these. There is no doubt that by marrying four of his ballerina muses – women over whom he exerted absolute professional control – he was making clear his own preferences regarding relationships and power. But he was also keenly aware of the limits of that power, and of the paradoxical way in which it depended on the consent of all concerned. In 1969, when his infatuation with his last muse Suzanne Farrell became unbearable to her, she simply left, and in Balanchine's works there is often a moment, as there is in the *pas de deux* in *Agon*, when the woman seems to escape the man's grasp – to slip away from him and to continue to dance unsupported.

Agon, par excellence, is the ballet which demands repeated viewing, repeated listening. A vast amount has been written about it by dance academics, but the piece elegantly evades the machinery of analysis. Instead – as Balanchine intended – it shimmers just beyond reach, its meaning vanishing in the face of the direct gaze. Elusive and extraordinary, *Agon* exists in the repertoires of many companies, including Stuttgart Ballet (1970), The Royal Ballet (1973), the Paris Opéra (1974) and Berlin Opera Ballet.

∿ View from the Wings

The first Balanchine ballet I danced, *Agon* brings me close to understanding the connection between music and maths which I've struggled to grasp ever since I read Hermann Hesse's *The Glass Bead Game*. It's geometry brought to life, its stark lines and ever changing groupings reminiscent of mathematical formulae. I danced both of the *pas de deux* in *Agon*: the first, two girls and a boy, when I was relatively new to the company; the second, one girl and two boys, later on in my career. Although Balanchine was choreographing at the same time as Ashton, his style – and the approach required to dance it properly – could not be more different. If Ashton's choreography seems to parallel the pastoral idyll of the English landscape as well as the charming haphazardness of English architecture, Balanchine's reflects America: its space, its aspirations, its brash brightness, the skyscrapers of New York as well as the open plains of the Midwest. The steps are big and are best made bigger: classical ballet keeps the hips, for instance, square and immobile while the legs describe shapes and patterns in the air. In Balanchine, the hips are released from this technical straitjacket. The line of the leg is made longer and a shape, consequently, bigger if the hip follows the action rather than stays resolutely in place. Similarly with the arms: elbows are allowed to straighten and wrists flex, breaking the rounded lines of classical ballet but adding a certain chic to the style.

A Midsummer Night's Dream

Two acts. Choreography by George Balanchine, music by Felix Mendelssohn, costumes by Karinska.
First performed at City Center, New York, 1962.

Balanchine had been choreographing for over forty years by the time he produced *A Midsummer Night's Dream* – his first original full-length ballet. As an eight-year-old, in 1912, he had appeared as an elf in a production of the play in St Petersburg. The piece is set to Mendelssohn's overture and incidental music for *A Midsummer Night's Dream*, the first three movements of his Symphony no. 9 for Strings, *The First Walpurgis Night*, and the overtures to *Athalie*, *The Fair Melusine* and *Son and Stranger*.

∼ Plot

ACT 1

In the forest near the palace of Theseus, Duke of Athens, Oberon and Titania have quarrelled over possession of an Indian child. To teach his queen a lesson, the fairy king dispatches the elf-child Puck for a magic flower. Puck brings the flower and anoints the sleeping Titania. When she wakes, she will fall in love with the first person she sees.

Two mortal couples, meanwhile, are lost in the forest. Helena loves Demetrius, but unrequitedly. Hermia and Lysander love each other equally. In the darkness, the couples have become separated. Observing Helena's plight, Oberon orders Puck to anoint Demetrius with the magic flower. Setting out to do so, Puck mistakenly anoints Lysander, who wakes and promptly falls in love with Helena (by now separated from Demetrius, whom Puck also anoints). Hermia is bewildered by Lysander's sudden abandonment of her, and by the fact that he and Demetrius are now fighting over Helena.

Oberon, meanwhile, has magicked a donkey's head onto Bottom, a member of a troupe of actors. Waking, Titania falls in love with the grotesque Bottom, and invites him into her bower. After a suitable period Oberon releases her from the spell, and commands Puck to separate the warring human couples and to correct the wrongly directed magic. In the morning the couples wake, all suitably enamoured, and a triple wedding is announced by the Duke, who is himself engaged to be married (to Hippolyta).

ACT 2

In the ducal palace in Athens the wedding celebrations are under way. Divertissements are performed for the entertainment of the three couples. When night falls and the humans retire, Oberon and Titania once more hold sway. Reunited, they order Puck to place their invisible kingdom in order.

∿ Notes

Shakespeare's play has prompted several ballet versions. The first were by Petipa (1876), and Fokine (1906); Balanchine's followed in 1962 and Ashton's in 1964. In North European folklore, Midsummer night was the one time in the year when mortals and supernaturals could interact, and it is the resultant overlapping of the real and magic worlds – echoing as it does the relationship between performers and audience in the theatre – which makes the story so compelling. Balanchine's real concern here is love. He presents love in its ludicrous aspect (the *pas de deux* for Bottom and Titania), love lost and found (Oberon and Titania) and at the heart of the Act 2 celebrations, Ideal Untroubled Love (a *pas de deux* for an unnamed couple). The principals – Oberon, Titania, Puck – are all given plenty of opportunity to shine, and there is a brief but dazzling display piece for Hippolyta, who appears in Act 1 as Artemis, goddess of the hunt, and in Act 2 as herself.

In its unalloyed romanticism and charm, the piece is true to the spirit of Mendelssohn's overture and incidental music, and it was this music rather than his affection for the play which inspired Balanchine to create the ballet. He is certainly less concerned with the drawing of character than with the creation of mood (Bottom's companions, for example, are barely glimpsed), and the lovers of Act 1 are essentially animated devices for setting up the enchanted splendour of Act 2, in which (in true Balanchine exhibition style) wave after bravura wave of dancers fills the stage. The ballet has been in the repertoire of New York City Ballet since its creation, and many of the smaller parts (bugs and fairies) are traditionally danced by students of the company's school. Since 1985 the ballet has also been danced by Pacific North Western Ballet.

Liebeslieder Walzer

Two parts. Choreography by George Balanchine, music by Johannes Brahms, costumes by Karinska, decor by David Hays.
First performed at City Center, New York, 1960.

∿ Outline

The decor suggests a private ballroom in nineteenth-century Vienna. A piano stands stage left, and there are four singers. As the music starts, four couples in formal evening dress begin to dance. The piece is plotless, and there is no overt indication as to the relationship between the dancers, but as the piece progresses through the first set of eighteen waltzes, the audience becomes aware of glances exchanged, words whispered, and gazes averted. Sometimes all of the couples dance, sometimes dancers wait at the edge of the floor. For the second part of the ballet the women exchange their satin evening dresses and heeled shoes for tutus and pointe shoes. The ballroom now has no walls, only the night skies. The dancing (to the second set of fourteen waltzes) is more abstract, and the dancers listen to the last song in motionless silence.

∿ Notes

From the audience's point of view *Liebeslieder Walzer* is a demanding piece. More than an hour long, and almost unvarying in tone, it can be a very hard sit for those not mentally prepared for it. Indeed, Balanchine himself conceded as much. 'But I felt I had to do dances set to this music.'

What the ballet establishes with extraordinary potency is an atmosphere. The songs' subject is love, its sweetness and its sadness, and to enjoy the piece as Balanchine intended one must yield to the music's fragrance and the sweep of the choreography and allow them to draw one into reverie. So that when the transfiguration occurs, and the walls of the ballroom are replaced by the starry skies, a kind of logic obtains. 'In the first section,' says Balanchine, 'those people are dancing. In the second section it's their souls.'

Since its revival in 1984 the ballet has been performed on occasion by New York City Ballet. It has never acquired a great following, and a 1979 staging by The Royal Ballet at Covent Garden was unsuccessful, but it is a masterwork nevertheless.

Jewels

Three parts. Choreography by George Balanchine, music by Gabriel Fauré, Igor Stravinsky and Pyotr Ilyich Tchaikovsky. Costumes by Karinska, decor by Peter Harvey.
First performed at the New York State Theater, Lincoln Center, New York, 1967.

Balanchine was inspired to create a ballet around the idea of gemstones when he met Claude Arpels, the jeweller. At the back of his mind was the possibility that Van Cleef and Arpels might be persuaded to bankroll the production, but in the event this did not happen. The ballet grew in scale from Balanchine's original one-act conception until it was full-evening length; it is often known as 'the first three-act plotless ballet'. Each of its three sections (often described in jewellers' language as 'panels') had its own composer: Fauré for Emeralds, Stravinsky for Rubies, Tchaikovsky for Diamonds. Balanchine considered a fourth panel (Sapphires, to the music of Arnold Schoenberg) but finally rejected the idea.

~ Outline

The ballet opens with Emeralds, and a stage washed and glittering in green. The colour relates to the Fauré score, much of which is made up of the composer's incidental music for *Pelléas and Mélisande*. This cryptic tale by Maeterlinck describes a mysterious girl who is discovered by a stream in a forest, and who refuses, even at the point of death, to divulge information about herself. Her affinity with water, however, and the place of her discovery, suggest that she may be a naiad, or water-spirit. The emerald-green set can be taken as a representation of both the forest and the undersea. The panel opens with a *pas de deux*, and an enigmatic solo by the leading woman (perhaps, or perhaps not, the watery Mélisande), which is then 'shadowed' by a woman who appears to be her spiritual deputy. A *pas de deux* and a further *pas de deux* follow, along with dances for the ensemble. The mood of the panel, echoed by Fauré's music and Karinska's medieval–fantastic costumes, is one of dreamy, courtly Romanticism.

With Rubies, the centre panel, the mood fast-forwards a millennium. Balanchine denied that Rubies was about America, or indeed about anything at all other than itself, but Stravinsky's *Capriccio* for piano and orchestra has a definite Manhattan buzz about it. The choreography is arranged to frame a central couple and their *pas de deux*. The ballerina role here is fast and slick, and once again there is a second woman – a rangy, temptress type – and she and the lead couple take it in turns to dance with the ensemble.

Diamonds is set to Tchaikovsky's Symphony no. 3 – his last composition before beginning work on *Swan Lake*. Although she is attended by soloists and an aristocratic partner, the piece isolates its ballerina in glacial, untouchable splendour. Her solo and partnered passages are studded, diamond-like, with classical complexities. Her leitmotif is the *pirouette*. She is a creature of the frozen north, a prefiguration of Odette, perhaps (as the music is to some degree a prefiguration of *Swan Lake*), but a free rather than a bound spirit. At one level, like *Symphony in C*, Diamonds is an elegy for the lost grandeur of Petipa's St Petersburg, but conceptually it refers back to the medievalism of Emeralds. Equine motifs are threaded throughout *Jewels* – the preux chevalier of Emeralds becomes the Broadway cowboy of Rubies – and in Diamonds the ballerina is given a curious pony-step which the US critic Arlene Croce identifies as a reference to the unicorn in the famous medieval tapestries at the Musée de Cluny (which Balanchine visited with Suzanne Farrell, on whom Diamonds was created). The ballerina of the final panel thus becomes both the Unicorn (a symbol of the heart's desire) and the Lady – the virgin in whose white samite-draped lap it lays its head.

More than any other of Balanchine's ballets, *Jewels* was composed around the personae of its original ballerina creators. Emeralds, with its pronounced French inflections, was first danced by the Paris Opéra-trained Violette Verdy (was there ever a greener, more flowers-of-the-forest name?), and Rubies by the petite, brilliant Patricia McBride. Diamonds, meanwhile, was created for the willowy Farrell, with whom (despite a forty-two-year age-gap) Balanchine was in love. Perhaps inevitably, it has been hard to achieve the depth and subtlety of the original performances. *Jewels* is a fragile piece. Shorn of nuance, it becomes a series of overdressed technical exercises, and the Karinska-designed glitter reduces to rhinestone tackiness. In the 1990s the work enjoyed a renaissance when it joined the repertoires of the Miami City Ballet (1992) and the Kirov Ballet (1999).

∼ View from the Wings

Another ballet with two principal leads. And yes, I danced the second. The most memorable thing for me about *Jewels* was a very silly leotard with the merest hint of a tutu – more Folies Bergère than Van Cleef and Arpels.

Who Cares?

Two parts. Choreography by George Balanchine, music by George Gershwin (orchestrated by Hershy Kay), original costumes by Karinska.

First performed at New York State Theater, Lincoln Center, New York, 1970.

Balanchine first heard Gershwin's music in Europe, during his Ballets Russes days. Later he met the composer when he was asked to choreograph the dances for the 1938 film *The*

Goldwyn Follies. Gershwin gave Balanchine a book of his songs, and one day Balanchine started playing them and 'there was no end to how beautiful they were'.

∾ Outline

The ballet is set to song-music composed between 1924 and 1931. The seventeen songs, in order, are as follows: Strike up the Band, Sweet and Low Down, Somebody Loves Me, Bidin' my Time, S'Wonderful, That Certain Feeling, Do Do Do, Lady be Good, The Man I Love, I'll Build a Stairway to Paradise, Embraceable You, Fascinatin' Rhythm, Who Cares, My One and Only, Liza, Clap Yo' Hands, I Got Rhythm.

∾ Notes

When Balanchine created *Who Cares?*, it was still unusual to set a classical ballet to a suite of show-tunes. Today it is a commonplace, but almost all such productions fail outright. Avid for the razzle-dazzle of Broadway, but constitutionally locked into balletic puritanism (and constrained by a balletic budget), choreographers come up with a hybrid product which plays to the strengths of neither. Balanchine avoided this trap because he knew both worlds well. He had worked on Broadway and he had worked in Hollywood, and had nothing to prove in either. In *Who Cares?* he was not creating show-dances, he was creating classical ballet to show-tunes, and it is as a ballet like any other that the piece must be approached. Choreographically it is witty, fluent and urbane, and Balanchine's moves cleverly underline the music's delicate structural complexity. Visually it is something else. The stage is dominated by a clichéd Manhattan skyline (by Jo Mielziner, 1970) and the costumes (redesigned in 1982 by Ben Benson) are cheap-looking pastels. Maybe some day some healing hand will strip the production back to its bones, and replace Hershy Kay's overstated orchestration with Gershwin's original piano score, but until then this choreographic gem will have to languish in an imperfect setting.

Ballet Theatre and the Other Americans

In 1933, the year before Balanchine founded his School of American Ballet, the Ballet Russe de Monte Carlo visited the United States. The company, headed by a former Cossack officer who styled himself Colonel de Basil and a French art critic named René Blum, was the successor to Diaghilev's Ballets Russes. In various forms, and under various names, this company would return to the USA annually until the outbreak of war in 1939, acquiring a keen coast-to-coast following. Classical dance was not unknown in America before 1933 – several nineteenth-century ballerinas had visited, most notably Fanny Elssler, and Anna Pavlova's company had toured the continent exhaustively in the 1920s – but it was de Basil's company who popularised it.

By 1940, the Ballet Russe had divided into two companies, and both were stranded in America by the war. Europe's loss was the USA's gain. Ballet thrived, and a new company was launched by Michael Mordkin (who had been Pavlova's partner), and one of his pupils, the heiress Lucia Chase. The company was named Ballet Theatre, later renamed American Ballet Theatre, and Chase's fortune would ensure its survival. From the outset the venture was grand-scale, and was able to call upon the services of many of the greatest choreographers of the day, including Fokine, Massine, Nijinska, Balanchine, and the British-born Antony Tudor. To begin with, the company's lead dancers were all former Ballet Russe stars. Soon, however, a generation of American-born dancers emerged – amongst them a young man named Jerome Robbins.

Robbins had danced on Broadway before joining Ballet Theatre in 1940, and was soon performing solo roles. Four years later, aged twenty-six, he choreographed the jazzy and hugely successful *Fancy Free*, about sailors on shore leave (the score was by Bernstein, and the ballet was later made into the musical *On the Town*; Robbins choreographed several musicals for Bernstein, and in 1957 the pair would collaborate on their masterwork, *West Side Story*). Already, American ballet had taken on a distinctly national flavour.

Another significant American presence at the creation of Ballet Theatre was Agnes de Mille. The niece of the famous film director, Cecil B. de Mille, Agnes had trained and performed extensively with companies in London before returning to the USA in 1938. She became Ballet Theatre's resident choreographer, creating *Black Ritual* in the year of the company's formation, and would continue to make ballets for them for the best part of half a century, dividing her attention between the worlds of classical dance and Broadway (amongst other shows, she choreographed *Oklahoma*, *Carousel*, and *Gentlemen Prefer Blondes*). Balletically speaking, her two most important works were the ebullient *Rodeo* (1942), created for the Ballet Russe de Monte Carlo, and *Fall River Legend* (1948) created for Ballet Theatre. Based on the tale of Lizzie Borden, the piece told of how a lonely, small-town spinster came to murder her parents with an axe, and represented a grimly intense coming-of-age for American classicism.

Jerome Robbins continued as a dancer–choreographer with Ballet Theatre until 1946, departed to work on Broadway for a three-year spell, and then joined Balanchine's newly established New York City Ballet as associate director. In the decade that followed he created several ballets for NYCB, including the wry *Afternoon of a Faun* (1953) and *The Concert* (1956), and made occasional appearances as a dancer. Departing NYCB to concentrate on musical and mainstream theatre, he returned in 1969 as ballet-master. A period of intense productivity followed. *Dances at a Gathering* (1969) and *In the Night* (1970) are romantic mood-pieces, tender but sophisticated, and *Goldberg Variations* (1971) is an interpretation of Bach's famous keyboard work.. The 1980s would see further elaboration of Robbins' creative imagination with the urbane, staccato *Glass Pieces* (1983) and *Ives Songs* (1988). Robbins retired from NYCB in 1990 and died eight years later. He was, and remains, America's greatest home-grown choreographer, and a mark of that greatness is the degree to which his oeuvre continues to evade any attempt to define or classify it.

New York City Ballet and American Ballet Theatre retain their complementary but separate identities today. NYCB remains, to a great degree, as Balanchine made it: high-minded, youthful and egalitarian. In it are combined the two great American counter-currents of positivism and puritanism, of austerity and rapture. ABT, meanwhile – as Lucia Chase always intended – is dramatic, starry and pluralistic. There's more than enough room for both of them.

Rodeo
The Courting at Burnt Ranch

Two scenes. Choreography by Agnes de Mille, music by Aaron Copland, decor by Oliver Smith, costumes by Kermit Love.
First performed at the Metropolitan Opera House, New York, 1942.

Rodeo was commissioned from de Mille by the Ballet Russe de Monte Carlo. The company had moved to New York as a result of the war in Europe (it would never return), and *Rodeo* was presented as a novelty piece of Americana. In 1950 it was remounted by Ballet Theatre, its classic status grew, and the ballet has remained in the repertoire of American companies ever since.

∾ Plot

The ballet is set on a ranch in the American south-west in around 1900. It is Saturday afternoon, and the weekly rodeo is about to begin. The tomboyish Cowgirl wants to join in, but the ranch-hands won't let her, because she is a girl. The rodeo begins, attended by a bunch of city girls, whom the cowboys vie to impress. The Champion Roper shows off his skills with a lasso. The Cowgirl tries to join in, partly to impress the

Head Wrangler, to whom she is attracted, and partly to emphasise her difference from the 'soft' city girls. But she is thrown by her bucking bronco, and everyone laughs at her. Evening falls. The Head Wrangler is eyeing up the Rancher's Daughter. The Cowgirl is in despair. She can't fit in with the men, and she doesn't want to fit in with the women. A traditional square dance begins, but she doesn't join in.

Later that evening, there is a hoe-down at the ranch. The only person not having a good time is the Cowgirl. The Champion Roper asks her to dance, and suggests she smarten herself up – she's still in her dusty rodeo pants – but she rebuffs him. He tries again, and seems to be cheering the Cowgirl up, when the reappearance of the Head Wrangler and the Rancher's Daughter upsets her. She runs out, and the dances continue. When the Cowgirl reappears, she is wearing a bright red dress. Her entry grabs the attention of all present. She and the Champion Roper begin a show-stopping hoe-down. The Head Wrangler makes a move for her, but the Champion Roper dazzles her with a tap dance, and kisses her hard on the lips. Amazed, the Cowgirl wakes to the realisation that the Champion Roper is the man for her.

~ Notes

In the original Ballet Russe production, Agnes de Mille danced the role of the Cowgirl herself. For an independent and creative woman in a man's world (as the world of classical choreography remains to this day) *Rodeo* was very much a personal statement. Its subject, de Mille wrote frankly, was 'how to get a suitable man'. Some feminist critics have deplored the way that the Cowgirl is shown as someone whose individuality is freakish and who has to be kissed into conformity, but such readings ignore the piece's almost Jane Austen-like irony. The Champion Roper is in his way as non-conformist as the Cowgirl (a tap-dancing cowboy!) and he is the only man who finds her attractive in her tomboy guise. He will, we guess, allow her to retain her individuality at the same time as answering her dream of love, and is therefore 'a suitable man' in the de Mille mould. Historically, the ballet is of interest because of its all-American subject. By incorporating folk-motifs like lariat-twirling and square-dancing, it helped define a classicism with its roots in American rather than Russian soil. First and foremost, however, *Rodeo* has survived because it is a fine romantic comedy, and a terrific vehicle for a dynamic dancer–actress. It is performed today by American Ballet Theatre and other US companies.

Fall River Legend

One act. Choreography by Agnes de Mille, music by Morton Gould, decor by Oliver Smith, costumes by Miles White.
First performed at the Metropolitan Opera House, New York, 1948.

The ballet is based on the real-life case of Lizzie Borden, who was accused of hacking her father and stepmother to death with an axe in 1892. As the ballet's title suggests, the story occupies an enduring place in the American consciousness. Making a possible murderess the subject of a ballet, and freely reworking her story in the process (in reality, Lizzie was acquitted of the double killing), was a characteristically audacious move on de Mille's part.

∼ Plot

Lizzie is standing by the gallows with the pastor, waiting passively for sentence of death to be carried out. Her life passes before her: a contented childhood in a small Massachusetts town shattered by the death of her beloved mother; her father's remarriage to the baleful stepmother, who persecutes her; the short-lived escape that she discovers in an extreme fundamentalist church; and finally – the moment that drives her to murder – when the stepmother scares away Lizzie's admirer by telling him that Lizzie is deranged. With the slaughter done, and the couple dead, Lizzie communes with the spirit of her dead mother. Before her, at the gallows, the townspeople pass curiously by. The pastor gives Lizzie what spiritual encouragement he can, and she is hanged.

∾ Notes

Fall River Legend is not, on the face of it, the most optimistic of ballets. But it is intensely dramatic, and Morton Gould's score does the dark subject matter full justice. As in *Rodeo*, the piece's heroine (or anti-heroine, or victim) is a misunderstood female outsider who is oppressed by the claustrophobic restraints of a small, conservatively minded community. Lizzie, like the Cowgirl of *Rodeo*, longs for love. When she is frustrated in this dream, and sees her last hope of escape evaporate, she becomes the deranged creature of the step-mother's accusations, and resorts to murder. De Mille makes the story's grim denouement seem predestined; at one point Lizzie raises an axe to chop logs, and her father and the step-mother exchange prescient glances. Structurally, and in its bleak humour, fatalistic tone and reliance on flashback, the piece owes much to early film noir (a similar mood would be striven for a half-century later by Mats Ek, whose *Carmen* opens with Don José standing before a firing squad, and ends with a fusillade of shots). *Fall River Legend* remains in the repertoire of American Ballet Theatre. It was revived for Dance Theatre of Harlem in 1983, and for Birmingham Royal Ballet in 1994.

Dances at a Gathering

One act. Choreography by Jerome Robbins, music by Frédéric Chopin, costumes by Joe Eula.
First performed at the New York State Theater, Lincoln Center, New York, 1969.

Dances at a Gathering started as an idea for a simple *pas de deux* for Patricia McBride and Edward Villela of New York City Ballet. Rehearsals started, and Robbins decided to add two more couples. The process gathered momentum, and soon he was working with five men and five women. As Balanchine did with *Serenade*, Robbins introduced a random element to the choreography, building the ballet on whichever of the dancers happened to be free from other rehearsal and performance commitments on a given day.

◇ Outline

The piece is plotless, but relationships clearly ebb and flow between the dancers – often in response to Thomas Skelton's lighting score. Dancers change partners regularly, illustrating the constantly changing nature of the relationships existing between them. As the choreographic process unrolled, Robbins told the American critic Edwin Denby in 1969, he began to feel that the dancers 'were all connected by some underlying sense of community'.

The eighteen Chopin pieces that make up the ballet's score are as follows: Mazurka, op. 63, no. 3, Waltz op. 69, no. 2, Mazurka op. 33, no. 3, Mazurka op. 6, no. 4, Mazurka op. 7, no. 5, Mazurka op. 7, no. 4, Mazurka op. 24, no. 2, Mazurka op. 6, no. 2, Waltz op. 42, Waltz op. 34, no. 2, Mazurka op. 56, no. 2, Etude op. 25, no. 4, Fourth Waltz op. 34, no. 1, Etude op. 25, no. 5, Etude op. 10, no. 2, Scherzo op. 20, no. 1, Nocturne op. 15, no. 1.

Until the final section, there are never more than six dancers on stage at once. During the Nocturne, however, all ten dancers appear. One touches the ground. They all watch the air intently, and then gradually leave the stage.

◇ Notes

In using Romantic music by Chopin, Robbins wanted to make a particular point. 'It is a revolt,' he said 'against the faddism of today'. By 'faddism', he meant the post-modern experiments of the Judson Church movement, which he felt were running counter to the spirit of the age, which was one of love, rather than disconnection. It is in the mystical light of late-1960s America, then, that this piece should be viewed, and the men's high boots and open shirts reflect the hippie fashions of the day. This does not mean, however, that *Dances at a Gathering* is sappy in any way, or an expression of hippie sentimentality. It is elemental and sweet-natured, but Robbins being Robbins, it is also satisfyingly precise in its construction. Much is unexplained, like the dancers' concerted upward gaze at the ballet's end, but nothing is wasted. Robbins described *Dances at a Gathering* as 'a Chekhov evening', and dedicated the piece to the lighting designer Jean Rosenthal, who died shortly before the premiere. The ballet was revived for The Royal Ballet in 1970, and the Paris Opéra Ballet in 1991.

In the Night

One act. Choreography by Jerome Robbins, music by Frédéric Chopin, costumes by Joe Eula.
First performed at the New York State Theater, Lincoln Center, New York, 1970.

In the Night, choreographed by Robbins for New York City Ballet the year after *Dances at a Gathering*, also uses music by Chopin (Nocturnes op. 27, no. 1; op. 55, nos 1 and 2; op. 9, no. 2) and a Thomas Skelton lighting score, and is regarded as a companion piece to the earlier ballet. Shorter and more overtly passionate, *In the Night* is set for three couples against a starlit cyclorama. It is danced by a number of companies including The Royal Ballet (1973), the Australian Ballet (1985), and the Paris Opéra Ballet (1989).

The English Tradition: Early Years

The English ballet was born of the efforts of two determined women, both of whom danced for the Ballets Russes. The first of these was Marie Rambert. A Polish-born dancer, she was engaged by Diaghilev in 1912 to help Nijinsky with the problematic rehearsals for *The Rite of Spring*. She joined the *corps de ballet* for a season, and then in 1914 moved to London, where in 1920 she opened her own school. A small performance group was born, and in 1926 a twenty-year-old student named Frederick Ashton created his first ballet for them – *A Tragedy of Fashion*. Ballet Rambert (as the group was eventually named) would never be more than a small touring company, but its indomitable, bullying founder would nurture several important choreographic careers. Apart from Ashton, the most important of the early Rambert choreographers was Antony Tudor, who in *Jardin aux Lilas* (1936) and *Dark Elegies* (1937) established the new genre of the psychological ballet.

In 1926, the year that Rambert showed *A Tragedy of Fashion*, another former Diaghilev dancer, Ninette de Valois, began producing ballet evenings in London. In 1931 de Valois was invited to establish a dance company and school at the newly rebuilt Sadler's Wells Theatre. The Vic-Wells Ballet took root, and by 1935 the sixteen-year-old Margot Fonteyn was dancing her first ballerina roles. The company's pre-war repertoire was built on St Petersburg classics reproduced from the notation brought out of Russia by Nicholas Sergeyev, and new works like *Les Rendezvous* (1933) and *Apparitions* (1935) by Frederick Ashton (who had by now parted company with Rambert to become de Valois's chief choreographer). The combination, as de Valois intended, was a happy one. While the Petipa ballets set the seal on the company's classicism, Ashton imbued the company and its dancers with a uniquely English wit, restraint and lyricism.

Les Rendezvous

One act. Choreography by Frederick Ashton, music by
Daniel Auber, designs by William Chappell.
First performed at Sadler's Wells Theatre, London,
1933.

Les Rendezvous was Ashton's first substantial classical work, and
was choreographed to show off the wit and brilliance of Alicia
Markova, then the company ballerina, and the extraordinary
technical accomplishment of the Polish phenomenon Stanislas
Idzikowski, who had danced with Markova in the Ballets
Russes. The nineteenth-century music by Auber was found
and arranged by Constant Lambert, the company's inspired
musical director (and for many years Margot Fonteyn's lover).

∼ Outline

The set evokes romantic parkland of the Regency era; the
mood is carefree and pastoral, suggesting the chance meeting
of a group of attractive young people. The ballet begins and
ends with ensemble dances (the *entrée des promeneurs* and the
sortie des promeneurs), and these frame a female *pas de quatre*, an
adagio duet and variations for the principal couple, a *pas de
deux* and a male *pas de six*.

∼ Notes

Like many of Ashton's works *Les Rendezvous* has a rose-
petalled, lighter-than-air quality about it, but it is far more
than just a romantic trifle. Ashton's brilliance lay in his ability
to bring classicism to vivid, sensuous life. The opening
sequence of *Les Rendezvous*, in which two party-dressed female
dancers interrupt their diagonals of *grand jetés* to exchange
affectionate air-kisses, gives the flavour of the piece. The
classicism is impeccable, but Ashton's wit makes it sing. By
means of quirky, naturalistic detailing and a fleeting economy
of gesture – the turn of a wrist, the inflection of a glance, the
tilt of a chin – he gives his dancers, and especially his female

dancers, character and back-story. When he was a thirteen-year-old boy in Peru, Ashton saw Anna Pavlova dance, and in her biography of Ashton (*Secret Muses*, 1996) the English writer Julie Kavanagh describes how 'all 'the carry-on' with her hands and eyes, never left him: every ballerina role he would go on to create was done so in the shadow of his muse'. *Les Rendezvous* is also an early example of an Ashton 'geometric' ballet, with entries, exits and corps patterns drawn with a fluent delicacy which recalls Petipa. Ashton's fascination with linear form would be brought to a peak of sophistication in *Scènes de Ballet* (1948). *Les Rendezvous* joined the repertoire of American Ballet Theatre in 1980 and was revived by The Royal Ballet in 2000.

Jardin aux Lilas
Lilac Garden
**One act. Choreography by Antony Tudor, music by
Ernest Chausson, designs by Hugh Stevenson.
First performed at the Mercury Theatre, London, 1936.**
The idea of a ballet set in a moonlit lilac garden came from its designer, Hugh Stevenson, who had created a painting of just such a scene and persuaded Tudor to use it as both his setting and his conceptual point of departure. As a *ballet psychologique*, in which its characters' interior monologues were played out in dance, the piece represented a radical new departure. The costumes seem unremarkable today, but when Tudor dressed his characters in the long evening gowns of the Edwardian era ('real' costumes) and then had them bare their emotions, he shocked early audiences of the piece – especially in the intimacy of the tiny Mercury Theatre.

∿ Plot
The narrative element of *Jardin aux Lilas* is effectively described by the titles given by Tudor to the four principal characters: Caroline the Bride-to-be, Her Lover, The Man

She Must Marry, and An Episode in his Past. The piece opens with Caroline and her fiancé discovered in the garden. Their body language makes it clear that there is no love between them, and that this is to be a marriage of convenience. As other guests enter and exit, they frustrate any attempt at real communication between the four protagonists. The fiancé's mistress and Caroline's lover come face to face, but the mistress is only interested in one man, and it is not this one. Her response is cold, and when the guests have regrouped and Caroline unknowingly greets her, it is colder still.

Caroline and her lover constantly strive to be alone together, but whenever they try to express their feelings they are interrupted by other guests, whose buoyant mood contrasts painfully with their own. Impossibly, the mistress arrives, and the three of them perform a strained trio, within which Caroline and her lover exchange charged touches and glances. With the mistress borne away by other guests, her lover exits, leaving Caroline to dance a desperate solo. Her lover returns and they manage an embrace, but hearing approaching footsteps, Caroline rushes off. She reappears dutifully to join a formal ensemble dance.

For the first time, the mistress and the fiancé dance together. Their duet is taut and inhibited, but not passionless. Caroline and her lover manage a further rendezvous but they are discovered, and Caroline is comforted by an older woman. A loveless marriage, the woman seems to suggest, is the lot of all women of their elevated caste. With increasing abandon, the two couples whom fate has separated seek each other out. They dance as a foursome, the rejected lovers shadowing the engaged couple, until finally Caroline is led from the garden by her husband-to-be, and the other guests depart.

∾ Notes

Lilacs, which bloom in the springtime, are a symbol of rebirth, of new life after winter's snows (hence the spirit of hope embodied in the Lilac Fairy in *The Sleeping Beauty*).

Here, of course, with all of the four protagonists victims of a society which places the observance of social convention above the feelings of the individual, their fragrant presence is sharply ironic. In *Jardin aux Lilas* Tudor presents us with a piece which is both more and less than a tragedy. Caroline, when all is said and done, is marrying her fiancé because she has elected to – presumably because only through an advantageous marriage can she continue to live as a lady of leisure. There is no suggestion throughout the ballet of compulsion. Nor, for all her wretchedness, does it ever occur to her that the marriage should not take place. By the same token we see from the bearing of the mistress that she is the outsider in this privileged gathering. Marriage to her is out of the question for someone of Caroline's fiancé's caste – assuming, that is, that he wishes to continue living in 'society'. The tragedy of Caroline and her Bridegroom-to-be is not that they are entering a loveless marriage: their tragedy is that they have chosen to.

Tudor's subtly muted choreography makes this abundantly clear. In a key moment of the ballet, towards the end, when it seems that both couples' secrets are finally out in the open, the action freezes. The music plays on, but no one moves. Slowly, Caroline seems to come to life, stepping away from the tableau to extend a yearning hand to her lover. It seems, for a long hopeful moment, that her decision is to be reversed. But slowly, reversing her steps, she returns voluntarily to the group – to society, in other words – and is subsumed.

In an ideal evening of ballet, *Jardin aux Lilas* would be performed alongside Agnes de Mille's *Rodeo*. Tudor and de Mille were both protégés of Marie Rambert, they were friends as well as colleagues, and both ballets addressed the subject of female autonomy at the turn of the twentieth century. That the dewy, repressed Caroline is swooning helplessly in the moonlight at the same moment that de Mille's yee-haw Cowgirl is kicking up a storm in the hoe-down and helping herself to the man of her choice says much about the contrast between the Old and the New World. An interesting footnote to Tudor's ballet is the fact that the choreographer was the lifelong partner of Hugh Laing, the original interpreter of the role of Caroline's lover. Their relationship was public, and probably known to many early audience members. *Jardin aux Lilas* has been revived all over the world, most recently for the Kirov Ballet (1991).

Dark Elegies

One act. Choreography by Antony Tudor, music by Gustav Mahler, designs by Nadia Benois.
First performed at the Duchess Theatre, London, 1937.
Dark Elegies was the last piece that Tudor choreographed for Ballet Rambert. He left the company that year, was involved in several brief touring ventures, and in 1939 departed for the United States (at the recommendation of Agnes de Mille) to become one of the resident choreographers of Ballet Theatre. He would spend most of the rest of his life in the United States.

∽ Outline

The piece is set to Mahler's *Kindertotenlieder* (*Songs on the Death of Children*), and the set shows a rough-hewn, inhospitable landscape. As an on-stage baritone sings, a group of men and women perform a dance of mourning for their children following some unspecified calamity. As the dancers express the agony of their loss, they lay the foundations for their ultimate acceptance of it.

∽ Notes

Tudor was the first choreographer to work with music by Mahler, widely thought to be 'un-choreographable' (the next significant interpreter of the composer's work would be Kenneth MacMillan, almost thirty years later). The ballet is a potent example of the choreographer's expressionistic style, in which naturalistic movements were combined with the classical vocabulary to produce an articulate, heartfelt language of the feelings. In the words of Jerome Robbins, who danced for him at Ballet Theatre, Tudor 'conveyed through movement emotions that could not be put into words'. *Dark Elegies* has been revived by many companies, most recently by the San Francisco Ballet (1991) and (in a version without pointe work) by the Limón Company (1999).

Checkmate
One act. Choreography by Ninette de Valois, libretto and music by Arthur Bliss, designs by Edward McKnight Kauffer.
First performed at the Théâtre des Champs-Elysées, Paris, 1937.

As war loomed in Europe, the young Vic-Wells Ballet under the directorship of de Valois was going from strength to strength. Until 1935, when they left to found their own company, the stars of the Vic-Wells were Anton Dolin and Alicia Markova. Thereafter their places were taken by Robert Helpmann and Margot Fonteyn. De Valois produced several important ballets for her fledgling company, including *La Création du Monde* and *Job* (1931), *The Rake's Progress* (1935), and *The Gods Go A-Begging* (1936). *Checkmate* was created for the company's first Paris season in 1937.

∼ Plot
In a short prologue, the figures of Love and Death are seen at a chessboard. Their battle will determine the destiny of the pieces they control.

The Red Pawns and Knights assemble; the Black Knights' entry heralds the arrival of the Black Queen. Through her power she bewitches one of the Red Knights. The retinue of the Red King then makes its appearence in the form of the stately Bishops and the implacable Castles. The frail Red King and his Queen enter.

The Black pieces launch a tactical assault on the Red

position and soon pin down the enfeebled Red King. Check. Various of his subjects attempt to defend him, but without success, and the Red Queen is taken. The last line of defence is represented by the Red Knight, but his counter-attack is fatally compromised by the fascination which the Black Queen exerts over him. Given the chance to kill her, he stays his sword-arm, and having hesitated, is quickly cut down himself and borne from the field of battle. The imperious Black Queen now controls the board. Humiliated, the Red King retreats to his throne, where he mounts a final impotent stand, but the Black Queen ruthlessly dispatches him. Checkmate.

∼ Notes

Given the date of its creation it is tempting to read references to Nazi Germany into de Valois's choreography, but there is no reason to suppose that she intended any. *Checkmate* remains a fascinating period piece, nevertheless, not least because of Bliss's score (his first for ballet) and McKnight Kauffer's arresting designs.

The Ashton Era

After the Second World War, Ninette de Valois's company (by then renamed the Sadler's Wells Ballet) opened in a new home – Covent Garden – and Frederick Ashton's choreography entered a new phase. His first ballet for the new house was *Symphonic Variations* (1946), a plotless work whose luminous, transcendent quality swiftly identified it as a masterpiece. Like *Scènes de Ballet*, which followed two years later, *Symphonic Variations* proved to British audiences what Balanchine's work had proved to the Americans: that classical dance could stand alone, unsupported by narrative.

In 1956, by royal charter, and in recognition of its status as a world-class ensemble, the Sadler's Wells Ballet was renamed The Royal Ballet. By then, Ashton was the company's associate director. In this middle period of his career, between the war and the 1960s, his principal muse remained Fonteyn. She was by no means a technically perfect dancer, but she embodied the qualities that he valued most in a ballerina: lyricism, *tendresse* and instinctive musicality. This period culminated in 1958 with the creation of *Ondine*, a ballet described as a 'concerto for Fonteyn'. In the 1960s and 1970s a new generation of Royal Ballet dancers including Anthony Dowell and Antoinette Sibley claimed Ashton's attention, and for these he created the works that represent the 'English' style in its purest distillation. Witty, poignant, and exquisitely light of touch, ballets like *La Fille Mal Gardée* (1960) and *The Dream* (1964) demanded unprecedented levels of technical finesse and dramatic refinement.

In 1961 a twenty-four-year-old dancer named Rudolf Nureyev made headlines when he defected from a Kirov Ballet touring party in Paris. Soon the young Russian was partnering Fonteyn at Covent Garden, rejuvenating her fading career and, by dint of his extraordinary magnetism, raising the stakes for male dancers everywhere. The oppositional

tension that was so evident between Nureyev and Fonteyn –
he so pantherine and devouring, she so elusively refined – was
reflected in Nureyev's long and uneven relationship with The
Royal Ballet. He blazed at Covent Garden – arrogantly mas-
culine in an environment which, in artistic tone, was essentially feminine – but unlike the brilliant and androgynous Anthony
Dowell, he never looked at home there. In 1963 Ashton
choreographed *Marguerite and Armand* for Nureyev and
Fonteyn. It is a beautiful piece but a short one, and notable for
the fact that in a period of creativity at The Royal Ballet
unsurpassed before or since, it is the only work of significance
created on Nureyev.

Rudolf Nureyev's most important contribution to dance
was as an inspirational performer, teacher and producer of the
Petipa classics. Having performed and memorised many of
these in Leningrad before his defection, he painstakingly
reconstructed them for companies in the West. These productions included *La Bayadère* (Act 3) and *Raymonda* (Act 3)
for The Royal Ballet, *Swan Lake* and *Don Quixote* for the
Vienna State Opera, *Sleeping Beauty* for the National Ballet of
Canada, *The Nutcracker* for the Royal Swedish Ballet, and a
full-length *La Bayadère* for the Paris Opéra.

Ashton learnt much from Petipa, and particularly from the
formal perfection of *The Sleeping Beauty*, and in the 1930s
he also worked in commercial theatre, composing dance-
numbers for revues. This broad base gave him a mastery of
balletic structure and geometry, displayed in its purest form in
the icily chic *Scènes de Ballet*. Like many of Ashton's works, this
has bitter-sweet undertones, and is haunted by a sense of loss.
A similar strain imbues his last great work, *A Month in the
Country* (1976). Like his *Enigma Variations*, made eight years
earlier, Ashton's treatment of the Turgenev story is a masterpiece of compression. A few brief steps and gestures, and his
subjects and their emotions are laid bare.

The late Ashton era (during which Kenneth MacMillan
also produced many of his greatest works) was The Royal
Ballet's golden age, just as the late periods of Petipa and

Balanchine represented the golden ages of their respective companies. In ballet-historical terms, there are preconditions for such times. They are born of unanimity, of companies submitting themselves at every level to an overriding artistic vision. Since the birth of English ballet Ashton had provided that vision, and when he died in 1988 he left behind him a body of work which ranks with the finest works of art – in any medium – of the twentieth century.

Symphonic Variations
One act. Choreography by Frederick Ashton, music by César Franck, designs by Sophie Fedorovitch.
First performed at the Royal Opera House, Covent Garden, 1946.

'I am frankly bored with too much characterisation in ballet,' said Ashton shortly after the war. 'I would personally prefer to see somebody moving beautifully and expressing nothing but 'line', than all the characterisation in the world.' *Symphonic Variations* is an uncompromising expression of this belief. Originally, according to Ashton, the piece was 'very complicated, with lots of people and a sort of seasonal theme'. An injury to principal dancer Michael Somes, however, caused a two-month postponement of the opening night. This gave Ashton the chance to revisit the choreography, and the result was a radical paring down to essentials.

∼ Outline
Three women and three men are discovered on stage in a meditative pose. In response to the piano's entry, the women begin to dance. One of the men steps forward, and in an echo of Apollo and the Muses in Balanchine's ballet, dances with the women in turn before allowing them to twine around him. The cast dance in different combinations; one of the flanking men dances a variation, followed by the principal woman. The principal couple dance a cool, lyrical *pas de deux*. As the music builds, the choreographic structures form and re-form

with increasing pace and momentum until all subsides, and the dancers restate the opening tableau.

∼ Notes

Ashton described *Symphonic Variations* as 'a kind of testament'. The war, during which he was drafted into the RAF, had given him ample time for reading, and he had immersed himself in books by St John of the Cross, St Teresa of Avila and other mystics. Franck's music also has a sense of the mystical, and the ballet's physical stillnesses and overall serenity were intended to echo what St John of the Cross calls the 'inward peace' of the soul. The set, a luminous green cyclorama inscribed with looping parabolas like the contour-lines on a map, evokes the English countryside in spring (for Julie Kavanagh, Ashton's biographer, this linking of classicism, covert religiosity and English landscape recalls T. S. Eliot's 'Little Gidding'). In choreographic terms the piece is quietly but persistently inventive, particularly in the partnered passages with their precise, vertiginous lifts. There is tenderness too: in the section where the three women cluster around the principal man like Apollo's muses, each gently reclines her head on the raised knee of the woman in front of her. In *Symphonic Variations* Ashton introduces motifs that would recur time after time in his later work. Low lifts, for example, in which the woman performs flickering airborne beats, often echoed in their turn by fleeting *terre-à-terre* diagonals. Watching the piece – certainly Ashton's greatest work – is to experience an almost tangible sense of peace after war, spring after winter, spaciousness after compression. In the words of the former Royal ballerina Antoinette Sibley, 'it's what heaven must be like.' The work remains in The Royal Ballet repertoire, and has been revived for Dutch National Ballet (1979) and American Ballet Theatre (1992).

∼ View from the Wings

As a member of the *corps de ballet*, you have very little choice about what you dance: you dance everything. You're needed to make up the numbers. But as you rise through the ranks, your repertoire becomes more selective and more appropriate: you're cast in those ballets which best suit your particular skills and style. As a dancer, I was considered to be more suited to MacMillan's, Balanchine's and, later, Forsythe's choreography and I always got on well with choreographers who came in to make ballets from 'outside'. So while, as a principal, I tackled a vast range of ballets by a wide range of choreographers, I danced very few by Frederick Ashton. I was particularly surprised, then, to be cast in Ashton's *Symphonic Variations* and looked forward to taking part in this, The Royal Ballet's crown jewel. Imagine how ungrateful I felt when I discovered that far from finding *Symphonic* the spiritual experience that many dancers reported it to be, I found it an absolute trial. Despite the beautiful music, the serene setting and the lyrical and logical choreography, for some reason *Symphonic* and I never saw eye to eye. As a ballet, it presents an unusual challenge: the six dancers, all principals or senior soloists, have to function as a *corps de ballet*. Yet the choreography is not *corps de ballet* material. Most ensemble dancing has a 'straightforwardness' which allows it to be performed en masse: it takes into account the fact that the dancer not only has to execute the steps well but must also keep a laser-sharp eye on the person next to her to ensure she's absolutely synchronised. Ashton's choreography for *Symphonic* is written for stars, exquisitely individual and idiosyncratic, yet he demands that three women and three men – years after they left the *corps de ballet* – perform it as a team. Perhaps it was this apparent dichotomy which had me foxed.

Scènes de Ballet

Choreography by Frederick Ashton, music by Igor
Stravinsky, designs by André Beaurepaire.
First performed at the Royal Opera House, Covent
Garden, 1948.

Ashton first heard Stravinsky's eighteen-minute score
(composed for a 1944 Ziegfeld revue), when he was lying in
the bath, listening to the radio. The music is sharply elegant –
'like a copy of *Vogue*' according to one critic – and although
the ballet was to be plotless, Ashton specified couture designs
in powder-grey, yellow and black, with diamond bracelets and
chokers and chic little head-dresses (and after a wearying
struggle with Beaurepaire, who was set on modernism, he got
them).

∼ Outline

Scènes de Ballet is set for four men, twelve women, and a
principal couple. Based on the patterns produced by Euclid's
geometric theorems – during the war, in the RAF, Ashton had
developed an interest in classical mathematics – it is designed
to be seen from any angle. As the curtain rises, the principal
male dancer is discovered centre-stage, flanked by the male
soloists. The female ensemble enters, and the female principal,
and a series of dances ensues (technically speaking, a conventionally structured *pas d'action*) in the course of which the ballerina is partnered and displayed by all five men. The
Petipa-derived classical *coda* terminates with an abrupt
flourish as the ballerina, supported by the male principal,
pirouettes into a steeply inclined *arabesque*.

∼ Notes

While Stravinsky's score and Ashton's choreography adhere
to a conventional balletic structure, both are stylised to an
oblique extreme. As Stravinsky's diverse rhythms pulse and
blare (the composer self-deprecatingly described his score as

'featherweight and sugared'), the dancers apply coolly idiosyncratic detailing to their steps. Heads switch and nod, wrists flick, *épaulement* is deployed at unexpected moments. The result is enigmatic. The male principal seems curiously underemployed compared to the soloists, whose elegant (and highly demanding) *tour en l'air*, *grand jeté* and multiple partnering sequences are intercut by languidly decorative groupings as if from a Cecil Beaton fashion spread. As the ballerina performs her icily controlled andantino solo, the four soloists sit around her in the pose of Michelangelo's Sistine Chapel Adam.

There are references here to the Rose Adagio in *The Sleeping Beauty*, and while *Scènes de Ballet* is a purely abstract piece we know from Ashton himself that the twelve-strong female ensemble relates to the number of months in the year and the four soloists to the four seasons. But the final piece has no seasonal resonance. Its bitter-sweet atmosphere is that of the 1930s, and the glamorous world that was swept away by the war. Much of Ashton's work is infused with a sense of the unrecoverability of time, but there is a mysterious quality about *Scènes de Ballet* which makes it much more than an exercise in nostalgia. Revealingly, Ashton claimed it was his favourite piece. 'If God said "you have one left" – that would be it.' The piece remains in The Royal Ballet repertoire and has been revived by several companies, most recently Dutch National Ballet (1992).

∼ View from the Wings

One of my favourite *corps de ballet* roles was in Ashton's *Scènes de Ballet*. Unusually for Fred, who favoured highly melodic and rhythmic music, it was set to a score which wasn't entirely regular and lacked obvious lyricism. I learnt it from my colleagues, dancers who'd been performing *Scènes* for years, and despite its irregular and complex phrases, no one ever counted a single bar. We sang the music and learnt the phrases accordingly. These days, when I hear it taught to dancers new to the company, it sounds like the room is full of people reciting phone numbers. It always worries me that when the dancers get on the stage and hear the music without the counts attached, they'll be completely lost.

Cinderella

Three acts. Choreography by Frederick Ashton, music by Sergei Prokofiev, designs by Jean-Denis Maclès. First performed at the Royal Opera House, Covent Garden, 1948.

Prokofiev completed the ballet's score in 1944 (in Russia *Cinderella* is known as *Zolushka*) and within two years both the Bolshoi and the Kirov companies had mounted full-scale productions. *Cinderella* was Britain's first three-act ballet, and in creating it Ashton risked damaging comparisons with Petipa and accusations that he had overreached himself. In the event, while one critic wrote that 'There is understandably less here for the adult mind than in Ashton's other works', the ballet was an immediate artistic and commercial success, and opened up the way for further new full-evening works.

∼ Plot

ACT I

The storyline follows the traditional fairy tale. The ballet opens in the house Cinderella shares with her father and the Ugly Sisters. The Sisters are sewing a scarf. They quarrel, ignoring their stepfather, and the scarf is torn. Left alone, the put-upon Cinderella dances before a portrait of her dead mother. The Sisters return, the stage darkens, and a crone enters. Cinderella prevails upon her father to give the old woman some money but one of the Sisters snatches it away, so Cinderella donates all that she has – a piece of bread. The crone vanishes and the Sisters' Dancing Master arrives, together with the costumier who has brought their ball-dresses and other service-providers. Despite the predatory attentions of the older Sister, the Dancing Master attempts instruction. Finally, rouged and costumed, the Sisters depart for the castle. Left alone once more, Cinderella dances sadly with her broom, as if with an elegant suitor. The walls seem to dissolve and the Fairy Godmother appears. She dances a variation, as do the accompanying fairies of Spring, Summer, Autumn and Winter. There is an ensemble dance, 'the *Cinderella* waltz', and the magical transformation of the mice and the pumpkin takes place. The Godmother reminds Cinderella, by now dressed in dazzling finery, that she must return by midnight.

Act 2

The ball has started. In the palace gardens a formal dance is under way. The sisters make a preposterous entry: the older grandiose, the younger visibly overwhelmed. They attempt to dance as they have been taught, with absurd results. The Prince enters with four male companions, who dance a *pas de quatre*. A newcomer arrives, and descends the steps on pointe. It is Cinderella, accompanied by her attendant fairies. The Prince, entranced, dances a variation, after which Cinderella and her fairies dance. The Prince and Cinderella dance a *pas de deux*. The Prince presents Cinderella with an orange, a rare fruit in the kingdom, and gives one to each of the Sisters too. Predictably, they squabble. A court dance begins, framing a lyrical duet for the Prince and Cinderella, but suddenly the clock begins to strike twelve. Leaving a slipper behind her, Cinderella flees into the night.

Act 3

Cinderella is at home, asleep by the fire. Waking, she discovers the remaining slipper and realises that the events of the previous night's ball were not just a dream. Remembering the Prince, she dances again with her broom. The Sisters return, exhausted, and exchange stories of their romantic conquests, and how they captivated the Prince. At this point the Prince himself is announced, and enters with the slipper.

Courteously he invites the Sisters to try it on. They do so, but without success. Cinderella is invited to do the same, the slipper fits, and the story is conventionally resolved with the Sisters forgiven. The scene changes to an enchanted garden, presided over by the Fairy Godmother. The Prince's four companions dance with the Fairies of the Seasons and the lovers dance a final *pas de deux*. Royally robed, the couple take ship and sail away.

∾ Notes

Two ballets are struggling to coexist in Ashton's *Cinderella*, and the fit is an uneasy one. The first ballet, a delicate, Petipa-style fairy tale, is magical. The fairy variations, the *pas de quatre*, the lovers' duets, and the big mises-en-scène represent Ashtonian classicism at its most generous and refined. The second ballet, starring the Ugly Sisters, is problematic. The roles of the Sisters were created on Robert Helpmann (the bossy older sister) and Ashton himself (the self-pitying younger one). The result was a series of pantomime sketches which, while legendary in their day, have started to look a little forced and over-busy. Dramatically speaking, they overbalance the production. The Sisters are not so much cruel as infantile, and because we cannot take them seriously as agents of repression, the pathos of Cinderella's situation (and in consequence all of the ballet's potential dramatic tension) is negated. There is also the fact that they are often – bizarrely – played as if a couple of decades older than Cinderella's father. The main Russian version of the story (choreographed for the Kirov Ballet by Sergeyev in 1946, and revised by him in 1964) presents a much steelier pair of Sisters named Krivlyaka (Affected) and Zlyuka (Furious), and this is to the plot's advantage.

Ashton had a signature sequence which he borrowed from Pavlova, and which he superstitiously included, in one form or another, in most of his ballets. In ballet-speak the Fred step, as it came to be known, goes as follows: *posé arabesque, coupé, developpé à la seconde, pas de bourrée, pas de chat*. The

Fred step is clearly visible in *Cinderella*. The Ugly Sisters attempt it (grotesquely) with the Dancing Master, and when they have gone to the ball Cinderella dances it beautifully on her own. Elements of the step also recur in Cinderella's later dances.

Apart from Ashton's, significant versions of the Cinderella story include Rudolf Nureyev's for the Paris Opéra Ballet (*Cendrillon*, 1986, set in Hollywood), Matthew Bourne's production for Adventures in Motion Pictures (1997, set in the London Blitz), and Michael Corder's 1996 staging for English National Ballet and Boston Ballet.

∿ View from the Wings

Cinderella gave me another of the few Ashton solos I danced: the Winter Fairy in the first act. It's a tough solo – exposed and hard edged as an icicle. I loved the opening moments: waiting behind a gauze, centre-stage, as Autumn blustered through her tornado steps, I'd prepare by imagining myself in the frozen north, picturing the arctic plains, hearing the silence which snow makes descend. And then, walking icily towards the audience, a step at a time, gaze unflinching, arms extended . . . the moment of suspense as my left leg closed into a tight fifth position, like the satisfactory clunk of a key turning in a lock. Is the key locking or unlocking? Is it the end or just beginning? It was the beginning: four sweeping circles of the legs, one after the other, which I'm not sure are actually possible to achieve. A hard solo to bring off, but immensely satisfying and I was always buoyed up, however badly or well it went, by the wonderful, lilting score.

Daphnis and Chloë

One act. Choreography by Frederick Ashton, music by Maurice Ravel, designs by John Craxton.
First performed at the Royal Opera House, Covent Garden, 1951.

Ravel's score for *Daphnis and Chloë*, composed for Diaghilev between 1909 and 1912, is one of the greatest pieces of music ever composed for dance. The choreography was by Fokine, but the original ballet was not successful – in part, at least, due to its overshadowing by Nijinsky's *L'Après-midi d'un Faune*, which opened three weeks before it. Ashton never saw Fokine's choreography, but fell in love with the score and reconceived the piece from scratch.

∾ Plot

In ancient Greece, the herdsmen and women present votive offerings to the Nymphs of Pan. Daphnis, a goatherd and Chloë, a shepherdess, vow eternal love to each other, but are interrupted by Dorkon, Daphnis's aggressive rival for Chloë's love. Dorkon proposes a dance contest between Daphnis and himself. Daphnis wins and is rewarded by Chloë with a kiss. With Chloë's departure, Lykanion (a married woman from the town) flirts with Daphnis, and seduces him. Too late, Daphnis sees a band of pirates make off with Chloë. He tries to follow them but is prevented from doing so by Dorkon. In a vision the Nymphs of Pan appear to Daphnis, and promise the aid of the god.

The pirates return to their anchorage. Bryaxis, their chief, is carrying Chloë, whom he later forces to dance, despite the fact that her hands are bound. She does so, but is saved from violation when her captors are seized with a paralysing terror. Chloë's tied hands are mysteriously freed, and Pan manifests himself, scattering the pirates.

At daybreak, Daphnis is discovered in an exhausted state on the sea-shore, and he and Chloë are tenderly reunited. The shepherds and shepherdesses dance.

∾ Notes

Chloë was one of the greatest roles that Ashton created for Fonteyn, and the sense of purity that she radiated has been the ballet's keynote ever since. In this work Ashton sets up a series of oppositions: the virginal Chloë and the libidinous Lykanion (whose sexual abandon is unambiguously portrayed); the gentle Daphnis and the belligerent Dorkon; the devout shepherds and the rapacious brigands. The choreography contains its own extremes, with Chloë's serene classicism set against the barely controlled savagery of Bryaxis and his pirates, and Ravel's impressionistic score perfectly captures the hazy timelessness of the Mediterranean. A major factor in the ballet's success was Ashton and Craxton's decision to costume the ballet in a version of modern dress – gathered skirts for the women, and belted trousers and shirtsleeves for the men. This slyly undercuts the tale's antique pastoralism, and eliminates its remoteness. Craxton's sets, stylised almost to the point of cartoonishness, perform the same function. The Ashton ballet remains in the repertoire of The Royal Ballet; other choreographers who have made ballets to Ravel's score include John Cranko (for Stuttgart Ballet, 1962), Glen Tetley (for Stuttgart Ballet, 1975), and John Taras (for New York City Ballet, 1975).

La Fille Mal Gardée

Two acts. Choreography by Frederick Ashton, music by Ferdinand Hérold (arr. John Lanchbery), designs by Osbert Lancaster.
First performed at the Royal Opera House, Covent Garden, 1960.

The original *La Fille Mal Gardée* was choreographed by Jean Dauberval in Bordeaux in 1789. Dauberval was a pupil of Noverre, and true to his master's precepts created a *ballet d'action*. In place of formal series of steps and measures, he presented lively dances which sprang from the plot, and instead of porcelain shepherds and shepherdesses, offered convincing country characters, born of observation. The ballet has remained popular and been presented in a multiplicity of versions ever since. Ashton was encouraged to create his own version by Tamara Karsavina, Nijinsky's former partner, who had danced Lise in St Petersburg, where it had been revived in 1885 by Lev Ivanov. Ashton agreed, but daunted by the scale of the task, procrastinated until Ninette de Valois forced his hand by announcing the ballet's upcoming premiere.

∾ Plot

In essence, Ashton's scenario follows Dauberval's. Lise (Lisette in the original), daughter of the Widow Simone, a landowner, loves Colas (Colin in the original), a young farmer. Simone, however, has ambitious plans for her daughter, and has set her sights on a match with Alain, the son of a wealthy local vineyard owner.

ACT I

When the curtain rises it is dawn, and the cock is crowing in the farmyard. Lise, searching for Colas, leaves him one of her ribbons, tied in a lovers' knot. The couple meet but are swiftly separated by Simone, who orders her daughter to churn the butter. Colas rejoins her, they declare their love and the butter-churn is abandoned. The other farm girls arrive and call Lise to join their dance, but her thoughts are still with Colas. Observing this, Simone warns her daughter that she must do as she is told. The vineyard owner, Thomas, arrives with his son Alain. The latter, it swiftly becomes clear, is somewhat simple-witted. Thomas asks Simone for her daughter's hand for his son, and Alain capers benignly, trying to impress his prospective bride. Lise is amused but not interested; her heart is spoken for.

It is harvest time, and at the day's end the workers dance in the fields. Alain dances with Lise, but she makes it clear that Colas is the man she loves. When Alain takes it upon himself to perform a turn, he makes such a spectacle of himself that he has to be rescued by Thomas. The two lovers dance, and even Simone joins in, until the celebrations are interrupted by a summer rainstorm.

ACT 2

Simone and Lise, soaked to the skin, return home. To take Lise's mind off Colas, Simone sets her daughter to spinning, and locks the gate. Within minutes, however, she becomes sleepy, and Lise tries to purloin the key. Colas, Lise knows, is waiting for her outside. As soon as Simone is well and truly asleep, she joins him at the gate. Simone is wakened, however, by the hired hands arriving for their day's pay, and returns her daughter to her spinning. Thinking herself alone, Lise muses on the joys of marriage – the clothes that she will wear and the babies that she will have. Colas, who unknown to Lise has been watching this little pantomime, reveals himself – much to her bashfulness and confusion. Once again, they exchange protestations of love. With Simone's reappearence, Lise hides Colas in her bedroom. Simone guesses that Colas has been in the house, and knowing that Thomas is on his way, hurries her daughter into the same bedroom. Thomas arrives with the village notary and a contract of marriage, and when the formalities are complete, Simone hands the hapless Alain the key to Lise's bedroom. He finally manages to get the door open, and out tumble the lovers, by now thoroughly compromised. Their union, Simone concedes, is now a fait accompli, and despite the splutterings of Thomas and Alain she gives them her blessing.

~ Notes

There exists in my imagination a life in the country of eternally late spring, a leafy pastorale of perpetual sunshine and the humming of bees . . . At some time or another, every artist pays his tribute to nature: my Fille Mal Gardée is my poor man's Pastoral Symphony.

So wrote Ashton of this happiest of ballets. *La Fille Mal Gardée* contains no princes or princesses, no fairies or magical transformations – it is a tale of ordinary people. Colas is a lusty young swain, Lise his brown-armed country girl, and together they ensure that love and desire prevail. The gathered harvest – that ever-useful bucolic metaphor – symbolises a ripeness and a sexual readiness which will not be constrained. On top of its sheer charm, the ballet offers a seamless dance narrative. There are no stoppages, just a fluent ribbon of dance invention. Ribbons, in fact, feature considerably in the piece (as they did in Ivanov's Maryinsky version). There is an extended ribbon-dance in Act 1, in which Lise and Colas weave each other into a cat's-cradle, and this leads to a much more elaborate sequence at the harvest celebrations.

The ballet is notionally set in eighteenth-century France, but its character and humour are entirely English. There are folk-dances and a very funny chicken dance, clog-dances and a maypole dance (more ribbons). The character of the Widow Simone is a tribute to the music-hall comic Dan Leno. Alain's signature prop, to which he is obsessively attached, is his umbrella. In a witty sign-off, Ashton ends the ballet with him hurrying back into Simone's house to retrieve it after his rejection by Lise. One of the piece's most appealing sequences is Lise's mime scene, which Ashton took directly from Karsavina's memory of the 1885 Ivanov production. In this Lise (watched, although she does not know it, by Colas) counts out the children she is going to have – one, two, three – tells one off and smacks its bottom, picks another up and rocks it in her arms, and sings gently to the third.

Osbert Lancaster's affectionate designs and John Lanchbery's genial orchestral arrangement both contribute to the piece's good humour. The original score for Dauberval's ballet was by an unknown hand, a later version was by Ferdinand Hérold, and the Maryinsky version by Peter Ludwig Hertel. Given carte blanche to construct a new score, Lanchbery drew principally on Hérold, although the clog-dance is a mixture of Hertel and Lanchbery's own composition. The whole makes for the easiest of listening.

Ashton's is much the most popular contemporary version of *La Fille Mal Gardée*, and has been staged by companies all over the world, but other significant productions include Oleg Vinogradov's for the Maly Theatre, Leningrad (1971), Heinz Spoerli's for the Paris Opéra Ballet (1981), and Ivo Cramér's reconstruction of the Dauberval original for Nantes Opera Ballet (1989).

∿ View from the Wings

Once, on a summer tour in Portugal whilst the company was on holiday, I had the chance to dance the *pas de deux* from the harvest scene in *La Fille Mal Gardée*. Written for Nadia Nerina, the dancing combined Ashton's customary detailed use of the upper body with big, bouncy jumps which exploited her natural elevation and sunny charm. The duet finishes with what is popularly known as a 'bum lift', which is pretty much as it sounds: the woman perches her bottom on the man's hand and he lifts her straight up above his head. She sits pretty, as if she was merely posing on a kitchen stool. Like a trip to the dentist, it sounds more frightening than it is.

More normally, I danced in the *corps de ballet* of *La Fille*, either as one of the many peasants or, later, as one of Lise's friends. As ever, Ashton inserts his hallmark 'Fred step' into the choreography: *posé, coupé, pas de bourrée dessous, pas de chat*. It's a simple, lilting series of steps which travels one way and then the other and takes just four counts to complete. It can be done on any number of rhythms and you'll see it in almost all of Ashton's ballets, danced large, small, fast and slow, in couples, alone and en masse.

Marguerite and Armand

One act. Choreography by Frederick Ashton, music by Franz Liszt (Piano Sonata in B minor), designs by Cecil Beaton.
First performed at the Royal Opera House, Covent Garden, 1963.

Ashton first had the idea of creating a ballet for Fonteyn on the theme of *La Dame aux Camélias* in 1961, after seeing a rehearsal of Alexandre Dumas's 1852 play (in 1853 the story became Verdi's opera, *La Traviata*). It was two years before the idea came to fruition, by which time Nureyev had defected and become Fonteyn's regular partner. For some time the right music for the piece evaded Ashton, until in the spring of 1962 he heard Liszt's piano sonata on the radio. 'Almost immediately,' he said, 'I could visualise the whole thing in it.'

∼ Outline

In the hallucinatory final stages of her illness, Marguerite Gautier – the Lady of the Camellias – remembers her love affair with Armand Duval. Her memories, which take the form of a series of dream-like *pas de deux*, divide into five episodes – Prologue, The Meeting, The Country, The Insult, Death of the Lady of the Camellias.

Dumas's story, from which these episodes are extracted, goes as follows. Marguerite is a courtesan – a kept woman – in fashionable Parisian society. Armand, a young man from a bourgeois family, falls passionately in love with her. Marguerite, secretly sick with tuberculosis, moves to the country, where a confrontation takes place between the jealous Armand and his lover's 'benefactors'. Marguerite agrees to dismiss her wealthy patrons and enjoys a rapturous affair with Armand, but is visited in secret by Armand's father, who begs her to leave his son and save his reputation. Out of love she agrees, and returns to Paris and her demi-mondaine life. Armand searches her out, and their affair briefly rekindles, but Marguerite is now deathly ill. For a second time, mindful of her undertaking to Armand's father, she leaves him. The next time they meet, it is at a fashionable ball. Approaching Marguerite, Armand publicly and contemptuously forces her to accept an envelope of money 'for her services'. As he walks out, Marguerite collapses. Shortly afterwards, abandoned by all the men who have used her, she dies.

∾ Notes

The rehearsal period for *Marguerite and Armand* was a turbulent time. Ashton was bitterly jealous of Nureyev's hold over Fonteyn – a muse whom he had previously thought of as his alone – and hated having to fit his rehearsals into their crowded international schedules. As the piece took shape in The Royal Ballet's studios, and rumours flew of an off-stage affair between the two stars, Nureyev indulged in regular tantrums and treated Fonteyn appallingly, constantly insulting her. The finished work – as much silent theatre as ballet – transmutes these tensions into melodramatic gold. Rapturous embraces, reckless lifts, rippling bourrés, melting surrender. Ashton at the time was much influenced by Alain Resnais's film *Last Year in Marienbad*, and the stylised, not-quite-real performances of the ballet's supporting cast (Marguerite's socialite admirers, Armand's father) strongly reflect the film's influence. The piece was Ashton's only work of substance for Nureyev, and his last full creation for Fonteyn. The pair performed it around the world to great acclaim and many said that it should never be danced by another cast. In 2000, however, The Royal Ballet revived the piece, with Sylvie Guillem inheriting the Fonteyn role.

The Dream

One act. Choreography by Frederick Ashton, music by Felix Mendelssohn (arr. John Lanchbery), sets by Henry Bardon, costumes by David Walker.
First performed at the Royal Opera House, Covent Garden, 1964.

Ashton choreographed this ballet in celebration of the four-hundredth anniversary of Shakespeare's birth. After considering *The Tempest* as a subject he settled on *A Midsummer Night's Dream*, a play he knew well. Ten years earlier he had choreographed a *pas de deux* to the Nocturne from Mendelssohn's incidental music for the play, and he now asked Lanchbery to construct a ballet score from the same incidental music (an Overture and Suite, twelve pieces in all). Rather than condense the entire play, Ashton concentrated the action on the events in the forest. He gave the leading role of Oberon to a then unknown *corps de ballet* dancer named Anthony Dowell, and that of Titania to a rising ballerina named Antoinette Sibley. By the ballet's first night, one of the twentieth century's great ballet partnerships had been born.

∾ Plot

Oberon, the Fairy King, is displeased with his consort, Titania, because she will not give him the Changeling Indian Boy (whom Oberon wants as his page). As the fairies flit hither and thither, he despatches Puck to bring him a magic plant. When the sleeping Titania's eyes are anointed with the plant's juice, she will fall in love with the first creature that she sees.

To the forest come two pairs of lovers: Hermia and Lysander and Demetrius and Helena. Demetrius has fallen out of love with Helena, and Oberon decides to intervene in their lives, ordering Puck to anoint Demetrius's eyes so that, when he awakes, his love for Helena is restored. The feckless Puck, however, anoints Lysander, who promptly falls in love with Helena and abandons Hermia. Oberon then anoints Demetrius's eyes himself, so that both men are in love with Helena. Titania, meanwhile, has awoken and fallen in love with Bottom, a buffoon whom Puck has half-transformed into an ass. To Bottom's mystified delight, Titania invites him into her bower.

At the night's end, wearying of this sport, Oberon releases the various lovers from their enchantment. Titania is shocked to discover that she has been dallying with the oafish Bottom, and in her relief at being reconciled with Oberon, gives him the Changeling. The two restate their love. Bottom, meanwhile, puzzles over the strangely intense dream from which he has awoken.

◇ Notes

The role of Oberon, with its extended *scherzo*, its brilliant footwork and its icily controlled *pirouette* sequences, is one of the most demanding in the male repertoire. Oberon is a king, with a king's pride, and his dancing is as calculated as his revenge on his wilful queen. Titania, of course, gives as good as she gets, and from her first imperious entrance to her final sensuous melting in Oberon's arms we never doubt her royalty. A character-defining moment occurs when Titania realises that she has been tricked into Bottom's embraces, permitting herself a second of wide-eyed and very human horror before the affectless faerie smile returns, and it is as if the incident had never been.

The atmosphere of the piece – prickling, exquisite, not quite human – is established immediately, and carried on the music. As the fairies flit and skim, their *épaulement* and delicately mannered *port de bras* a subtle Ashtonian homage to Taglioni (whom Mendelssohn much admired), the forest glints with unearthly light. Yet this is a very English magic. The fairies are not a faceless Petipa-style *corps de ballet*: they have characters, as Shakespeare intended, and react with dry understated wit to events around them. The human lovers, whose emotional vagaries could have acted as a drag on the action, are given poignant comic business, and the 'rude mechanicals' (Snug, Quince, and company, who could have killed it stone-dead) come and go with gratifying swiftness. The ballet's highlight is the reconciliation duet. Its brilliance lies in the fact that for all its *tendresse* – and Ashton gives the scene a sweet profundity of feeling that Shakespeare only hinted at – we never for an instant think of the royal couple as human. They remain supernaturals, and their love, for all its combative nature, remains a supernatural love. The ballet (which Ashton willed to Dowell, along with *A Month in the Country*) is regularly danced by The Royal Ballet, and has joined the repertoire of several other companies, most recently American Ballet Theatre (2003).

Monotones

One act. Choreography and designs by Frederick Ashton, music by Erik Satie (*Trois Gymnopédies*, *Trois Gnossiennes*).
A short Ashton dance named *Monotones*, to the *Trois Gymnopédies*, was shown at a Covent Garden gala in 1965. The following year Ashton added a second *pas de deux*, which he named *Monotones I*. The earlier section was renamed *Monotones II*, and the two sections have been shown together, in the reverse order of their creation, ever since.

∾ Outline/Notes

The choreography of *Monotones* is of limpid simplicity – a neo-classical statement of Ashton's most fundamental beliefs concerning dance. In it we see his style at its most distilled, expressing, he said, 'nothing but itself, and thereby expressing a thousand degrees and facets of emotion'. According to the choreographer, the *Gnossiennes* dancers (one man and two women in olive-green) are 'terrestrials', while the *Gymnopédies* dancers (two men and one woman in white), are 'heavenly bodies'. That, however, is the limit of the characterisation. There is no trace of a story. *Symphonic Variations* and *Scènes de Ballet* have narratives embedded deep within them, even if only abstract narratives. *Monotones* is glass-clear.

Throughout the ballet, the choreography adheres to the lunar pulse of Satie's music, with the shining lines of the dancers' bodies in constant evolution against inky space. Nothing in it is new; for the most part the ballet calmly states and restates the *attitude* and *arabesque* positions. The groupings and the circling runs are simplicity itself. *Monotones I*, danced by the terrestrials, is the less detached of the two, and its music is marginally less unruffled.

The costumes' vibrant green, in harmony with the *Gnossiennes*' eastern inflexions, suggests the organic world. By *Monotones II*, however, we have moved light years forward, and the dancers move with the calm inexorability of the stars in their courses. There is a sense of displacement, of witnessing something at an infinite remove from human emotion. The work has been taken into the repertoires of a number of companies, most recently the San Francisco Ballet (1981).

A Month in the Country

One act. Choreography by Frederick Ashton, music by Frédéric Chopin (arr. John Lanchbery), designs by Julia Trevelyan Oman.
First performed at the Royal Opera House, Covent Garden, 1976.

A Month in the Country was choreographed after a long period of creative inactivity on Ashton's part. Once he had made the decision to adapt Turgenev's play, a long search for music followed. It was Sir Isaiah Berlin, an expert on Russian literature, who eventually suggested Chopin. The piece draws on the composer's Variations on 'Là ci darem' (from *Don Giovanni*), the Fantasia on Polish Airs, the Andante Spianato and the Grande Polonaise.

∾ Plot

The action takes place in the country house of Yslaev around 1850. It is summer, and for Yslaev's wife Natalia Petrovna, there is little to relieve the long days' torpor. Her husband's friend Rakitin maintains an unrequited passion for her; she finds his attentions sometimes amusing, sometimes irritating. Also present in the house are Natalia and Yslaev's son Kolia, and their ward Vera. A tutor, Beliaev, has been engaged for Kolia. Natalia has conceived an infatuation for the handsome young tutor, but to her distress he seems more interested in Vera. Matters worsen for Natalia when Vera innocently confesses that she is in love with Beliaev, and when Natalia sees what she takes to be a passionate scene between the couple she reacts by slapping Vera. In fact, Beliaev's interest in Vera is purely brotherly, and he secretly reciprocates Natalia's feelings. Their attraction for each other is finally given expression in a *pas de deux*, culminating in a kiss. This is witnessed – to her despair – by Vera. The household, previously so smooth-running, is now in a state of emotional disorder. Misunderstanding the true state of affairs, and under the impression that he is one of the causes of the upset, Rakitin insists that both he and the tutor depart. Beliaev reluctantly agrees, and after a passionate and abandoned farewell, takes his leave of Natalia. Before his final exit, unseen by the weeping Natalia, he pauses, and kisses one of the long ribbons that trail from her robe. He leaves behind a rose that she has given him. A moment later – too late – she finds the rose, and lets it fall.

∼ Notes

In his ballet, Ashton leaves out all but the essentials of Turgenev's original play. This has the desired effect of distilling the action but also simplifies the central characters. In the play, for example, Natalia decides that the best way to separate Vera and Beliaev is to encourage her young ward to marry a much older man whom she does not love, and with Beliaev's departure, the ingenuous Vera does exactly this. Ashton's Natalia is not quite as viciously manipulative as this. She is indolent, jealous, and self-dramatising (as the choreographer himself could be), and her love for Beliaev is essentially selfish. It is still love, however, and for its duration she is transfigured. Ashton's Beliaev, by the same token, is a much less equivocal figure than Turgenev's. He loves Natalia in return.

The ballet, perhaps thirty-five minutes long, is an object-lesson in the construction of dramatic tension. The lethargy and inertia of the opening minutes is so extreme that the search for a key becomes a noteworthy event. Gradually, however, the pace builds. Beliaev's entry is signalled by the wind billowing the curtains. He has a kite for Kolia, a symbol of his association with the elemental 'outside' rather than the airless interior, and of the emotions that he will cause to blow through the household. The theatricality of the final *pas de deux* is intense. Natalia is swooning, gracile and histrionic – a self-aware tragic heroine of the kind that Ashton understood perfectly. It is possible that she was modelled on the Spanish opera singer Pauline Viardot with whom – in the full knowledge of her Yslaev-like husband – Turgenev conducted an extended romance. Choreographically the ballet is full of Ashton motifs, from the 'Fred step' that Rakitin and Natalia perform on their way out to the garden, to Natalia's wafting, heartbroken *bourrées* in the final duet. *A Month in the Country* was a notable triumph for Lynn Seymour, who created the ballerina role, and the piece remains in The Royal Ballet repertoire.

Absent Friends: Tudor and Cranko

In 1939, with the threat of war in the air, the dancer–choreographer Antony Tudor departed Britain for the USA. He had left Ballet Rambert, where he had made his name, in 1937, and in the interim had directed two companies, both short-lived. In New York, thanks to the lavish purse of Lucia Chase, Ballet Theatre was being formed, and Tudor was invited to be one of its resident choreographers and principal dancers. He moved swiftly into his creative stride, and in 1942 produced *Pillar of Fire*, a landmark production in the new psychological genre.

Other works followed for Ballet Theatre, New York City Ballet, and the Royal Swedish Ballet. Inexplicably, however, given his early success in Britain with *Jardin aux Lilas* and *Dark Elegies*, Tudor was ignored by The Royal Ballet. In 1963 he became the director of the Royal Swedish Ballet, and in the same year created the dark, anti-war *Echoing of Trumpets* for them.

In 1967, by now in demand worldwide in consequence of the grace, compassion and emotional truth of his work, Tudor finally returned to London to create *Shadowplay* for The Royal Ballet. His final appointment, in 1974, was as associate director of American Ballet Theatre.

John Cranko was eighteen years Antony Tudor's junior, and arrived in England from South Africa in 1946. Aged nineteen, he had trained at the Cape Town ballet school, where he had also choreographed two early works. Within four years he had stopped dancing but had embarked on a prolific decade of ballet-making for The Royal Ballet and Sadler's Wells companies. The breezy *Pineapple Poll* (1951) is probably his best-remembered work from this time. Commissions from the New York City Ballet, Paris Opéra and La Scala companies followed, and in 1961, following the failure of his *Antigone* (1960) for The Royal Ballet, and a period of turbulence in his personal life, he accepted the directorship of the Stuttgart Ballet.

As for many creative artists before him, relocation spurred Cranko's finest work. In Stuttgart, he took a long-established but faded ensemble and turned it into Germany's leading ballet company. He created more than twenty pieces for the company, of which the best known are the three-act narrative works *Romeo and Juliet* (1962), *Onegin* (1965), and *The Taming of the Shrew* (1969), and made international stars of his principal dancers, Richard Cragun and Marcia Haydée.

In his move to Germany and his embracing of the full-length dramatic ballet, Cranko can be said to have had much in common with his immediate contemporary, Kenneth MacMillan. But his career, undoubtedly one of the most significant of the late twentieth century, was to be cut short. In 1973, returning to Stuttgart from Philadelphia, Cranko suffered a fatal heart attack. He was forty-six.

The Leaves are Fading

One act. Choreography By Antony Tudor, Music by Antonin Dvořak, sets by Ming Cho Lee, costumes by Patricia Zipprodt.
First performed at New York State Theater, New York, 1975.

At the age of thirty, having been ignored by Ninette de Valois, who failed to recognise his talent (and cold-shouldered into the bargain by Frederick Ashton, who disliked him), Tudor effectively left Britain for good. British ballet's loss was American ballet's gain. Except for brief periods in which he worked as director and choreographer for the Royal Swedish Ballet, Tudor would spend the rest of his life in the United States. *The Leaves are Fading* was made for American Ballet Theatre when the choreographer was sixty-six – almost forty years after the creation of *Jardin aux Lilas*. The principal female role was created for ABT's troubled prodigy Gelsey Kirkland.

∽ Plot

The piece opens and closes with a woman moving pensively across the stage, and the elegiac sequences which follow seem to express her memories. From an ensemble of fifteen – six men, nine women – four couples dance expressive duets in turn. The first duet is playful and tentative, the second sees attraction burst into love, the third suggests shared contentment, and the fourth reprises elements of all these emotional states.

∽ Notes

The Leaves are Fading is a delicately emotive piece whose springtime friendships and passions are given an edge of sadness by the suggestion that they are in the past. Airi Hyninnen, who worked with Tudor for many years, describes the work as the choreographer's retrospective look at his own career, with the emotions expressed by the dancers representing Tudor's love for ballet itself, and the fading leaves of the title representing his waning physical and creative powers. The ballet was Tudor's first and last to music by Dvořák. Much of it is set to a chamber piece named *Cypresses*, recalling the fact that this tree is often to be found in graveyards, and is a symbol of sadness. Choreographically, however, no waning of powers is evident. Tudor's classicism is sharply inscribed, evoking love's fears and dangers as vividly as its ecstasies. Even as desire is expressed in a series of rapturous lifts and space-devouring leaps, we sense its finite nature. All changes, all passes. If the piece has a weakness, it is its over-emphatic and over-literal set (bright green leaves!) and its dated tie-dye costumes. These elements, however, do not detract too much from the subtle edge of Tudor's choreography. *The Leaves are Fading* was his last important work. It remains in the repertoire of American Ballet Theatre (for whom Tudor created it) and was revived by The Royal Ballet in 2002.

Onegin

Three acts. Choreography by John Cranko, music by Pyotr Tchaikovsky (arr. Kurt-Heinz Stolze), designs by Jürgen Rose.

First performed at the Württemberg State Theatre, Stuttgart, 1965.

John Cranko was a prolific choreographer, and had created more than fifty ballets when, as director of the Stuttgart Ballet, he turned his attention to Pushkin's verse poem. Cranko had first encountered the story of Evgeny Onegin thirteen years earlier when choreographing the dances for the Tchaikovsky opera at Sadler's Wells, and there is evidence that he had considered using the opera music for a ballet version for Fonteyn and Nureyev at Covent Garden. The General-intendant at Stuttgart considered this score sacrosanct, however, and commissioned Stolze to create an alternative score from other less well-known Tchaikovsky pieces. The sources Stolze drew from include the piano cycle *The Seasons*, the opera *Vakula the Smith* and the symphonic poem *Francesca da Rimini*.

∾ Plot

ACT 1

Tatiana Larina's birthday is approaching, and the family is assembled in the garden. Lensky, a well-born poet engaged to Tatiana's younger sister Olga, arrives with his dilettante friend Evgeny Onegin. The bookish Tatiana quickly falls for the elegant, supercilious young stranger, and that night, sleepless with love, declares her feelings for him in a letter.

ACT 2

It is Tatiana's birthday. The Larina family is holding a ball, and the local gentry are in attendance. Onegin makes no attempt to conceal the fact that he considers the company provincial. He is irritated rather than charmed by Tatiana's letter, and seeking her out, tells her that he feels nothing for her and tears up the letter. Tatiana, distraught, does not notice the attentions of Prince Gremin, with whom her socially ambitious mother is attempting to matchmake her. Bored, Evgeny decides to flirt with the pretty, empty-headed Olga. Ignoring Lensky's visible distress, Olga flirts back. In a paroxysm of jealousy, Lensky challenges Evgeny to a duel. Early the following morning the two sisters attempt to reconcile the two men, but Lensky is unrelenting. The duel takes place, and Evgeny shoots his friend dead.

ACT 3
Evgeny, his life empty of meaning, has wandered the world. Finally he returns to St Petersburg and attends a ball given by Prince Gremin. Presented to his hostess, the beautiful, *soignée* Princess Tatiana, Onegin recognises the country girl he once considered so gauche. His amazement at her transformation turns to a crushing sense of loss. He writes a note to Tatiana, but she refuses to meet him. Making his way to her boudoir, he pleads his love for her. Tatiana is torn between the urgings of passion and loyalty to her husband, but through her distress she recognises the self-centred nature of Evgeny's behaviour. Tearing up his note, she demands that he leave her for ever.

∽ Notes
Every Russian schoolchild reads Pushkin's Romantic master-piece, and Tatiana is undoubtedly Russia's best-loved heroine. Cranko serves her well in his ballet, and she is given ample opportunity to display her passionate character. The ballet's twin peaks are the gorgeously crafted duets at the end of Act 1 and Act 3. In the first of these, in a brilliant *coup de théâtre*, the Evgeny of Tatiana's adolescent yearnings steps from the mirror in her bedroom and sweeps her tremulous form into his arms – what more romantic scenario could be imagined? The second of the great duets, culminating in Tatiana's rejection of

Evgeny, is equally sensuous in its construction. By its end Tatiana's limbs are taut with anguish, her *cabrioles* fluttering in mute despair. Like Ashton, Cranko was a choreographer who passionately identified with his heroines.

While Tatiana is a wonderfully realised character, however, Evgeny is less so. Rather than the complex, narcissistic young man of Pushkin's verse poem, Cranko's Evgeny is an emotional sadist who hurts Tatiana simply because he can (the public rejection of Tatiana and the tearing-up of her letter are Cranko inventions; in the book Evgeny lets her down gently, and in private). Nor are we permitted to know that a large part of the reason for Evgeny's flirting with Olga is to demonstrate to Lensky just how vacuous and faithless she is. These omissions mean that we are considerably less sympathetic to Evgeny when he reappears than we might be. It is in the duel scene, however, that Cranko's vision leads him furthest adrift. His insistence on seeing events through his heroine's eyes means that Tatiana has to be present, and to balance things, Olga too. The women dominate the scene, and their silent-movie histrionics rob it of all dramatic potential.

These shortcomings, however, are largely swept away on the ballet's emotional flood-tide. *Onegin* is a wonderfully entertaining and romantic piece, well served by Rose's sensitive designs and (despite continued misgivings amongst Tchaikovsky purists) Stolze's cleverly constructed score. The ballet has been revived for several companies, most recently (in 2002) for The Royal Ballet.

The Taming of the Shrew

Two acts. Choreography by John Cranko, music by Kurt-Heinz Stolze after Domenico Scarlatti, designs by Elizabeth Dalton.
First performed at the Württemberg State Theatre, Stuttgart, 1969.

The Taming of the Shrew, choreographed four years before the choreographer's early death, was the last of his great trio of works for Stuttgart Ballet, and cemented the company's international reputation.

ᕦ Plot

ACT I

The setting is the Italian Renaissance. Hortensio, Gremio and Lucentio are raucously serenading Bianca, the beautiful younger daughter of the wealthy Baptista. They are interrupted by the appearence of Kate, Bianca's bad-tempered elder sister, and by Baptista. Before there is any question of Bianca marrying any of them, Baptista informs the suitors, a husband must be found for Kate. Pooling their resources, the three repair to a tavern, where they persuade the penniless roué Petruchio to seek Kate's hand in marriage. Learning that there is a dowry involved, Petruchio agrees to try his luck.

Bianca, to the jealous fury of Kate, is wondering which of her three suitors she prefers. When Petruchio and the suitors enter, they discover a full-blown row. Petruchio pleads his case, but his ironic manner further infuriates Kate, who thinks that he is mocking her, and she slaps him in the face. When Petruchio persists, however, Kate begins to thaw, and she agrees somewhat shakily to marry him. Bianca, meanwhile, treated to an absurd display of singing and dancing by her suitors, determines that the student Lucentio (rather than the vain, foolish Hortensio or the ageing Gremio) is the man for her. Amidst much commotion, and chaotic scenes instigated by Petruchio, who arrives late, terrorises the priest, and then carries his furious bride away by force, Kate's marriage takes place.

ACT 2

In Petruchio's house the newly-weds lose no time in coming to blows. Deciding to bring matters to a head, Petruchio picks a fight with Kate over the food and determines to starve her into submission. Kate, in return, refuses to sleep with him and spends the night on the kitchen floor. In the town, meanwhile, it is carnival time. Amongst the festivities Gremio and Hortensio each encounter a disguised figure, and in the belief that this is Bianca, each agrees to marry her. In truth, as the pair discover too late, the women are whores, put up to the deceit by Lucentio.

At Petruchio's house, Kate is still furious, but pretends to submit to Petruchio in order to be allowed to eat. The fighting between the pair finally resolves itself into a wary truce, and from there, by stages, to the appreciation that each has given as good as he or she has got, and that they are indeed made for each other. By the time that Bianca and Lucentio are married, the pair are the most loving of spouses. Gremio and Hortensio, meanwhile, have discovered that marriage is not all unalloyed joy.

∿ Notes

Cheerfully sexist and often described as a 'comedy' or 'slapstick' ballet, *The Taming of the Shrew* does not at first sound as if it has much going for it in the twenty-first century. But Cranko knew what he was about when he adapted Shakespeare's play. He has substituted dance for words with extraordinary effectiveness and the piece remains hugely popular whenever it is revived. Originally mounted on Stuttgart Ballet's star couple Richard Cragun and Marcia Haydée, the ballet relies on a magnetic principal pair. Kate must be a frumpy, vile-tempered bitch, but she must also have the capacity to enchant us. Petruchio, by the same token, must be simultaneously a boozy rakehell and a perfect gentleman.

Cranko, as this ballet demonstrates, was a past master at delineating character through movement. Kate is all clenched fists and darting feet and rigidly in-turned *pirouettes*, punching and stamping her way through the ballet in *staccato* fury. Petruchio, by contrast, expresses himself through spectacular, outgoing leaps, whipping off elaborate *jetés* and *tours en l'air* with raffish insouciance. When, in the big Act 2 *pas de deux*, the couple's close-quarters combat finally begins to shade into a love duet, the choreography's erotic charge is considerable. (The interchanges between Lucentio and Bianca, by contrast, are highly controlled; the pair dance a conventional *pas de deux* in a manicured topiary garden, and by the ballet's end we are not convinced that their 'perfect match' is any such thing.)

Since 1969 *The Taming of the Shrew* has dated in parts, and the pratfalls and the pantomime clowning of the suitors and other minor characters will not be to all tastes, but these are made up for by the fluency of Cranko's choreography and – in the right hands – the adorability of his heroine. The music, composed by Stolze after themes by Scarlatti, is orchestral chamber music in the baroque style, and features a harpsichord. The ballet has been revived for many major companies since its creation, most recently for the National Ballet of Canada in 1992.

Kenneth MacMillan

In 1955, a twenty-six-year-old dancer was commissioned by Ninette de Valois to produce a piece for the Sadler's Wells Theatre Ballet (the touring section of what was to become The Royal Ballet). The result was the highly unusual *Danses Concertantes*, which was so successful that it remained in the company's repertoire for seventeen years. As a dancer Kenneth MacMillan suffered from debilitating stage fright, but as a choreographer he would prove himself one of the most audacious in twentieth-century ballet. By the 1960s, few dance-makers were still creating full-length story ballets – in his entire career, Ashton choreographed just four – and many considered the form antithetical to modern classicism. With serene confidence, MacMillan proved the untruth of this. His *Romeo and Juliet* (1965) is a dramatic masterpiece of such authority that no production of the story since has escaped its shadow, and *Anastasia* (1971), *Manon* (1974) and *Mayerling* (1978) – while all arguably flawed to some degree – are huge landmarks in late twentieth-century dance.

MacMillan created *Romeo and Juliet* on his young Canadian muse Lynn Seymour and Christopher Gable, but the pair were then compelled to relinquish the premiere to Nureyev and Fonteyn. The consequent rift between MacMillan and The Royal Ballet widened when the choreographer was informed that the music that he had selected for a subsequent work – Mahler's *Das Lied von der Erde* – was unsuitable for ballet. Determined to see the piece staged, MacMillan took his ideas to the Stuttgart Ballet, then run by John Cranko. *Song of the Earth* (1965) was a huge success in Germany, and in a reconciliatory gesture was taken into The Royal Ballet repertoire six months later. Disenchanted with the Covent Garden management, however, MacMillan accepted the directorship of the Deutsche Oper Ballet in Berlin.

When MacMillan returned to The Royal Ballet in 1970 it was to take over the artistic directorship of the company from Ashton. The contrast between the two men could not have been greater. If Ashton's choreography drew on a lyrical classicism which had been born in France and Italy and flowered in St Petersburg, MacMillan's work had its roots in the darker soil of Middle European expressionism. Angst-ridden, hyper-dramatic and hyper-physical, it represented the Teutonic rather than the Mediterranean strain of the British character. MacMillan remained in the post for seven years, creating *Anastasia*, *Manon* and *Requiem* (1976), and in 1977 he resigned in order to concentrate on choreography. In the years that followed, his fascination with humanity's dark side was given full rein. *Mayerling* depicts the double suicide of the psychotic Crown Prince Rudolf of Austro-Hungary and his mistress; *My Brother My Sisters* (1978) examines the murderous fantasies of children; *Valley of Shadows* (1983, based on Bassani's *The Garden of the Finzi-Continis*) includes scenes set in Nazi concentration camps, and *Different Drummer* (based on Büchner's *Wozzeck*), is a tale of bullying and sadistic medical experimentation.

Under MacMillan's influence, The Royal Ballet moved away from the precisely schooled classicism that de Valois and Ashton had fostered so assiduously, and into a no man's land from which it has yet to emerge with any clear identity. The best of MacMillan's late works is probably *Gloria* (1980) an elegy to the dead of the First World War. In 1990 the arrival from Moscow of the former Bolshoi dancer Irek Mukhamedov spurred the choreographer to a final burst of creativity. For Mukhamedov and the young Darcey Bussell, MacMillan created *Winter Dreams* (1991) and in 1992 he made his last ballet, *The Judas Tree*, again with Mukhamedov in the lead role. He died the same year.

Song of the Earth is MacMillan's most significant artistic achievement, but it is his narrative works – vivid, intense and sexually explicit – which remain his most important legacy to dance. He gave blazing new life to the full-length

ballet, and roles like those of Juliet, Manon Lescaut and
Maria Vetsera (in *Mayerling*) are amongst the most spectacular dramatic challenges in the classical repertoire.

Danses Concertantes

**One act. Choreography by Kenneth MacMillan, music
by Igor Stravinsky, designs by Nicholas Georgiadis.
First performed at Sadler's Wells Theatre, London,
1955.**

Kenneth MacMillan was twenty-six when he received his first
ballet commission from Ninette de Valois. His original choice
of music was Stravinsky's *Le Baiser de la Fée*, which he owned
on record. The piece required more musicians than the
touring Sadler's Wells Theatre Ballet could afford, however,
and MacMillan eventually chose the piece on the other side of
the record – the much more sparingly orchestrated *Danses
Concertantes*.

∼ Outline

Stravinsky's sharp-edged score is in five movements, and to
complement its fractured structures MacMillan developed a
brittle, angular style of startling originality. Fingers are
pointed, sphinx-like profiles are presented, feet flicker like
knives. The piece has a pronounced atmosphere, with
Georgiadis's set suggesting the antechamber to some palatial
but not-quite-real domain. Its aquarium tones, against which
the dancers in their turquoise, lime and gold costumes flash
and shimmer like tropical fish, seem to submerge us. Even the
lighting is unexpected, with day turning whimsically to night
and back again. The structure of the piece has hierarchical
references. Six women represent a *corps de ballet*. A principal
couple performs an extended *pas de deux*. Another man and
two women perform a *pas de deux*. No note of the personal,
however, touches these encounters. Emotionally speaking,
the dancers seem to glance off each other.

∼ Notes

Although futuristic (for its day) rather than retrospective in atmosphere, *Danses Concertantes* has elements in common with Frederick Ashton's *Scènes de Ballet*, made six years earlier. One of MacMillan's men's poses (sitting, with arm extended and finger pointing) is markedly similar to Ashton's 'Adam' pose, and the 1950s cocktail smoulder of MacMillan's ballerina contrasts interestingly with the 1930s glamour of Ashton's. That said, *Danses Concertantes* makes it clear that the younger choreographer was his own man, with his own style, from the start. MacMillan's steps and lines work almost aggressively against expectation. The lifts are highly unusual, and prefigure the complex physicality that, in the longer later works, would become his signature.

∼ View from the Wings

I never cease to be amazed by *Danses Concertantes*. It feels so fresh and young, and yet it was choreographed half a century ago. Maryon Lane, who originally danced the central role, taught me when I was at school and seemed, even then, to be a piece of living history. (Apologies, but young people think anyone over thirty is old.) I danced the *pas de deux*, a quirky little number which starts, oddly, side on to the audience in the front corner: not a normal starting position in ballet as it gives you only one choice as to subsequent moves. You're forced to move across the stage, profile to the audience – hardly the best angle from which to see the steps and certainly not the most flattering. Most ballet variations begin on the centre or in the back corner of the stage, positions which give you far more options about where to go next. The *pas de deux* is fairly typical of *Danses Concertantes*, with its seemingly unscheduled and abrupt pauses, mechanical body dips and acutely pointed fingers. It has a tongue-in-cheek chic, which suited me down to the ground.

Song of the Earth
Das Lied von der Erde
One act. Choreography by Kenneth MacMillan, music by Gustav Mahler, designs by Nicholas Georgiadis. First performed at the Württemberg State Theatre, Stuttgart, 1965.

In 1907 Mahler learned that he was suffering from incurable heart disease, and when the following year he was sent a book of T'ang dynasty poems whose subject was life's sadness and transience, he began setting them to music in the knowledge that his own end was near. MacMillan had long wished to create a danced realisation of Mahler's symphonic song cycle, but when he proposed the project in early 1965, the Royal Opera House Board refused him – on the grounds, apparently, that *Das Lied von der Erde* was 'a masterpiece that should not be touched'. The Board's high-handedness had immediate consequences. MacMillan took the project to John Cranko at Stuttgart, who immediately invited him to mount the piece for the company there. Both the critical and the public reactions were rapturous, confirming MacMillan as the most important new choreographer on the world stage. Within six months Frederick Ashton had invited MacMillan to stage *Song of the Earth* at Covent Garden, where it was received with further superlatives. The choreographer, however, would not return to The Royal Ballet until 1970.

∼ Outline
Mahler used six of the Chinese poems, which are sung in their German translation by an on-stage tenor and mezzo-soprano. Prominent amongst MacMillan's nineteen-strong cast of dancers are the Woman (in white), the Man (in grey), and the Messenger (masked, in black). The Messenger is an ambiguous figure. He is the Messenger of Death – eternal – but he is also at different stages of the ballet a companion and a guide. In the early part of the piece the Man and the Woman are

portrayed as profoundly attached to each other and to the things of this life, transient though these are. But the Messenger shadows the pair from the first. He is inexorable – magisterial in his authority – and he is not to be denied. By the ballet's end the Man has assumed another state. Like the Messenger, he is masked. He and the Messenger are one.

MacMillan's spare, beautiful choreography for *Song of the Earth* has no direct connection to the T'ang songs; MacMillan merely uses their imagery as a point of departure. He makes a couple of specific choreographic references: the song 'Of Youth' describes a pavilion reflected in a pool whose occupants can be seen in the water, upside-down (MacMillan briefly stands his cast on their heads) and flower-gathering gestures are incorporated into the dance to 'Of Beauty', which describes a party of women picking lotus flowers on a riverside. But these are fleeting details in another, wordless narrative. The story the dancers tell is one of love, loss and the inevitability of death.

～ Notes

Song of the Earth, one of the greatest ballets of the twentieth century, is Kenneth MacMillan's masterwork. In its apparent simplicity, and in the unblinking directness of its gaze, MacMillan's choreography perfectly echoes Mahler's austere symphonic composition. Yet the piece is profoundly moving and uplifting, for both composer and choreographer express the certainty of life's renewal. Death is the companion who awaits us all, the ballet tells us, but his embrace is not to be feared.

Although the Royal Opera House Board were almost certainly unaware of the fact, MacMillan's was not the first realisation in dance of *Das Lied von der Erde*: Antony Tudor had set a ballet to Mahler's score as early as 1948 (*Shadow of the Wind*, for American Ballet Theatre). The piece did not thrive, however, and MacMillan's is the definitive version. The ballet is in the repertoires of the Stuttgart Ballet, the

Paris Opéra Ballet, the Australian Ballet, and the National Ballet of Canada.

∽ View from the Wings

There are certain ballets in a company's repertoire which are so special, so revered and so prized that to be cast in them is like a blessing from above. Seeing your name listed as a potential interpreter of these ballets is a valediction of everything you have always tried to be. You've made it. *Song of the Earth* is one such ballet. So you can imagine – or, more probably, you can't – my total and utter shock, my disbelief, my stunned amazement, when I saw my name – MY NAME – listed to understudy the lead role in *Song of the Earth*. And then, when one of the casts was injured and I was shunted up and given two performances . . . Well, even now, I look back on that time as if it was someone else, not me, in the white leotard with its simple skirt, my hair tightly pulled back. But it was me, and it was an extraordinary experience as well as an honour, to be on stage as an unequal partner to MacMillan's masterful choreography, Mahler's great music and poetry passed down from the T'ang Dynasty.

Romeo and Juliet
Three acts. Choreography by Kenneth MacMillan, music by Sergei Prokofiev, designs by Nicholas Georgiadis.
First performed at the Royal Opera House, Covent Garden, 1965.

MacMillan was inspired to undertake *Romeo and Juliet* by John Cranko's 1962 version for Stuttgart Ballet. He created the title roles on Christopher Gable and Lynn Seymour, but in the event casting control was denied him, and Nureyev and Fonteyn danced on the first night (Seymour was relegated to fourth cast).

∿ Plot

ACT 1

Romeo, a Montague, accompanied by his friends Mercutio and Benvolio, is flirting with Rosaline. A quarrel with the Montagues is provoked by Tybalt, a Capulet, and the marketplace of Verona is soon ringing with the clash of rapiers. By the time that fight is halted by the arrival of the Prince of Verona, several young men lie dead. Juliet, meanwhile, who is playing with her nurse, is introduced by her parents to Paris, a well-born young man of the Capulet clan.

Guests arrive for a ball at the Capulets' house. Amongst them, in disguise, are Romeo and his friends. They participate in the formal dances, and Romeo sees and is entranced by Juliet, who is smitten in return. Recognising Romeo, Tybalt orders him to leave, but is restrained by Lord Capulet, who is determined to heed the Prince's plea for peace between the two houses. The guests depart – the Montagues with them – but Juliet is unable to sleep. Stepping on to her balcony she sees Romeo below. She descends, and the couple declare their love in a rapturous *pas de deux*.

ACT 2

Romeo, in the marketplace with his friends, can think only of Juliet. A wedding procession passes, further concentrating his thoughts. Juliet's nurse pushes through the crowd with a letter. When he is finally allowed to read it by Mercutio and Benvolio, Romeo learns that Juliet has agreed to marry him. Because of the enmity of their families, this must occur in secret.

The pair are duly married by Friar Lawrence, who prays for conciliation between the two clans. Romeo returns to his friends, but with no further desire to antagonise the Capulets, disassociates himself from their provocative behaviour. His companions are surprised by this uncharacteristic attitude, and finally Tybalt – still furious at the Montagues' incursion of the night before – takes advantage of the situation to challenge and kill Mercutio. The conventions of honour demand that Romeo avenge his friend, and he does so.

ACT 3

Romeo, compelled to exile himself to Mantua, leaves Juliet's bed at dawn. Shortly afterwards her parents enter with Paris but Juliet, distraught, refuses to receive him. Paris's pride is stung, and Lord and Lady Capulet, furious at her disobedience, threaten to disown her. In despair, Juliet races out and throws herself at Friar Lawrence's feet. The priest gives her a potion which will make her fall into an extended, deathlike sleep, and undertakes to warn Romeo that he must rescue her from the family tomb.

Returning with the vial of potion, Juliet returns home, apologises to her parents, and agrees to marry Paris. Then, fearfully, she drinks the potion. When her friends and the nurse enter the following morning to dress her for her wedding, they find her on the bed, unmoving. Her parents arrive with Paris, and Lord Capulet sorrowfully declares his daughter dead.

Friar Lawrence's message has not reached Mantua. Hearing of Juliet's death, Romeo returns to Verona in the disguise of a monk and enters the Capulet crypt. Finding Paris there, he kills him. He lifts Juliet's body from the bier but his worst fears seem to be confirmed, and he takes the poison that he has brought with him. Shortly afterwards, Juliet wakes from her long sleep. To her horror and confusion, the first thing that she encounters is the dead body of Romeo. Snatching up his dagger, she stabs herself in the heart, and as she dies, embraces Romeo for the last time.

∿ Notes

It is hard to imagine a more dramatic or romantic story than that of Shakespeare's young lovers, and countless versions of the ballet have been created. The most significant of these, pre-MacMillan, are Leonid Lavrovsky's for the Kirov Ballet in 1940 and John Cranko's for the Stuttgart Ballet in 1962. Both were set to Prokofiev's grand, lyrical score, which was composed in 1935. The Lavrovsky production, majestic but old-fashioned, starred the great Galina Ulanova, and Cranko's Juliet was Marcia Haydée. By the time that Nureyev and Fonteyn took the stage at Covent Garden in 1965, the ballet already had a considerable performance history.

MacMillan places his passionate young heroine squarely at the centre of his production. His choreography is dazzlingly inventive and his staging bristles with machismo – tempers are short, and rapiers fly from their scabbards at the least provocation – but it is Juliet who makes the ballet unforgettable. MacMillan, always fascinated by psychological extremes, was clearly profoundly engaged by her impetuosity, her wilful resisting of the stiff formalities of the Capulet houshold, and her final, pitiful fracturing. Every last nuance of her feelings is communicated through dance – the character's transparency is almost shocking. Juliet is the dance-actress role par excellence – the role that every ballerina covets.

Given the *quattrocento* setting, it is easy to forget just how expressionistic rather than classical MacMillan's *Romeo and Juliet* is. There are large-scale spectacles – the sword-fights, the Capulets' ball – but there are no balletic formalities like solos. Instead, dance, character, narrative and emotion are woven into a seamless continuum. When Romeo and Juliet dance the balcony *pas de deux*, one of the most heartstopping evocations of mutual desire in all ballet, time does not stand still. Time passes, dangerous and urgent, and discovery is possible at any moment. MacMillan, like Shakespeare, draws a contrast throughout between the formal safety of the interior world and the violence and moral disorder of the exterior; the balcony scene, with calculated ambiguity, takes place between these two worlds. With this *pas de deux*, MacMillan made his first major statement of the ultra-physical choreographic style that in later ballets would become his hallmark.

Romeo and Juliet is not a perfect ballet. Prokofiev's score is fabulously dramatic and lyrical, but it is also very long, and the

Act 2 marketplace scenes become a repetitive parade of strutting swordsmen and capering whores. In Act 3 the stage seems very sparsely populated after the dazzle and bustle of the previous two acts (a problem some choreographers, including Nureyev and Tudor, have solved with a funeral procession for Juliet). But these are minor shortcomings. This is a truly exciting, truly moving piece, drenched in colour and atmosphere, and framing one of the most exquisitely drawn of ballet heroines.

∿ View from the Wings

Aside from an apparently unavoidable tendency to be cast as the second female lead, I had another recurring theme throughout my dancing career: being cast as the whore. If there was a lady of the night, a tart, a harlot or a prostitute to be played, you can bet I was up there doing it. I have no idea why this might be except that usually, the whores in ballet are good-time girls, resolutely cheerful and responsible for leading the assembled crowds in dancing and merriment. *Romeo and Juliet* was no exception. The three harlots, each one paired with the three principal male characters, Romeo, Mercutio and Benvolio, are tarts with hearts, rays of sunshine who ply their trade, you might think, simply because they like to make people smile. They certainly never seem to collect any money and while the womenfolk of Verona are none too keen, the men seem more than happy to have them around. The harlots have great fun: leading the dancing in the Town Square scenes, getting Juliet's nurse all flustered as she tries to deliver her letter and then playing a key role in Mercutio's death. I danced two of the three harlots – Romeo's and Mercutio's. Dancing Mercutio's harlot may yet prove to be my biggest claim to fame: when Rudolf Nureyev danced for the last time at Covent Garden, it was not in the leading role but as Mercutio, in a performance of *Romeo and Juliet* staged specially to

benefit Margot Fonteyn who was, by then, in poor
health. That evening, I danced Mercutio's harlot, making
me, technically, his very final partner on the Royal Opera
House stage.

Anastasia

**Three acts. Choreography by Kenneth MacMillan,
music by Pyotr Ilyich Tchaikovsky (Symphonies nos. 1
and 3), Bohuslav Martinů *Fantaisies Symphoniques*), Fritz
Winckel Rudiger Rufer (electronic music), designs by
Barry Kay.**
**First performed at the Royal Opera House, Covent
Garden, 1971.**

In 1967, for the Deutsche Oper Ballet (of which he was then
director) MacMillan choreographed a one-act version of the
story of Anna Anderson, an unidentified woman in a Berlin
hospital who claimed that she was the Grand Duchess Anastasia
(the daughter of Tsar Nicholas II who had been murdered
with his family by the Bolsheviks in 1918). When MacMillan
came back to London as director of The Royal Ballet he
choreographed two further acts to precede the earlier one. A
revised version of the three-act ballet appeared in 1996.

∾ Plot

ACT I
It is 1914. The Imperial family is holding a picnic on their
yacht, the *Standart*. The party includes the Tsarina's friend
Anna Vyrubova, Rasputin, and several naval officers. The
Tsarina is concerned for the health of her son, who is a
haemophiliac, and trusts Rasputin to keep him from harm.
The thirteen-year-old Anastasia enters in her sailor-suit,
and dances with the naval officers and her mother. The out-
ing ends with the arrival of a telegram bringing news of war.

ACT 2

It is 1917. Despite street demonstrations and growing social unrest, the Tsar has determined to give a ball in Petrograd to celebrate the coming out of his daughter Anastasia, now sixteen. As guest of honour he has invited the Maryinsky ballerina Mathilde Kchessinska. Outside in the streets, an angry crowd is gathering. The forty-five-year-old Kchessinska enters, and with her partner performs a spectacular *pas de deux*. The scene is a fashionable one, but the naive Anastasia is bewildered by the air of promiscuity. The ball is brought to a catastrophic end when agitators from the street invade the ballroom.

ACT 3

In a Berlin hospital, some years later, a woman sits on an iron bed. As the consequence of unknown events she has lost her memory, and her identity is in doubt. Is she a woman named Anna Anderson, or is she the Grand Duchess Anastasia, who somehow escaped the slaughter at Ekaterinburg which claimed her parents, sisters and brother? Danced flashbacks combine with back-projected newsreel footage to show a possible version of events: Anastasia's rescue, her love affair, the birth of her child, the death of her husband by firing squad, the disappearance of her child, her suicide attempt, her struggle to prove the validity of her claims, and her confrontations with the surviving Romanovs.

If we remain uncertain of the woman's identity, she herself is not. Shining through the darkness of these recollections is a luminous memory of the past – that of a thirteen-year-old child in a sailor-suit. This child is as certain of the security of the world that she inhabits as she is of her parents' love for her. The bed in the Berlin hospital begins to move downstage like an open carriage, and the Grand Duchess Anastasia graciously receives the tributes of the crowds.

∾ Notes

When this ballet was created, there was genuine uncertainty as to the validity or otherwise of Anna Anderson's claims. Since then, however, DNA evidence has proved them to be fantasy, and we are no longer free to give the ballet's central character the benefit of the doubt. These are no longer possible scenes from her life, they are the dramatisation of her psychiatric case-notes. While this closure changes the nature of our relationship with the piece, it does not reduce the scale of MacMillan's achievement. *Anastasia*'s subject is ambiguity and the meta-life, but its formal structure is that of the three-act story ballet. If the result is only partly successful in dramatic terms, this is hardly surprising. Choreographically, too, the piece is peculiar. The first two acts are conventionally classical, but the third act draws on the dark, raw-boned expressionism to which, at this stage of his career, MacMillan gave only occasional rein.

All of these are reasons to see *Anastasia*, rather than reasons not to see it. The piece, undoubtedly flawed, divides audiences to this day. When it first appeared in 1971, as the first major work of MacMillan's directorship, it was accorded a very hostile critical reception. Unsurprisingly, the viciousness of the reviews stung the choreographer, and his next work was the seamless *Manon*, from which all traces of the darker MacMillan strain have been banished. A generation later, however, *Anastasia* can be seen in a less hysterical light, and almost as a personal manifesto. We are none of us quite who we seem, MacMillan tells us, and we are defined, rather than obscured, by the conflicted elements in our natures.

∾ View from the Wings

Anastasia presented me with one of the few nightmare moments from my career at The Royal Ballet. I danced Mathilde Kchessinska on a few occasions – a 'gala' *pas de deux* on the occasion of Anastasia's 'coming out' ball which makes up a section of the second act. It's fiendishly tricky and while I managed a couple of good shows, there was one, memorable, performance where everything that could possibly have gone wrong did so. In my diary that night I wrote: 'It's a strange number, as it comes out of nowhere; no preamble, no chance to build up a character. You walk on, the music starts, and off you go. Tonight, right from the beginning, it fell apart. The lights were dazzling and I couldn't seem to make firm contact with the floor. It was like one of those anxiety dreams made flesh, where everything you touch turns to dust and slips through your fingers. And we had done so well last time. Tonight, everyone on stage knew we'd blown it. It was all pretty depressing and afterwards I slunk towards the stage door in dark glasses clutching my ill deserved flowers.' Not everything at the ballet is always beautiful.

Manon

Three acts. Choreography by Kenneth MacMillan, music by Jules Massenet (*Le Cid*, *Esclarmonde*, *La Navarraise et al.*, arr. Leighton Lucas), designs by Nicholas Georgiadis.
First performed at the Royal Opera House, Covent Garden, 1974.

According to MacMillan, what attracted him to the heroine of the Abbé Prévost's great eighteenth-century romantic novel was her amoral, changeable nature. The ballet's first night came three years after the critical assault on *Anastasia*. During the interim the choreographer had created six short pieces, none of them especially memorable (although a *pas de deux* to Fauré's *Pavane* was praised). *Manon*, however, was an instant hit, and along with *Romeo and Juliet*, is the ballet for which MacMillan is best remembered.

∾ Plot

ACT I

In the courtyard of an inn near Paris, a favoured spot for assignations, the louche young Lescaut awaits the arrival of his sister, Manon, who is on her way to enter a convent. Also present is Des Grieux, whose broad-brimmed hat marks him out as a student of divinity. A coach arrives. Inside are Manon and the Old Gentleman, who makes no secret of his desire for her. Noting this, Lescaut steers the Old Gentleman into the inn to settle the price of Manon's virtue. She, meanwhile, encounters Des Grieux, who falls in love with her. Equally attracted, Manon reveals that she has stolen money from the Old Gentleman, and the couple decide to flee to Paris. Having struck a bargain with the Old Gentleman, Lescaut exits the inn, but too late – Manon has gone. Monsieur GM, a wealthy onlooker, informs Lescaut that he too would be prepared to enter into negotiations concerning Manon. Lescaut, scenting a fortune, promises to find her.

In his modest lodgings in Paris, Des Grieux is writing a letter to his father – a request for money. Manon, impatient for love, interrupts him, and a passionate interlude ensues. Des Grieux leaves with his letter, and in his absence Lescaut arrives with Monsieur GM. Childishly dazzled by the gown and the trinkets that he has brought for her, Manon succumbs to GM's advances, and leaves with him. When Des Grieux returns, Lescaut informs the earnest young student that there will be money for all of them if Manon is made available to GM. Presented with the fait accompli of Manon's absence, Des Grieux unhappily consents.

ACT 2

Manon, now glitteringly arrayed, arrives at a party hosted by Monsieur GM. The salon is a decadent hall of mirrors, with tables laid out for gambling and scantily clad prostitutes in attendance. Des Grieux, uncomfortable and out of place, is present with Lescaut, who is boisterously drunk. Manon, it is clear, still loves Des Grieux, but she cannot resist the promise of wealth represented by GM. She dances with her many admirers, and is passed amongst them like a toy. Des Grieux begs her to leave, but she prevaricates, insisting that he extract money from GM at cards. GM is not stupid, however. He catches the student cheating, and Des Grieux and Manon rush from the salon.

Back at his lodgings, Des Grieux and Manon declare their love for each other, but are soon interrupted by the arrival of the vengeful GM, who seeks the return of the jewellery that he has given Manon. The police follow GM into Des Grieux's room. Accompanying them, his wrists bound, is Lescaut, who has been arrested as a procurer. On GM's orders, the police arrest Manon as a prostitute. A struggle ensues, and to the horror of Manon and Des Grieux (and the satisfaction of GM), Lescaut is killed.

ACT 3

In the penal colony of New Orleans, the Jailer awaits the next consignment of convicts from France. In the port, ships are unloaded of their cargoes and passengers. Amongst these is a sad column of women – convicted prostitutes like Manon. The Jailer casts an eye over them and his attention alights on Manon, who has been followed to New Orleans by Des Grieux (who has pretended to be her husband). The Jailer summons Manon to his office, and in an attempt to persuade her to leave Des Grieux places a bracelet on her wrist. Des Grieux enters and stabs the Jailer to death.

Manon and Des Grieux have fled into the Louisiana swampland. Exhausted, Manon sinks to the misty ground, and incidents from her short life pass before her eyes. Des Grieux attempts to console her, and she gives herself to him in a last abandoned dance. Her dreams of wealth and position have all evaporated; only her lover remains, constant to the last. Flying one last time into his arms she dies.

~ Notes

Manon is the most sumptuously decadent of ballets. Georgiadis places the stiff finery of the rich – blood-red, black, dull gold – in jarring adjacency to the greasy monotoned rags of the poor, and the rancid sheen of corruption lingers over all. Manon's motivation is thus made clear at a glance: there is the world of the rich, soulless though it may be, and there is the abyss.

The story unfolds with seamless fluency. Manon and Des Grieux's *pas de deux* in his lodgings is as precipitous as it is passionate. Manon is adorable, but we quickly see flashes of the inconstancy that will lead her into the arms of Monsieur GM. The *pas de deux* for GM, Lescaut and Manon which follows is one of the ballet's most inspired passages. Lescaut's near-incestuous manipulation of his sister and GM's connoisseurial examination of her as she swings artlessly between them are brilliantly repulsive, and brilliantly illustrative of each protagonist's character. An equally memorable sequence takes place at Monsieur GM's party when, in a Hogarthian précis of her demi-mondaine career, Manon is partnered, and her charms coldly savoured, by all of the eight 'Gentlemen' present.

The character who is drawn with the least precision, and who remains a cypher throughout, is Des Grieux. In his first meeting with Manon outside the inn he dances a highly precise (and notoriously difficult) *adagio* solo. By the solo's end, and for all its exquisite fashioning, we know no more about Des Grieux than we did when we first saw him – nor are the duets which follow any more revealing. They could be danced by any pair of lovers, from any period. These vaguenesses notwithstanding, *Manon* is a ravishing ballet. The music, for all the multiplicity of its sources (at least a dozen Massenet works went into its creation) has a gorgeous sweep to it, and Manon herself – avaricious, feckless, feminine to the core – is one of ballet's most irresistible heroines. The piece is regularly performed by The Royal Ballet and has been taken into the repertoire of no fewer than twelve of the world's major companies, including the Paris Opéra Ballet, American Ballet Theatre, and the Kirov Ballet.

∿ View from the Wings

Manon is one of my Desert Island ballets, one of the few I'd like to sneak into my metaphorical pocket and take with me if I was ever shipwrecked. As ever, I danced not Manon but the secondary role, the mistress of Manon's brother, Lescaut. Created for one of my mentors, the former ballerina and now Director of The Royal Ballet, Monica Mason, Lescaut's Mistress is a joyful, sincere, warm-blooded woman: another prostitute, yes, but with a heart of gold (and an eye for the same) who truly loves her man. She dances three times: two supremely musical, intelligently constructed and highly challenging solos and a *pas de deux* with her drunken lover which can bring the house down. (It can also fall dreadfully flat, depending entirely on the chemistry between the couple and his ability to play drunk.) I danced Lescaut's Mistress with several wonderful partners but for the last five or six years, I was cast with Irek Mukhamedov and enjoyed sharing the delighted laughter of the audience which was, I'm certain, directed primarily towards him. It was a dream.

Mayerling

Three acts. Choreography by Kenneth MacMillan, scenario by Gillian Freeman, music by Franz Liszt (*Faust Symphony*, *Mephisto Waltz* no. 1, *Transcendental Studies et al.*, arr. John Lanchbery), designs by Nicholas Georgiadis.
First performed at the Royal Opera House, Covent Garden, 1978.

In 1977 MacMillan resigned his directorship of The Royal Ballet in order to concentrate on choreography. The result was *Mayerling*, his fourth full-evening ballet for the company.

In 1992, during the course of a performance of *Mayerling* at Covent Garden (Irek Mukhamedov's debut as Rudolf) MacMillan died.

⤳ Plot

A prologue is set in the Heiligenkreuz cemetery before dawn.

ACT 1.

At the Imperial Palace, Vienna (the Hofburg), Crown Prince Rudolf of Austria-Hungary is celebrating his marriage to Princess Stephanie of Belgium. The marriage is an arranged one, and Rudolf flirts openly with another woman, angering his parents, Emperor Franz Josef II and Empress Elisabeth. Later Rudolf meets Countess Marie Larisch and her friend Baroness Helene Vetsera, who introduces her daughter Mary to him (Larisch is Rudolf's ex-mistress, who latterly has been acting as his procurer and go-between). After four Hungarian officers plead the cause of their country's separatist movement (to which Rudolf is sympathetic), Larisch makes clear her own sexual availability, should Rudolf wish to resurrect their relationship. The Emperor, however, interrupts the rendezvous and orders Rudolf to attend to his wife.

After the ball, Rudolf visits his mother's apartments in the Palace, where she is preparing for the night. Rudolf pleads his unhappiness at his forced marriage, but the Empress is unresponsive. Retiring in despair to his own apartments, Rudolf terrifies his bride with his revolver and a human skull before violently and lovelessly consummating their marriage.

ACT 2

With his wife Stephanie and his driver Bratfisch (who is also a nightclub entertainer) Rudolf arrives at a notorious tavern. This is full of whores, and despite the attempts of Bratfisch to amuse her, it is clear that Stephanie is deeply unhappy to find herself in such a place. She leaves, and Rudolf switches his attention to his demi-mondaine mistress Mitzi Caspar, and to his Hungarian separatist friends. There is a police raid, and the royal party hides. Morbidly depressed, Rudolf suggests to Mitzi that they commit suicide together – she declines. Count Taafe, the Prime Minister, enters the tavern, searching for the Crown Prince. Rudolf departs with his friends and Mitzi leaves with Taafe. Outside the tavern, the intrigue-loving Countess Larisch engineers a meeting between Rudolf and Mary Vetsera, whom she is supposedly chaperoning.

Calling at the Vetsera house at a later date, Larisch finds Mary gazing at a portrait of Rudolf. Taking a pack of cards, she tells Mary's fortune and assures her that her romantic dreams will come true. To this end she agrees to deliver a letter from Mary to Rudolf.

It is the Emperor Franz Josef's birthday. During the celebrations Count Taafe confronts Rudolf about his unsuitable political affiliations. Also present is 'Bay' Middleton, the Empress Elisabeth's bluff English lover, who to Rudolf's vast amusement offers Taafe an exploding cigar. As a birthday present the Empress gives her husband a portrait of an actress named Katherina Schratt, whom everyone knows to be his mistress. There are fireworks, which Middleton and the Empress take advantage of to conduct an amorous tryst. Witnessing this, Rudolf (who has been forbidden a separation from his unloved wife Stephanie), is overcome with anger at the hypocrisy which surrounds and confines him. He is diverted from these bitter thoughts by Countess Larisch, who bears Mary Vetsera's letter. In his private apartments, Rudolf conducts the first of his secret rendezvous with Mary.

ACT 3
The royal family are enjoying a shoot in the countryside, but catastrophe strikes when Rudolf unexplainedly discharges his gun, killing a member of the court and narrowly missing his father. Back at the palace his mother encounters Larisch with Rudolf in his apartments, and sends her away. Rudolf, however, is quickly joined by Mary, and in the course of their highly

charged meeting the couple make a suicide pact.

At the hunting lodge at Mayerling, Rudolf is drinking with two companions, but tells them that he is unwell and wishes to be left alone. Bratfisch arrives with Mary, unsuccessfully attempts to entertain the couple, and withdraws. Rudolf's behaviour becomes increasingly deranged. He makes violent love to Mary and then injects himself with morphine. Dragging Mary into his arms one last time he shoots her dead. Hearing the shot, Rudolf's companions enter. Rudolf allays their concerns, and then, alone once more, shoots himself.

An epilogue returns to the Heiligenkreuz cemetery, final resting place of Mary Vetsera.

∾ Notes

Based as it is on real historical events, *Mayerling* lacks the narrative arc that the creator of a ballet plot would normally seek. Real events have no symmetry; they are rough and uneven, and this is reflected in *Mayerling*'s episodic nature and sprawling cast of characters. Without a foreknowledge of the political background to the story and of the complex web of relationships linking its central characters, it can be hard to know what is going on. Balanchine famously stated that 'there are no mothers-in-law in ballet', meaning that there are certain set-ups which it is beyond the non-verbal medium of ballet to establish. The back-story of the Countess Marie Larisch – former royal mistress turned procurer, and ostensible chaperone of the daughter of the social-climbing Helene Vetsera (who may or may not, at some earlier date, have relieved the Crown Prince of his virginity) – would seem to be a case in point, as would the issue of Rudolf's separatist sympathies, or for that matter his venereal diseases. *Mayerling* groans beneath the weight of all of this information.

But it is necessary information. If we are to understand the pressures leading Rudolf to murder and suicide, we have to identify them. They include (amongst deeper-buried issues) his loveless marriage, syphilis, his morphine addiction (and consequent paranoia), and the accusations of murder and treason that are shortly to be levelled against him. As the pressures mount, the Crown Prince's damaged character is revealed through a series of anguished duets with the women in his life – Stephanie, Larisch, Mitzi, Mary – and these escalate to a rawness and an erotic power which takes ballet into previously unvisited territory. Seventeen-year-old Mary, winding her body around her lover's like a viper, is recklessly, ruttishly unhinged. Rudolf – his emotions veering frenziedly between desire and hatred – is ultimately demonic.

On balance, the ends of this work – its horror, pathos, and shattering darkness – justify its sometimes laborious means. This is MacMillan at full stretch, unrestrained by all considerations except for those of emotional truth, and for all its longueurs and its structural imperfections, *Mayerling* is his greatest narrative ballet. The piece continues to be performed at Covent Garden.

∼ View from the Wings

Mayerling is a ballet which boasts not two principal women but five. I was cast as Mitzi Caspar, a favourite of Prince Rudolf, adding yet another prostitute to my collection. It's another sunny role which combines a languid and seductive solo with a feisty *pas de cinq*, to Liszt's *Mephisto Waltz*, in which Mitzi flirts energetically with the four Hungarian officers. There's lots of throwing around, from partner to partner, and quick direction changes and if you're not all on the ball it can go horribly, horribly wrong. At the end of the dance, when you're panting for breath, Rudolf catches your hand and locks you in a full-on, mouth to mouth embrace. Amongst the many casts of Rudolf, the kinder ones faked the kiss and gave you a few millimetres of space in which to pant for breath. The less kind delighted in watching you turn slowly blue.

The Judas Tree

Choreography by Kenneth MacMillan, music by Brian Elias, designs by Jock McFadyen.
First performed at the Royal Opera House, Covent Garden, 1992.

Deborah MacMillan, the choreographer's wife, recommended that her husband listen to a recording by Elias after she attended a performance of his work. In consequence Elias was given an unusual open commission: to compose a piece of any kind that he chose, unencumbered by a scenario. This work would then provide the impetus for a new MacMillan ballet. The choreographer created the piece on his final muse, the Russian dancer Irek Mukhamedov.

～ Plot

A team of mechanics assembles on a South London work-site. The area is clearly a deprived one, with battered cars, graffiti, and scaffolding strewn around. Red lights shine in the sky, against which stands the looming bulk of Canary Wharf Tower. A figure is brought on, wrapped in a sheet. A skimpily dressed woman emerges. She struts around provocatively, and in return is treated with casual contempt by the Foreman, with whom she appears to have some sort of sado-masochistic relationship. Turning her attention to the Foreman's friend, she flirts with him in an aggressive and obvious fashion. The friend responds to her advances, and in consequence the Foreman and the other workers gang-rape the woman and murder the Foreman's friend. Afterwards the Foreman climbs up onto the scaffolding and hangs himself.

～ Notes

The Judas Tree has been much criticised in the years since its creation. The case for the prosecution is that the ballet is prurient, misogynistic and if not a little silly. The Woman, dressed in a sort of swimsuit, exists only to be punished for her vagrant sexuality, while the Workmen in their cutoffs and ripped jeans are fetishised male stereotypes. The piece displays an almost nineteenth-century fearfulness of (and fascination with) untrammelled working-class desire.

The case for the defence is that there is a biblical subtext. The Workmen, twelve in number, are the disciples of Christ, and a Workman who stands by during the rape and killing is Simon Peter. The psychotic Foreman, meanwhile, represents the twin brother of Jesus (a figure named in the gnostic texts as Judas Thomas), and the Woman is the Magdalen of the same apocryphal gospel. Her revival after the rape, when she appears veiled and Giselle-like next to a wrecked car (a symbol of the tomb of Christ), represents the indestructability of the purified soul. My personal feelings are that whatever MacMillan's allegorical and religious intentions, the absurdity of the onstage scenario makes it difficult to take them seriously.

Soviet Ballet: Leningrad

The October Revolution of 1917 found St Petersburg's ballet in a severely weakened state. The 'dancers' revolt' of 1905 had been a cry of protest against the conservatism of the Imperial Ballet establishment, Anna Pavlova departed on the first of her foreign tours in 1908, and from then on there was a steady exodus of choreographic and dancing talent from St Petersburg – mostly to Europe and Diaghilev's Ballets Russes. Those that left – dancers like Pavlova and Karsavina, choreographers like Fokine – were the most adventurous and forward-looking of their generation. They were the ones who, had they stayed, might have acted as catalysts for change. But they did not stay, and while the Maryinsky's technical standards remained high, the creative energy of the Petipa days was spent.

The Revolution caused a further spate of departures to the West, but initiated change. Lenin favoured ballet as an entertainment for the masses, despite its Tsarist roots, and in the early 1920s the former Maryinsky company (which in 1935 would be renamed the Kirov Ballet) embarked on an experimental period, presenting Evenings of Young Ballet, of which George Balanchine was one of the leading lights. Unfortunately for Soviet ballet, the young choreographer did not see a future for himself with the company, and in 1924, having secured permission to leave Russia in order to undertake a German tour, he defected to Diaghilev's company.

There were many who stayed, however, and one of these was a dancer named Agrippina Vaganova. Although technically highly accomplished, her plain looks and lack of social connections denied her ballerina status at the Maryinsky until the age of thirty-six. Vaganova retired from the stage shortly before the October Revolution, and in 1920 joined the staff of the Leningrad Ballet School. A woman of vision and determination, she spent the following decade reforming the teaching system. Discarding all that was superfluous, she took the best elements of the French, Italian and Russian styles, and distilled them into an impeccable classicism. As Vaganova's pupils rose through the hierarchy, and she herself became the company's artistic director, so the Kirov Ballet assumed the style – noble of bearing, supple of back, serenely pure of line – with which it is associated to this day. Almost all of the greatest twentieth-century Russian dancers – Ulanova, Soloviev, Nureyev, Kolpakova, Baryshnikov, Makarova, Asylmuratova – were or are Vaganova Academy graduates.

In the decade before the Second World War, the Kirov Ballet flourished. With Vaganova's encouragement, ballets like Vainonen's *Flames of Paris* (1932) and Zakharov's *Fountain of Bakhchisarai* (1934) were created. Dramatic in style, these ballets were ideal vehicles for the new virtuosity, and although clearly compatible with Party ideals (especially *Flames of Paris*, set at the time of the French Revolution), they were free of the deadening political correctness which would afflict later Soviet work.

During these years, the first great Soviet ballerina emerged. Galina Ulanova was a pupil of Vaganova. Unremarkable-looking in person, she proved to be a mesmerising dancer–actress with whom audiences immediately and passionately identified. In 1938 Vaganova handed over the Kirov's directorship to the choreographer Leonid Lavrovsky, who in 1940 produced an epic staging of *Romeo and Juliet*. The thirty-year-old Ulanova created the role of Juliet – Prokofiev is said to have been inspired by her in his writing of the score – and many consider her interpretation of the role more moving and profound than any that have followed it. Her Romeo was the elegant Konstantin Sergeyev, two months her junior, who as the company's artistic director would lead the Kirov through the Cold War years of the 1950s and 60s.

After the Second World War it became clear that the artistic centre of gravity was shifting. Moscow, not Leningrad (a city which Stalin had always distrusted for its Tsarist associations), was the USSR's capital, and henceforth Moscow's ballet – the Bolshoi – was to be pre-eminent. The

Kirov and the Bolshoi were very different in character. If the supremely refined, heritage-conscious Kirov represented the female principle in Russian ballet, the Bolshoi – big, bold and bravura – represented the male. With the war won at bitter cost, and its ideological enemies re-arming themselves, it was the latter image that the Soviet state wished to present to the world.

In 1944 Lavrovsky and Ulanova departed Leningrad for Moscow. The transfer of its most important artists to the Bolshoi marked the beginning of a period of artistic purdah for the Kirov. Until the 1960s the company would remain immured in Leningrad, and thereafter its tours to the West would be infrequent. Since the earliest days of the Revolution the company had remained committed to the preservation of its nineteenth-century repertoire, and this now became its principal *raison d'être*. Perceiving that some updating was needed, Konstantin Sergeyev produced highly successful new stagings of *Swan Lake* (1950), *Sleeping Beauty* (1952) and other classics. A less conservative profile for the Kirov became a possibility in the late 1950s with the emergence of an energetic young choreographer named Yuri Grigorovitch, but after making two important new works for the company – *The Stone Flower* (1957) and *Legend of Love* (1961) – Grigorovitch was transfered to the Bolshoi as artistic director.

Lacking any forward momentum, the Kirov entered a period of artistic stagnation. By then, like all Soviet organisations, the company had become intensely politicised. The Party had eyes and ears everywhere – several dancers (including a company ballerina) were known to be KGB informers – and distrust was endemic. In 1961, with Sergeyev at its head, and accompanied by a substantial team of KGB minders, the Kirov undertook a tour to the West. The principal dancers were Sergeyev himself, then fifty-one, and his wife Natalia Dudinskaya, who was forty-nine (the ages alone give an idea of the Kirov's hermetic and anachronistic nature during that era). Other featured artists were Irina Kolpakova and Alla Sizova ('Flying Sizova'), the brilliant but mordant

Yuri Soloviev, and a comparatively inexperienced twenty-three-year-old named Rudolf Nureyev. In Paris, Nureyev proved a sensation. Technically speaking, he was no match for the classically impeccable Soloviev, but his wild beauty and electrifying charisma won him cult status almost overnight. In open defiance of official policy Nureyev met and talked to Westerners. A summons was issued for his immediate return to Leningrad (and, without question, severe punishment), but at the last moment he gave his minders the slip at Le Bourget airport.

Nureyev's defection had lasting consequences for his teachers, friends and family – all of whom were publicly and vindictively denounced. Until her death, decades later, Nureyev's mother would never be allowed out of Russia to visit him. For his colleagues at the Kirov, as they returned to an unbroken diet of Sovietised classics, the hatches were battened down more tightly than ever. Despite the best efforts of the KGB, however, Nureyev would be followed to the West by Natalia Makarova in 1970, and by Mikhail Baryshnikov in 1974. Throughout the course of the twentieth century it was the Leningrad company's melancholy destiny to form the greatest talents in world ballet, and then – one by one – to see them depart.

The era's saddest postscript concerns Yuri Soloviev, whose seamless virtuosity Nureyev was always swift to acknowledge ('You think I'm good? You should see Soloviev!'). Some now think that the Kirov star was planning to defect at the same time as Nureyev, but failed to go through with it. In 1977, at a snowbound dacha outside Leningrad, Soloviev was found shot, apparently by his own hand. Perhaps he saw no other chance of escape from the political and artistic prison that his country had become.

The Fountain of Bakhchisarai

Four acts. Choreography by Rotislav Zakharov, music by
Boris Asafiev, designs by Vera Khodasevich.
First performed at the Kirov Theatre, Leningrad, 1934.

 Plot

PROLOGUE

A fountain stands beneath the palace at Bakhchisarai. Cold
water drips onto cold marble, and an atmosphere of sadness
prevails. On the steps of the fountain, motionless, kneels
Khan Girei.

ACT 1

In a Polish castle, music is playing, and knights are dancing.
Princess Maria and her bridegroom Vaslav descend the castle
steps and exchange words of love. The ball continues – a
polonaise, a *mazurka*, a *cracovienne* – and Maria dances for the
assembled guests. Then a wounded Polish warrior staggers in
with news that the Tartar hordes of Khan Girei are approaching. The Khan's warriors kill the guards and rush in, slaugh-
tering as they come. Vaslav tries to lead Maria to safety, but at
every turn their way is barred. Khan Girei appears, kills
Vaslav, and approaches Maria. Her beauty astounds him.

ACT 2

In Khan Girei's harem, Zarema is the most beautiful and
favoured of the wives. So when the Khan leads his new trophy
– Maria – into the palace, Zarema is desperate. The Khan,
meanwhile, is seized by melancholy. He realises that for the
first time in his life he has fallen in love – with Maria. Observing this, the other wives become openly contemptuous of
Zarema.

ACT 3

Maria spends the days in solitude. All at Bakhchisarai is alien to her. Khan Girei appears at the door of Maria's chamber. He has come to tell Maria of his love, but she turns away from him in terror, and the Khan leaves. Night falls. Zarema steals into Maria's chamber and pleads with Maria to return the Khan to her. Her entreaties become threats, waking a servant girl who runs for Khan Girei. The Khan hurries to the chamber where Zarema, in an agony of jealousy, plunges her dagger into Maria. Aghast, Girei stands over the body of his beloved. His first reaction is to kill Zarema, but when she willingly moves forward to meet the blade, he lowers his weapon.

ACT 4

The Khan is inconsolable. Neither the beautiful female captives brought to him by his chieftains nor the splendid dances of his warriors can assuage his grief. He watches unflinching as his guards hurl Zarema to her death off the palace walls.

EPILOGUE

Before the fountain erected in Maria's memory, Khan Girei's days are passed in sad contemplation.

∾ Notes

The Fountain of Bakhchisarai was the first work choreographed by Zakharov, and is based on a poem by Pushkin. A pioneer of new Soviet ballet, who would later become a harsh critic of the works of Grigorovitch, Zakharov became known for ballets with literary sources, colourful and dramatic, the piece remains in the repertoire of the Kirov and other Russian companies.

The Stone Flower

Three acts. Choreography by Yuri Grigorovitch, music by Sergei Prokofiev, designs by Simon Virsiladze.
First performed at the Kirov Theatre, Leningrad, 1957.

1957 was the year when, on the other side of the world, Balanchine created *Agon*. In the light of this knowledge *The Stone Flower* does not look so radical, but in Soviet terms it was a considerable advance on Mikhail Lavrovsky's mime-heavy 1954 version, and a major personal success for Grigorovitch.

∾ Plot

ACT 1

Danila, a stone carver in the Ural Mountains, wishes to create a vase as perfect as a living flower. This dream preoccupies him even at the party to celebrate his engagement to Katerina. The party is interrupted by the hated overseer Severian, who admires one of Danila's vases. When Danila refuses to give it to him Severian is enraged, and a fight is only prevented by the intervention of Katerina. Inflamed by her beauty, Severian importunes Katerina, but is ejected by the other guests.

In a reverie, Danila encounters the Mistress of the Copper Mountain. She is the guardian of the underground treasures, and she alone possesses the secret of working stone. She shows Danila an exquisite Stone Flower and then vanishes. Danila, realising how far his work falls short of this artistry, smashes the vase that he has made and runs in pursuit of her. The Mistress of the Copper Mountain leads Danila to the Hill of the Serpent and into her malachite-green kingdom, where the glittering stones dance before his eyes. High above them, an image of perfection, is the Stone Flower.

ACT 2

Katerina is bewildered by her fiancé's disappearance. She sees the smashed vase, and attempts to piece it together again. Once again Severian importunes her, but Katerina threatens him with a sickle, and he leaves.

Outside Severian meets a party of gypsies, whom he accompanies to a fair, where they dance. In the course of the dance Severian catches sight of Katerina, who is searching for

Danila, but his attempt to seize her is foiled, and his way barred by the Mistress of the Copper Mountain. As the crowd watches in amazement he falls to the ground, and completely in her thrall, is led away. Severian begs forgiveness, but the Mistress of the Copper Mountain is implacable, and the earth opens up and swallows him.

Act 3

In her search for Danila, Katerina has wandered into the forest. Exhausted, she halts and lights a fire. From the flames leaps a Fire-maiden, who leads her to the Hill of the Serpent. In the underground kingdom, meanwhile, Danila is carving his Stone Flower. He has learnt the secrets of his art, and perfection is within his reach. The Mistress of the Copper Mountain, realising that Danila will eventually wish to return to the world, casts a spell on him, for she has fallen in love with him. Katerina enters, and is received angrily. She pleads for her fiancé's return. Touched by her devotion, the Mistress of the Copper Mountain relents, and the couple are permitted to go free. Exiting the underground kingdom, they dance together in a tender celebration of their reunion.

Epilogue

All celebrate the wanderers' return, and the gift of artistry with which Danila, through his travails, is now endowed.

～ Notes

Its integration of drama, design and dance into a unified and modernistically inclined whole made *The Stone Flower* a landmark Soviet production, and with Vasiliev as the idealistic Danila and Maximova as his faithful Katerina, the piece was a huge hit when, in 1959, it was revived for the Bolshoi. The former Kirov dancer Mikhail Baryshnikov (who never danced in it), describes *The Stone Flower* as 'a beautiful work', and his favourite of the Grigorovitch ballets. On the debit side Prokofiev's score is a long one – a good three hours – and not one of his best. The ballet's symbolism tends to a lack of subtlety, and the virtuous, sickle-wielding Katerina needs a dancer of Maximova's charisma to bring her to any kind of dramatic life.

Legend of Love

Three acts. Choreography by Yuri Grigorovitch, music by Arif Melikov, designs by Simon Virsiladze.
First performed at the Kirov Theatre, Leningrad, 1961.
Grigorovitch intended the principal role of Ferkhad in *Legend of Love* for Rudolf Nureyev, and the ballet was in rehearsal when Nureyev departed on the Kirov's 1961 European tour. When the dancer's luggage was returned from Paris to Leningrad after his defection, it was found to contain a bolt of blue material that he had bought for Ferkhad's costume.

∼ Plot

ACT I
Princess Shirin, the younger sister of Queen Mekmeneh Banu, is seriously ill, and the doctors are helpless. The Queen and her attendants are in despair, when an unknown man in pauper's clothes is led in. He has learnt of the Princess's condition and is certain that he can help. For the first time in many months the Queen's face lights up. She offers the man precious stones, but he refuses them, as he does a golden crown. When asked what payment he will accept, he tells the Queen that his price is that she must sacrifice her beauty. This demand causes Mekmeneh Banu great anguish, but for the love of her sister she agrees. The man casts a spell, and Princess Shirin rises from her bed. She looks at her sister, once so beautiful, and fails to recognise her.

Mekmeneh Banu and Shirin (now cured) visit a palace which is under construction. Both sisters are attracted to the artist Ferkhad, and when the royal retinue has moved on, Shirin approaches him. At first he believes her to be just a simple girl, and a tender interlude ensues. When Ferkhad realises that the girl with whom he is falling in love with is in fact the Princess Shirin, however, he retreats. Outside the palace, meanwhile, a crowd gathers round a dry spring. There has been no water for months except for a dwindling supply kept in the palace. The only way to irrigate the area is to carve a water-course through the mountains. But who would undertake such a task?

ACT 2

Mekmeneh Banu thinks sadly of Ferkhad, for she too loves him. Only now does she fully understand the extent of the sacrifice she has made. Shirin, by contrast, is in love and is loved in return, and in order not to be separated from Ferkhad, departs the court. Mekmeneh Banu, angry at her sister's dereliction of duty, summons the lovers. When they are brought before her, Ferkhad proves his own sense of duty by vowing that he will not marry Shirin until he has built a water-course through the mountains.

ACT 3

Mekmeneh Banu dreams – impossibly – of a life in which she is still beautiful, and Ferkhad is passionately in love with her. Shirin, meanwhile, is chafing at her separation from the young artist. She implores her sister to accompany her into the mountains so that she can see him. Mekmeneh Banu agrees, and on reaching the summit suggests to Ferkhad that he should down tools and attend to Shirin. As expected, Ferkhad tells her that although he loves Shirin, he will not let down those who are relying on him. Shirin understands that her duty is to accept this. She bids farewell to Ferkhad and departs with Mekmeneh Banu. Ferkhad leaves to fulfil his vow.

In a vision Ferkhad sees torrents of water, and standing nearby the figure of Shirin. He returns to his work with renewed vigour.

Notes

After *The Stone Flower*, more symbolic mountains. *Legend of Love* was adapted from Hikmet's Turkish play, and allowed Grigorovitch to position a colourful orientalist spectacle in an ideologically impeccable setting. The choreographer would revisit the theme of hydrology in 1976 (with rather less enjoyable results) in *Angara*, set on a dam-construction site in Irkutsk.

Soviet Ballet: Moscow

In 1918 Lenin made Moscow the Bolshevik capital, establishing the seat of government in the city's Kremlin Palace. At the time the Bolshoi – very much the Maryinsky's junior in terms of status and heritage – had been for two decades under the leadership of Alexander Gorsky, a prolific choreographer, and the architect of the dramatic, larger-than-life Bolshoi style.

Gorsky was succeeded by Vassily Tikhomirov, who in 1927 created *The Red Poppy*. The ballet, set in a Chinese shipyard, was a response to the Communist regime's demand for Social-ist Realist ballet. In years to come this genre would embrace such subject matter as the evils of industrial sabotage (*The Bolt*, Lopukhov, 1931), the adulterous temptations of an agronomist (*The Bright Stream*, Lopukhov, 1935) the politics of an Armenian cotton collective (*Gayané*, Anisimova, 1942), the moral courage of a team of geological surveyors (*Heroic Poem*, Kasatkina/Vasiliov, 1964), and the ups and downs of life on a construction site in Irkutsk (*Angara*, Grigorovitch, 1976). Despite their beyond-pastiche political correctness, these pieces are not without interest or choreographic worth. Tikhomirov, a former partner of Pavlova's, was a courageous fighter for the conservation of the classics under early Communism, and while *The Red Poppy* certainly represented a symbolic offering to the authorities in terms of theme, its construction reflected the nineteenth-century works of Petipa. In consequence, despite its great success, the piece was con-demned by the authorities as 'archaic'. The Leningrad choreo-grapher Fyodor Lopukhov, another great custodian of the classics, was similarly damned when he essayed Socialist Realism – in the case of *The Bolt* for portraying the workers as crude and subhuman, and in *The Bright Stream* for inappropriate 'formalism'.

In 1956, under the directorship of Leonid Lavrovsky, the Bolshoi visited London for a season, proving a sensation, and in 1959 they repeated the triumph in New York. Galina Ulanova, now the USSR's prima ballerina assoluta, enjoyed a personal triumph on both occasions, as did the passionate, sexually dazzling Maya Plisetskaya (who enjoyed a close, if somewhat circumscribed friendship with John F. Kennedy). The virtuosity of the male performers stunned the West, with the sheer athleticism of dancers like Nicolai Fadeyechev exceeding anything that Europe or America could offer.

These overseas successes signalled the beginning of a brilliant if often volatile era at the Bolshoi. In 1964, Lavrovsky was succeeded as artistic director by Yuri Grigorovitch, and over the next decade, during which Grigorovitch produced *Legend of Love*, *Spartacus* and *Ivan the Terrible*, as well as his own stagings of *Sleeping Beauty*, *The Nutcracker* and *Swan Lake*, the company became an inimitable presence on the world stage. Grigorovitch's work updated Soviet dance, banishing the static mime and expository sequences that had been a feature of his predecessors' work in favour of much faster-moving dance narratives. His productions were often dark and fatalistic, with much emphasis on heroic sacrifice, and their sweep and scale were unequalled. The foreign tours continued, and the Bolshoi stars became cult figures. The best known of these were Maya Plisetskaya, Natalia Bessmertnova (whom Grigorovitch married), Ekaterina Maximova, and Vladimir Vasiliev. Noble and sombre, Vasiliev was the perfect instrument of Grigorovitch's virile choreography, and the captivatingly pretty Maximova was his perfect ballerina counterpart. The couple married straight out of MAKHU (the Moscow Ballet Academy), and riding the flood-tide of Grigorovitch's inventiveness, embarked on one of the great partnerships of dance history.

But there was a dark side to the story, and the glory-days of the 1960s would give way to bitterness and recrimination. The Bolshoi Ballet was the supreme instrument of Soviet cultural propaganda, and while the company was lavishly funded, an iron control was exercised over its affairs. For a time, Grigorovitch was allowed a certain creative freedom, but he was never permitted to forget that his function was to express the grand themes of Communism. His attempts to retain artistic integrity at the same time as pleasing the Party apparatchiks on whom he depended for his position became increasingly desperate, and in 1968 he was forced to make drastic changes to his new *Swan Lake*, including the insertion of an ideologically sound happy ending (religion was banned under Communism, and the Party censors regarded the original denouement as having unacceptably spiritual overtones).

In 1975 Grigorovitch produced *Ivan the Terrible*, whose choreography was praised, but whose theme of good born of evil was damned as Stalinist by the Moscow intelligentsia, and in 1976 the near-unwatchable construction-site epic *Angara*. In their wake Grigorovitch was assailed on all sides. Plisetskaya and Vasiliev both harboured choreographic ambitions, which he refused to indulge. Instead he sidelined them, and they and Maximova became the leaders of a faction which denounced their artistic director as a power-crazed autocrat.

The atmosphere in the company, previously so optimistic, became poisoned by intrigue. Factionalism – for generations a feature of Bolshoi life – became rife, with the casting of principal and solo roles controlled by a self-serving cabal of company members over whom Grigorovitch admitted he had no control. As a result promising careers were stifled, and second-raters flourished. Adverse criticism was censored, but Moscow audiences had ways of making their feelings known. During one performance a broom was thrown on stage, indicating that the ballerina in question would have been more suitably employed sweeping the stage than dancing on it.

At MAKHU, the decline was similarly drastic. In the entire three decades of Grigorovitch's directorship at the Bolshoi Theatre, the school failed to produce a single lyric ballerina comparable to Maximova or Bessmertnova. The only contender of real promise was Nadezhda Pavlova, who was trained in Perm. A dancer of prodigious natural gifts, who promised to become one of the greatest dancers of her generation, Pavlova joined the Bolshoi in 1973, aged seventeen.

Within a few years, however – overworked, unhappily married, and shattered by the viciousness of company politics – she was burnt out.

There were other casualties. In 1984 Maximova was discovered unconscious, her wrists slashed, in a hotel bathroom (she survived). There were several defections to the West, and there would have been more had not the KGB kept the dancers in check by means of threats against their families. The Grigorovitch era would stagger on until 1995. By the time that he was finally ousted Communism was dead, and Grigorovitch himself had not produced a major ballet for thirteen years. The Bolshoi Ballet was still alive – just – but the world in which it had flourished was gone for ever.

Spartacus
Three acts. Choreography by Yuri Grigorovitch, music by Aram Khachaturian, designs by Simon Virsiladze.
First performed at the Bolshoi Theatre, Moscow, 1968.
The ballet is set against the background of the unsuccessful slave uprising led by a Thracian gladiator against Roman oppressors in AD 71.

∼ Plot

ACT 1
Spartacus and his wife Phrygia are captured in battle by Crassus, a cruel and arrogant Roman General. The couple are chained, sold as slaves and separated. Phrygia is taken to the villa of Crassus, where she is taunted by his whorish mistress, Aegina, and forced to attend an orgy. Two blindfolded gladiators are thrown into the room, and compelled to fight to the death. When the victor removes his mask we recognise Spartacus. He is horrified when he discovers he has killed a fellow slave, and encourages his fellow captives to escape to the hills and form an army against Rome.

Act 2

Spartacus is proclaimed leader of the uprising. He saves Phrygia from Crassus's villa and the couple reaffirm their love. The rebel army captures Crassus, but in a duel with Spartacus, he shows himself a coward and begs for mercy. Spartacus releases him and Crassus flees ignominiously.

Act 3

Crassus determines to defeat Spartacus and regroups his legions. Aegina, meanwhile, vowing to avenge her lover's disgrace, enters the rebel camp with a band of prostitutes. Spartacus and Phrygia bid each other a tender farewell and Spartacus prepares for battle. His men, however, in the throes of a debauch with Aegina's women, are surprised and over-powered by the Romans. Spartacus is captured and at Crassus's command is put to death by the legionaries, while Phrygia is left to mourn alone.

∾ Notes

Spartacus enjoyed immediate success and quickly became a flagship Bolshoi production. The ballet displays the four-sided construction favoured by Grigorovitch – good man, good woman; evil man, evil woman – and his signature themes of power and the necessity of sacrifice. Choreographically the ballet delivers stage-devouring leaps, pyrotechnic lifts and a goose-stepping corps of Roman legionaries. In an unforgettable final tableau – a secular crucifixion – Spartacus is lifted high above his executioners, his body impaled on the points of countless spears.

Colourful and dramatic, the piece remains a Bolshoi favourite; its original cast has never been bettered. Vasiliev and Maximova danced Spartacus and Phrygia, Nina Timo-feyeva was the sultry Aegina, and Maris Liepa was Crassus. Liepa was a particularly flamboyant character; one of the most charismatic dancers of his day, he married two of his ballerinas

(Plisetskaya and Semizorova), drank with the KGB, and was the lover of Stalin's daughter, Svetlana. Despite the instant success of *Spartacus*, it was acknowledged by the Moscow intelligentsia that Grigorovitch was playing dangerous games. Just who was it that represented the Soviet state in the ballet, they wondered. The brave Thracians, or the fascistic legions of Rome?

Ivan the Terrible

Two acts. Choreography by Yuri Grigorovitch, music by Sergei Prokofiev (from the score of Eisenstein's film *Ivan the Terrible*, with excerpts from his Symphony no. 3 and *Alexander Nevsky*, arr. Mikhail Chaluki), designs Simon Virsiladze.
First performed at the Bolshoi Theatre, Moscow, 1975.

∼ Plot

The scenes of the ballet are prefaced by bellringers who toll the mood of the action – joy, war, peace and death.

ACT 1

The bells announce the new Tsar's accession, and a black-clad Ivan assumes his throne. Below him are gathered the Boyars – rich barons who deeply resent his control. To secure his position, Ivan knows that he must choose a bride. A procession of young girls is summoned, they dance before him, and Ivan selects the beautiful Anastasia. Prince Kurbsky, the leader of the Boyars, also loves Anastasia, and is made wretched by the Tsar's choice. Determined to avenge the loss of the woman he loves, he plots with the other Boyars against Ivan.

The bells announce a Tartar invasion, and the Russians ride into battle with Ivan and Kurbsky at their head. A frenzied battle scene ensues. Anastasia is fearful for her husband but finally the bellringers announce a hard-won victory. The Tsar becomes sick. The Boyars wonder if this is their chance to overthrow him, but Ivan suddenly reappears. Hurling a spear into their midst, he demonstrates that he is still in control.

ACT 2

As Ivan and Anastasia exchange protestations of love, the Boyars continue to plot. They decide that the most effective way to destroy the Tsar is by poisoning Anastasia. Kurbsky cannot bring himself to hand her the fatal cup but orders one of the Boyars to do so. The bellringers solemnly toll the news of Anastasia's death.

Ivan, distraught, vows to avenge her death. In his imagination, Anastasia returns from the dead and blesses his vow. Energised by thoughts of revenge, Ivan forms the Oprichnina – the secret police – who track down the guilty Boyars. A play is staged before them, in which the murder of Anastasia is re-enacted. Kurbsky is then forced to drink a cup of poison and the other Boyars are brutally executed. Much cheered, Ivan returns to the business of unifying his country, and in a gesture expressive of his supreme power, gathers to himself the ropes of the bells.

∼ Notes

In this grim and fatalistic work, Grigorovitch returns to his favourite theme of the corrupting nature of power. Choreographically the ballet was praised, but elements of the Moscow intelligentsia damned its theme – stability won at the price of wholesale domestic slaughter – as Stalinist. Disapproval of the ballet served to unite a caucus of dancers (led by Maximova, Vasiliev and Plisetskaya) who resented Grigorovitch's 'Ivan-like' grip over the Bolshoi's affairs. They publicly accused the director of favouritism, blacklisting, artistic conservatism and collusion with the 'forces of repression'.

The Golden Age

Three acts. Choreography by Yuri Grigorovitch, music by Dmitri Shostakovich, designs by Simon Virsiladze. First performed at the Bolshoi Theatre, Moscow, 1982.

～ Plot

The setting is a small resort on the Black Sea in 1923 at the time of Lenin's New Economic Policy.

ACT 1

It is festival time. In the town, a performance by the Young Workers' Propaganda Theatre is beginning. Its actors are young fishermen, led by the idealistic Boris. In the watching crowd is Rita. Boris and Rita meet, but she disappears before he can catch her name. He sets off to look for her, and the search leads him to a nightclub named 'The Golden Age', where he discovers that the girl he is seeking is one of the performers. The couple's pleasure in finding each other does not escape the attention of Rita's stage-partner Yashka, a thief. Outside the club Yashka's girlfriend Lyushka intercepts two drunken revellers whom Yashka and his gang attack and rob. Returning to the restaurant Yashka sees Rita and Boris dancing together. He attacks Boris but Rita throws herself between them. Left alone together, the couple confess their love.

ACT 2

Smarting, Yashka attempts to charm Rita, but she rejects him and leaves. Yashka and his gang hide the spoils of their robbery. On the shore, meanwhile, the fishermen are working. Rita arrives looking for Boris and finding him, is introduced to his friends. Yashka's thugs appear, and launch an unprovoked attack on the fishermen. Boris is overpowered but Rita runs for help and he is saved.

ACT 3

The fishermen discover the hideout where Yashka's men are carousing, and send them fleeing. At The Golden Age it is almost time for Rita's act. Rita is not in the mood, her thoughts are with Boris, but she is obliged nevertheless to perform her tango. Afterwards, she begins to leave The Golden

Age but Yashka blocks her way, protesting his love. Watching this scene, Lyushka is overcome with jealousy and hurls a knife at Yashka. It misses him, but in his fury and frustration he kills her. Grabbing Rita, he attempts to use her as a hostage, but is finally overcome. Reunited, Rita and Boris celebrate their happiness.

∾ Notes

The Golden Age was a considerable success, and was much toured in Communism's final decade. Grigorovitch's detractors claimed that it smacked of Soviet orthodoxy, but in fact the piece can just as easily be read as a critique of the Soviet state. Choreographically, the piece has many points of interest, and the jazzy Shostakovich score (which includes the composer's orchestration of 'Tea for Two'), is unusual and atmospheric. Grigorovitch's ballet is a reworking of a 1930 Soviet Realist ballet of the same name by Vainonen, which starred Ulanova. The earlier version showed the adventures of a Soviet football team in the West, and ended with the capitalist workers and the Soviet footballers joining together in a dance in praise of work. Considered 'ideologically destructive', the piece was mothballed after one season.

∾ View from the Wings

While the great Russian classics of the late nineteenth century make up the core repertoire of many major ballet companies, the big twentieth-century Soviet ballets, for obvious reasons, didn't travel quite so well. For much of the twentieth century, there was little crossover between Russian and British ballet beyond the highly public defections of the 1960s and 70s. The influence of Soviet ballet was felt most strongly, at The Royal Ballet, in the presence of Rudolf Nureyev, following his defection to the West in 1961. Overnight, it seemed, ballet changed. Whereas the English style was intimate, embroidered, almost curlicue in its detail, the Soviet style, as exemplified by Nureyev and the dancers who followed – Natalia Makarova and Mikhail Baryshnikov – was vast: huge swathes of movement ricocheting through the body and designed, it seemed, to mirror the endless expanse of the Russian continent. The Soviet dancers' footwork might have been less immaculate than that of their English counterparts, but their sheer energy, physical strength and technical prowess was nothing short of astonishing. The ante was officially upped.

I only once tried to master the expansive style of the Soviets, in *Laurencia*, a ballet created in 1939 by Chaboukiani, which received a handful of performances at Covent Garden in the 1990s. *Laurencia*, like *Don Quixote*, takes you to Spain as viewed in a Moscow travel agent's window, and like *Don Quixote*, it's fantastic fun to dance: great leaps incorporating such generous back bends that from time to time, I'd feel my back foot making contact with my bun. And a grand circle around the entire stage of single and double turns, sixteen in succession which, when achieved, left you feeling on top of the world.

Modern to Post-Modern

By the turn of the millennium the giants of twentieth-century classical choreography – Ashton, Balanchine, Cranko, MacMillan, Nijinska and Tudor – were dead. Communism, which for all its artistic failures had been an assiduous curator of the classical repertoire, had fallen. In Europe, companies that had once performed the classics were now stripped-down contemporary ensembles, and in the USA the senior choreographic figures – Merce Cunningham, Paul Taylor, Twyla Tharp, Mark Morris – were all products of modern dance. The prevailing view of the ballet-going public seemed to be that of Mikhail Baryshnikov. As a young Kirov and ABT dancer he had been the most technically accomplished classicist the world had ever seen; now, as a born-again contemporary performer, he no longer seemed to find it relevant. This is not to say that classical ballet was not being performed and enjoyed all over the world. It was, but there was a sense that directors were marking time, waiting for the signs that would indicate a new direction. There was no shortage of choreographers prepared to create single-act works – plotless, abstract, decorative, vaguely thematic – but very few were realising large-scale classical projects with any conviction.

In private, behind the doors of the great ballet theatres, some were asking themselves if the game was up – if the creative arc launched by the Sun King had not finally completed its trajectory. If it had not been for Diaghilev, the fatalist argument went, ballet would have faded from view in the early twentieth century. At best, it would have been mothballed in the USSR for a few decades. But Diaghilev temporarily revived it in the West – gave it another half-century of meaningful life – and the careers of twentieth-century Western choreographers like Ashton and Balanchine were the final expression of that revival. With their passing ballet will continue to exist as a 'museum' art, but in terms of meaningful new work we are now witnessing the slide towards oblivion. There will no more be another Ashton or Balanchine than there will be another Ravel or Stravinsky. We have entered a post-modern era in which creativity has been reduced to the emotionless reworking of old ideas – *vide* the work of Mats Ek, William Forsythe, Jiri Kylian, Angelin Preljocaj and others.

This is the alarmist view, and many vigorously refute it. Classical ballet, the optimists insist, far from being in decline, has never been healthier. Ballet is fashionable, its stars enjoy mainstream celebrity status, and the world's opera houses sell out with a speed that leaves the 'straight' theatre open-mouthed with envy. No longer the elitist pursuit of old, classical ballet is now the expression of a vibrant pluralism, and its doors have been thrown open to all. The strict division between classicism and contemporary dance is a thing of the past, as is the mutual antipathy between the two forms. Each borrows freely from the other to the benefit of both, and the resultant cross-fertilisation has produced a fascinating crop of international dance-makers – *vide* the work of Mats Ek, William Forsythe, Jiri Kylian, Angelin Preljocaj and others.

Both arguments contain elements of the truth. The second half of the twentieth century saw ballet spread to every corner of the globe. Hundreds of companies have come into existence – national, regional, and independent – and a vast amount of new work is commissioned and performed every year, with the most successful choreographers booked many seasons in advance. Most ballet companies (that is companies whose repertoire is mostly or entirely performed on pointe) rely on a base of classical standards – *Swan Lake*, *Giselle*, *Romeo and Juliet*, et cetera – which they supplement with new or recent work. The directors of great 'heritage' companies like The Royal Ballet, The Royal Danish Ballet, and New York City Ballet, however, are faced with a complex task, in that they have to be innovators as well as respectful curators of their historic repertoires. If they are too impermeable to outside influence, their companies end up as shrines to the dead. If they are too promiscuous, they sacrifice all that makes them unique on the altar of a bland internationalism.

Choreographers, meanwhile, continue to pursue a variety of paths. Although worldwide the momentum has been away from 'story ballets', several important dance-makers continue to work in a representational, narrative vein. The British choreographer David Bintley (currently director of the Birmingham Royal Ballet), has produced several dramatic full-length works including *Cyrano* (1991), *Far From the Madding Crowd* (1996), *Edward II* (1995), and *Arthur* (2001), as well as a host of shorter pieces like the witty *'Still Life' at the Penguin Café*, and the more abstract *Tombeaux*. The work of James Kudelka (director of the National Ballet of Canada) is more modernist in tone, but the Ontario-born choreographer is equally prolific. His dramatic work includes *Washington Square* (1977), *Dracula* (1985), *The Heart of the Matter* (1986), *Hedda* (1993), and *The Contract* (2002). Amongst the full-evening works of Australia's Stanton Welch (director of the Houston Ballet) are *Of Blessed Memory* (1991), *Madame Butterfly* (1995), *Hereafter* (2003) and *Tales of Texas* (2004). Although all of these choreographers also work with non-narrative forms, their high-profile careers are testament to the continuing popularity of storytelling through dance.

To understand the more complex currents flowing through present-day ballet, it is helpful to look at the evolution of modern dance. A key moment occurred in 1957 with the performance of an early work by the contemporary choreographer Paul Taylor. In *Duet*, Taylor and his pianist remained motionless and silent on stage for the duration of a 'non-score' by the composer John Cage (to which one reviewer's response was a blank column). The work represented the logical conclusion of reductive modernism; no further progress was possible in that particular direction and the deconstructive experiments in American dance which followed – particularly those of the (New York) Judson Church school of the 1960s, whose exponents included Lucinda Childs, Trisha Brown and Twyla Tharp – are generally characterised as post-modern in character.

Classical ballet assumes a post-modern character when it starts to question its own narrative and formal structures – an impulse central to the structuralist movement of the 1960s and 70s, which also called into question ideas of fixed meaning, authorship and empirical truth. The result is a fracturing of familiar forms, often accompanied by layers of historical reference (the vestigial court-dance forms in Balanchine's *The Four Temperaments* and *Agon* are an early example of this). Theatrically, post-modern narratives gain their power from an associative process not unlike déjà vu. The audience is drawn into events on stage not by a conventional, linear process of identification, but through flashes of recognition and association. Dance, as we have seen, has a potent ability to illustrate dream states, and there are clear parallels between the fractured post-modern perspective and the workings of the subconscious. With its concern for deep structures, the work of choreographers like Mats Ek and Angelin Preljocaj sometimes appears to echo that of Marx and Freud, both of whom saw the world in terms of underlying causes and transpersonal forces. Critics of the approach have claimed that, like Marxism and Freudianism, structuralism is 'anti-humanistic', and presents the individual self as a helpless victim, washed through life by tides and forces which he cannot control.

Mats Ek is a prolific Swedish choreographer who has found international fame for his radical reworking of the classical ballets, amongst them *Giselle*, *Swan Lake* (1987) and *Sleeping Beauty* (1996). His style fuses elements of classical and modern dance into fractured narratives which are often highly surreal and disturbing. Thus his Giselle is an artless country simpleton, and the wilis of the original Romantic ballet become her fellow inmates in a lunatic asylum. In Ek's *Swan Lake*, the prince is the timorous Oedipal child of a domineering single mother, and in *The Sleeping Beauty*, the cloistered princess succumbs not to the prick of a spindle but to hard drugs. Ek's ballets are invariably searches for the psychological truths underpinning human relationships. The old stories, he believes, contain hidden and often subversive truths, and it is necessary to find 'the Mystical Door, which one must open in order to see what is behind'. The subsequent discovery may not always be a heartening one. 'A fairy-tale is like a pretty little cottage,' Ek has said. 'But there's a sign on the door saying mined area.'

The French choreographer Angelin Preljocaj, a one-time student of Merce Cunningham, has explored similar territory in a series of 'revisitations' of iconic ballets. His 1989 version of *Les Noces* was followed by *Romeo and Juliet* (1990), *Parade*, *Spectre de la Rose* (1993), *Firebird* (1995) and *Rite of Spring* (2001). These versions tend to a gritty corporeality: the relationship between his Romeo and his Juliet contains strong elements of sado-masochism and is set in a fascistic future state prowled by guard dogs. His Spectre, unlike the creature of romantic reverie created by Fokine and danced by Nijinsky, is the spectre of rape.

In reworking *Rite of Spring* as a representation of carnality, of sex as an act 'literally dictated by the very molecules of our being', Preljocaj was arriving at the same conclusion as had another French choreographer, more than forty years earlier. Maurice Béjart's sexually explicit *Sacre du Printemps* was created for the Brussels Opéra in 1959, and its huge popularity launched Béjart's career, which continues to this day. Béjart is a hippy prophet in the 1970s mould. In the course of a vast body of work which over the years has veered between hyper-drama and Euro-kitsch, he too has been moved to revisit several of the Diaghilev ballets.

Swan Lake has long been a popular subject for revisionist choreographers. One of the most successful works of the American choreographer John Neumeier (since 1973 the director of the Hamburg Ballet) is his *Illusions – Like Swan Lake* (1976), in which he transposes the story to the castle of Ludwig II at Neuschwanstein (like Prince Siegfried in the original ballet, with whom he passionately identified, Ludwig died by drowning). In 1987 Mats Ek took the story further into the realms of psychoanalysis, including male swans as objects of desire, and in 1995 Matthew Bourne, who had already radically updated *The Nutcracker* (1992) and *La Sylphide* (as *Highland Fling*, 1994), created a hugely successful version featuring Odette and the entire *corps de ballet* as male swans.

Central to many of these ballets is the theme of mental disturbance. The poignancy with which ballet could portray the unravelling of the mind was first demonstrated in Giselle's famous 'mad scene', and in his *Red Giselle* (1998), the Russian choreographer Boris Eifman told the story of the brilliant but troubled Maryinsky ballerina Olga Spessivtseva (1895–1991), and the mental decline of her later years. Eifman, who at the height of the Brezhnev era was working to Pink Floyd scores, is probably the longest-serving of the Russian new-ballet choreographers. Unafraid of the big themes, he has produced dramatic, highly coloured versions of – amongst other literary works – *The Brothers Karamazov* and *Hamlet*. The same texts have been interpreted by another choreographer, Danish-born Kim Brandstrup, whose British-based Arc Dance Company has been touring since 1985. Brandstrup's background is in contemporary dance, but in recent years he has worked widely with classical dancers and companies. To a greater or lesser extent, all of the choreographers mentioned above are working within an essentially narrative strand. One of the principal tenets of this strand is that old texts, if questioned and deconstructed, can offer new meanings.

Other European choreographers, most importantly Hans van Manen, have concerned themselves with balletic form rather than balletic narrative. A founder member of Netherlands Dance Theatre in 1960, and a prolific contributor since that date to NDT and to Dutch National Ballet, van Manen's work is classically based but non-representational. Although highly atmospheric, and often powerfully suggestive of interpersonal tension, it offers little detectable story or incident. Amongst his best-known pieces are *Twilight* (1972), a rebarbative and ultimately inconclusive duet for a man and a woman in an industrial setting; *Adagio Hammerklavier* (1973), an emotionless slow-motion suite for three couples, and the mordant *Black Cake* (1989), in which the performers indulge in coldly antagonistic ballroom routines. In a van Manen piece those on stage are not to be viewed as representations of other people in other contexts, but as themselves – as dancers, dancing. For van Manen, as a modernist, the true subject of dance is dance itself. Just as grammar represents the set of constraints within which meaning is generated through language, so classical form represents the constraints within which meaning is generated through ballet. All of van Manen's works, whatever their emotional content or non-content, are rigorous examinations of classical form. His audiences thus become spectators not only of the dance itself, but of the process of communication through dance.

The Czech choreographer Jiri Kylian is particularly associated with Netherlands Dance Theatre, having been the company's artistic director from 1977 to 1999. Like Hans van Manen, Kylian avoids specific narratives in his work, preferring to construct layers of emotional tone through the very precise deployment of his dancers. Historically, his pieces have tended to religiosity; *Return to the Strange Land* (1975) concerns the journey of the spirit after death, and *Soldiers Mass* (1980), was inspired by the fate of recruits in the First World War. Stylistically, Kylian's work is informed by a pliant classicism, but also borrows freely from contemporary dance. The resultant hybrid form – easily digestible, aesthetic rather than intellectual in nature – has been enormously influential. And much imitated – pastiche Kylian is now one of the most recognisable strands of European neo-classicism. In recent years he has introduced increasingly ludic elements into his work: in *Sweet Dreams* (1990), performers dance with tennis balls in their mouths, while in *Arcimboldo* (1995, revised 2000) the audience is presented with a food fight, with tomatoes hurled at the stage from the pit.

When in the late 1960s the American choreographer Twyla Tharp moved away from the austerity and anti-ballet posture of the Judson Church school, and towards a more audience-friendly blend of art-dance and showbiz hoofing, she did not leave her post-modern sensibilities behind her. In 1973 she choreographed *Deuce Coupe* (1973) for the Joffrey Ballet to music by the Beach Boys, and in 1976 she made the sharp, self-aware *Push Comes to Shove* for Mikhail Baryshnikov and American Ballet Theatre. The marriage of classicism and loose-limbed Broadway vernacular that Tharp achieved in these pieces was a happy one, and her unexpected choreographic juxtapositions and frequent knowing quotes from other choreographers (theorists talk of her oeuvre's 'inter-textuality') quickly marked her out from the mainstream of US dance. Tharp has never considered herself part of the classical establishment, and her principal body of work – eclectic, athletic, highly precise in construction – has been choreographed on her own contemporary-styled ensembles. Tharp has long been in demand by classical companies, however, and in the decades since *Deuce Coupe*, she has created fusion pieces for ensembles as diverse as American Ballet Theatre, The Royal Ballet, and the Paris Opéra Ballet.

Another contemporary choreographer who has worked widely with classical companies is Mark Morris. The Seattle-born choreographer founded his own troupe in 1980, and in 1988 the Mark Morris Dance Group became the resident company at the Théâtre Royal de la Monnaie in Brussels, succeeding Maurice Béjart. The French choreographer's broad-brush style had been popular in Belgium, and the apparent simplicity and naivety of Morris's work – his dancers hardly seemed to be dancing at all, just unforcedly running and leaping and turning – found extreme disfavour. 'Morris Go Home,' read the headlines, and the American became the object of a concerted hate-campaign (to which, baited beyond endurance, he responded with the words 'Béjart is shit', thus winning himself further opprobrium). Against this nightmare background, Morris created and premiered series of works including *L'Allegro, il Penseroso ed il Moderato* (1988), and *Dido and Aeneas* (1989), which are now considered masterpieces. In 1991 the company returned home, and today Morris is probably the United States' most popular choreographer. His range is vast, from the carnivalesque weirdness of *Dogtown* (1983), to the folksy cowboy kitsch of *Going Away Party* (1990) to the sweeping mystery of *V* (2002), but the musical style in which he has worked most extensively and successfully – in response, perhaps, to the purity of its internal structure – is the Baroque. Morris has choreographed work on pointe and made ballets for a dozen classical companies, but he is not generally described as a classical choreographer. Like Tharp, he is one of a generation of highly eclectic choreographers whose post-modern instincts do not admit hard and fast category boundaries.

The most influential choreographer working in or alongside the classical idiom today is William Forsythe. New York born and trained, Forsythe danced with the Stuttgart Ballet before assuming the directorship of the Frankfurt Ballet in 1982. In the years between that date and his highly acrimonious resignation in 2003, Forsythe smashed classicism through the walls of what he describes as its 'faux fantasy of decorum', and imprinted his ballet-trained dancers with an extreme – and some would say brutal – new physical vocabulary. In pieces like *Steptext* (1984), *in the middle, somewhat elevated* (1988) and *Herman Shmerman* (1992), the classical underpinnings remain in place, but the dancers' bodies are subjected to extreme articulations, super-fast distortions and wrenching imbalances – an approach developed by Forsythe from the geometric principles of the Hungarian dance theorist Rudolf von Laban (1879–1958). The results are arrestingly powerful, especially when combined with the crashing electronic scores of Forsythe's regular collaborator, the composer Thom Willems, and large-scale pieces like *Artifact* (1984) and *Impressing the Czar* (1988) are often thrilling in their sweep and strangeness.

A distinction can be made between Forsythe's 'opera-house' pieces, like those referred to above (which have been performed by companies like The Royal Ballet, New York City Ballet and Paris Opéra Ballet) and the more eclectically inspired pieces, often involving spoken text, surreal props and film, which Forsythe created specifically for the Frankfurt

Ballet. As a post-structuralist, who has aligned himself with philosophers like Jacques Derrida and Jacques Lacan, Forsythe seeks a vibrant choreographic impermanence, embedding improvisational passages into his work in order to undermine its stability and ideas of its fixed authorship. In order to acclimatise his dancers to these ideas Forsythe produced a CD-ROM entitled *Improvisation Technologies* (1995), which morphed into the piece *Self Meant to Govern*, which in its turn became the opening section of one of his most important Frankfurt pieces – *Eidos: Telos* (1995).

Forsythe's assaults on structure and permanence have the effect of keeping both dancers and audiences on their toes. At the Paris Opéra premiere of *in the middle, somewhat elevated* the choreographer 'let the linear formations disentegrate' by informing the dancers just before curtain-up that he had reset the order of the sequences. In *Kammer/Kammer* (2000), members of the Frankfurt company were filmed as they interacted behind moving barriers, and the resultant images were then projected onto screens so that the audience could extract whatever meaning it chose. Little movement and no dance (in the usual sense of the word) was involved. It was this sort of activity which, in 1999, led the New York critic Laura Jacobs to label Forsythe 'pretentious as hell', and bemoaning the technical mediocrity of the Frankfurt dancers, to suggest that he 'get his nose out of Derrida and start tending to his tendus'. Frankfurt councillors evidently agreed, and in 2002 announced that Forsythe's government-subsidised troupe was to be closed down in favour of a more conventional ballet company. A worldwide protest eventually led the council to reverse its decision, but by then Forsythe had decided to move on. A letter of farewell written to the people of Frankfurt gives a good idea of his choreographic style:

> For the present I feel strongly that my own methodological evolution would be best served if conducted in a context less integrated into a field of political practice that is, understandably, challenged by the task of establishing

primary descriptive models of cultural policy that can be accurately represented by numbers. It is extremely difficult, perhaps impossible, to objectively translate or reduce intrinsic, multiple values as are typically embedded in art, into interest-maximising numbers that explicate its relevance in political models of cultural well-being.

The message couldn't have been clearer. Forsythe didn't want to be answerable to an authority wielding a balance-sheet, nor to sponsors or patrons who, as he once put it, 'want ballet as part of the fine-dining experience'. The controversy throws into relief the whole question of ballet's future. The post-modern cat is out of the bag, and the current mood, as defined by Forsythe and his contemporaries, is one of bracing cerebrality and aggressive challenge to the old hierarchies. To ask whether classical ballet will survive the deconstructive process is a little like asking whether painting will survive Cubism. It will, but there will be casualties. The histrionic and unnecessary transposition of 'literary classics' to dance; wishy-washy neo-classicism; stale representationalism; pastiche Petipa, pastiche Balanchine, pastiche Kylian – all of this will go by the board. The good news is that nothing of lasting worth will be lost. Classical ballet can only gain from the broadening of the discourse. The classical canon will stand.

Push Comes to Shove
Choreography by Twyla Tharp, music by Franz Joseph Haydn (Symphony no. 82) and Joseph Lamb ('Bohemia' and other rags, arr. David Bourne), costumes by Santo Loquasto.
First performed by American Ballet Theatre at the Uris Theatre, New York, 1976.

∾ Outline
Considered a breakthrough in the development of contem-

porary ballet, as well as in the career of its star, Mikhail Baryshnikov, Tharp's piece marries classical ballet and Broadway jazz to cool, super-smart effect. The piece is full-company scale, and divided into six movements – solos, duets, group numbers – in which the music swings in archetypal postmodern fashion between Haydn's 'Bear' Symphony and Lamb's syncopated rags. The women are dressed in loose flapperish dresses, the men in bizarre outfits featuring legwarmers and mid-calf pants. The piece's central conceit – the 'joke' by which it stands and falls – is that at the time of the piece's creation Baryshnikov was thought of as the Russian classicist par excellence. To see him in Loquasto's extraordinary bowler-hatted costume (based on Tharp's own outfit from her Charlie-Chaplinesque 1975 piece *Sue's Leg*) performing Tharp's funky swivels and slouches alongside his own Kirov-perfect tendus and pirouettes was to see the artform's certainties slickly and irresistibly subverted. Baryshnikov was also known in the dance world as a tireless womaniser – Tharp herself had an affair with him – and so the piece surrounds him with a *corps de ballet* of women and has its two female principals competing for his attention. Around this close-focus portrait, meanwhile, is arranged a wider-angle comedy – that of a ballet company in meltdown, with spoof references to *Giselle* and *Swan Lake*. The message was clear: henceforth the barriers are down. The new dancer is, as Tharp says, 'the one who can do it all'.

∾ View from the Wings

Twyla Tharp's arrival at The Royal Ballet came at a particularly good time for me. Recently promoted to principal and enjoying what felt like my best years, I was immediately captivated by Twyla's fierce intelligence and her free-ranging choreography in which a single phrase could take you from Broadway to the Bolshoi. I loved the latitude she took with classical ballet, cheekily ending a textbook sequence with an unexpectedly flexed foot, or slipping in a soft shoe shuffle. It was liberating and challenging and a delight to find someone asking such rigorous questions about where this age-old art-form might go next – whilst simultaneously having so much fun.

Live

Choreography by Hans van Manen, designs by Keso Dekker, music (*Sospiri, Wiegenlied et al.*) by Franz Liszt. First performed by the Dutch National Ballet at the Carré Theatre, Amsterdam, 1979.

∿ Outline

A female dancer enters, followed by a cameraman, and begins to dance to the Liszt piano music. As she does so, she is filmed by the cameraman, and her image is simultaneously projected onto a giant screen behind her. As the camera's focus narrows, so that we note every eyelid flutter, every muscle reaction, every tautening of her pointe-shoe ribbons, the performancere takes on an increasingly exhibitionistic and voyeuristic character. The woman is performing a duet with herself, and through the camera lens, with her audience's collective gaze.

A male dancer enters. He approaches the woman and remonstrates with her. After a time the woman walks off stage. The male dancer and the cameraman follow her through the auditorium – their dispute continuing – and out into the foyer. In the auditorium, meanwhile, we watch their progress on the screen. Evading the man, the woman marches out of the theatre and into the street. The camera follows her for some distance – we see her amongst pedestrians, through the traffic – and then finally she is lost to us.

∿ Notes

If van Manen's ballets have a subject, it is the disconnections that occur between men and women. If they have a conclusion, it is that women usually come off best, and this elegant conceptual piece is no exception to the rule. In it van Manen takes theatrical space and makes it elastic, stretching it far out into the public domain. Only when the dancer reappears on stage to take her bow, often with damp hair and rain-spattered pointe-shoes (in Holland there have been rumours that she returns to the theatre by bicycle) does the illusion finally snap to a close.

Steptext
One act. Choreography by William Forsythe, music Johann Sebastian Bach (Chaconne from Partita in D minor for solo violin), designs by Raymond Dragon Design Inc. and William Forsythe.
First performed by Aterballetto at the Teatro Municipale, Reggio Emilia, 1985.

∽ Outline
Forsythe describes *Steptext* as 'a short narrative of signs from the language of theatre. A movement, a gesture, a sound, a picture, a word, a light.' The work, for one female and three male dancers, is a combative examination of classical form. The cast break the conventional ballet vocabulary down to its constituent parts, and then, through a process of close-focused scrutiny and extreme articulation, test it to destruction. In a typically Forsytheian blurring of boundaries, the curtain rises and the dancing begins when the house-lights are still on and the audience are filing in to take their seats. Rejecting the modernist dance convention whereby faces remain neutral, the *Steptext* dancers visibly evince passionate emotions – resentment, sadness, anger – particularly in the male–female partnered passages. When not dancing they often behave anti-balletically – pacing the stage, folding their arms defensively, looking away. The piece is not danced to an orchestra but to a disjointed audiotape. The fractured form in which Bach's Chaconne is rendered seems to echo the difficulties of personal connection described by the choreography.

∿ View from the Wings

It's hard to dance Forsythe. At least it's hard to dance it well. It's all to do with language. Forsythe once said 'Je parle ballet mieux que je parle français,' and he was right. His French is good, but he has always spoken ballet beautifully, albeit with a Forsytheian accent. Since the mid-1980s, however, Forsythe has developed that accent until it is almost a language of its own, derived from classical ballet but no longer automatically intelligible by classical dancers who, however hard-working and well-intentioned, parle ballet pretty much as Petipa, the great nineteenth-century choreographer, wrote it.

Of all the Forsythe ballets I danced, the one in which I worked most intimately with the choreographer was *Steptext*. When ballets are acquired second-hand, they are usually taught by a repetiteur. But on *Steptext*, I worked in the studio with Forsythe for around six weeks, his sensitive coaching and clever corrections becoming part of the choreography itself, a kind of route map to which I could refer, on stage, when nerves threatened to take over.

Steptext is a ballet which provokes extreme reactions. You either love it or you hate it. In several ways, the ballet is a challenge to both the audience and the dancers. It opens with a section of improvisation within set guidelines which allow freedom without ever being totally free. But even with guiding principles, improvisation is a bizarre experience for a dancer unused to working outside a script. It takes a lot of courage and, for that reason, dancers often shy away from trying out improvisation, leaving it until the last possible moment, when they get on the stage. This, of course, is the worst place to be testing new techniques. The experience needs to be rehearsed over and over before it begins to feel natural. Chance favours the prepared mind.

From the moment you start dancing *Steptext*, there is no holding back. There are very few sections where the choreography doesn't suffer if the dancer is less than 'full out'. Yet physically, it has much less to do with cracking joints and wrenching ligaments than with a deep, constant muscularity. All of the movement starts from within, from a small instigation somewhere deep inside the body. Where that instigation ends up will depend on the dancer and their particular physique. Not everyone has 180-degree extensions. What is more important is that the impetus starts in the right place and continues to the end of its natural life. This may involve shifting the pelvis, distorting off-balance, or tilting the body to those famously precarious angles. Whereas in classical ballet the torso is generally held quiet, resisting the influence of the movement of the limbs, in Forsythe the torso follows suit. There are occasions where the body seems to defy its own anatomy. Certain movements appear to have joints operating contrary to the laws of nature, an effect achieved through optical illusion, not physical abuse. The body learns to move in greater detail; isolated sections of it will explore one idea while the body as a whole explores another.

The steps, too, are broken down and reformed in a way which defies established sequences of movement. Just because assemblé usually follows glissade, for instance, is not a good enough reason for it always to do so. Accepted classical formulae are turned on their head. Forsythe's ballets, without these habitual patterns, are slightly more difficult to learn; the irregular sentence construction tends to confuse. (Perhaps it's closer to German: you could dance an entire Forsythe variation and leave the stage with the verb still in your mouth.)

This endless denial of our expectations is pure Forsythe – it runs through the whole experience, from curtain-up (if there is one) to curtain-down. Even though the controversial aspects of Forsythe's staging are, for many, central to his work, what interested me as a dancer was the idea of going against the grain physically –

something which is raised to an art-form by the dancers of the company he directed in Germany, Frankfurt Ballet, who appear to achieve the impossible. They fall to the right and somehow land on the left. They seem to stand on their shins. They propel themselves into the air from a prone position and, with a quirky flexibility beyond the average dancer, they appear to move parts of the body which anatomy books would swear are immobile.

Yet for all its anatomy-defying elements, *Steptext* doesn't feel tricksy or dangerous. There is a logic and flow to the choreography which drives the dance from one step to the next. If you asked me to draw the movement, I would cover the paper with great, sweeping, interconnected circles. That same circularity exists within the dancer, in the ever-present, all-pervading sense of *en dedans*, or turn-out, which starts in the pelvis, continues up through the ribcage and extends out into the arms.

The no-nonsense look of the dancers, often described as 'arrogance' or 'attitude', also has less to do with posturing than with the physicality of the piece. The dancer's gaze is generally decided by the precarious angle of their body or the dynamic force of the movement. It's very hard (and probably not appropriate) to maintain the serenity of a Swan Queen while your legs are doing a heptathlon. When the focus is straight at, or through the audience, it can be mistaken for arrogance, but more often than not, I was barely aware that the audience was there, let alone intent on staring them out.

Steptext is without doubt a physical feat. It is relatively short, about fourteen minutes in all, yet I started out each time knowing that I would be absolutely drained by the time it was over. It required a different sort of stamina from most classical ballets, which separate bouts of exertion on stage with recovery periods in the wings and out of view of the audience. *Steptext* offers very little in the way of recovery time. Each entrance, each renewed push comes not from a normal heart rate, where 'energy' is available, but from a greatly elevated one, where 'energy' is not. The entire ballet hovers on the cusp of aerobic and anaerobic activity, just at the point where lactic acid starts to build up in the muscles. Fourteen minutes is a very long time to sustain this type of exercise, making it a tour de force more akin to athletics than ballet dancing. Throughout, I felt I was having to push myself onwards when I was already close to the point where, under normal circumstances, I'd be able to leave the stage and pant shamelessly. To make things worse, in *Steptext*, Forsythe has his exhausted ballerina stand centre stage, back to the audience, and watch the action whilst struggling to recover her breath. The first time I performed the ballet, my ribcage was expanding and contracting like a pair of bellows and my arms, hanging down by my sides, were going along for the ride. I must have looked like I was trying to take off.

One of the real revelations about dancing Forsythe was to discover my inbuilt fear of failure had totally evaporated. The great and liberating essence of the choreography is that within reason, and if the intention is right, it's very hard to be wrong. Falling over isn't a crime, and pirouettes which don't quite happen can legitimately become something else. Because there are no real absolutes, a dancer can find and set her own standards. A performance doesn't fail because a single balance goes awry. Paradoxically, with the fear of failure removed, one tends to fail much less frequently than normal.

I was once asked by a senior figure in the dance world whether I thought Forsythe was valid in major classical companies, whether there is anything in his choreography which requires the particular strengths of classical dancers. I would argue that it is more than valid; it is an essential part of today's repertoire. Forsythe has stretched the language of dance, and with it the dancers, moving ballet in new directions whilst continuing to employ the full range of classical technique. And we dancers of the 1990s needed to dance Forsythe. For the first half of my career, despite the fact that I was performing much of the Royal's repertoire, I never really felt I was speaking my own language. Margot Fonteyn and her generation had Ashton. Lynn Seymour had MacMillan. Yet there was an entire breed of 1990s dancers, me included, who didn't seem to have a repertoire which we could own. For me, Forsythe's ballets were exactly what I needed. They represented the moment which Forsythe himself claims he is striving for: the moment where I surprised myself.

in the middle, somewhat elevated

One act. Choreography and designs by William Forsythe, music by Thom Willems.
First performed at the Opéra de Paris, 1988.

This work, a highly precise deconstruction of formal French classicism, was originally created on the Paris Opéra Ballet, but later the same year Forsythe mounted it for the Frankfurt Ballet as the central section of a full-evening work entitled *Impressing the Czar*. The first part of *Impressing the Czar* is entitled *Potemkin's Signature*, and its decor includes a pair of outsize black cherries. These recur, as a pair of miniature gold cherries, in *in the middle, somewhat elevated*, and the section's title is taken from Forsythe's stage direction as to where on the stage they should be hung. The third and fourth sections of the compellingly weird *Impressing the Czar* are *The House of Mezzo-Prezzo* and *Bongo Bongo Nageela*.

∾ Outline

in the middle, somewhat elevated is almost conventional compared to the rest of *Impressing the Czar*. Unlike much of Forsythe's later work, the piece lends itself perfectly to the talents of a classical company – or at least a classical company whose dancers are prepared to take risks, and explore the outer limits of their technique. Structurally it is built around a single, highly demanding sequence in Forsythe's drastic, dislocated post-classical style. The principal female dancer performs the whole of this sequence in the course of the piece, while the other eight male and female dancers perform greater or smaller parts of it. Every dancer has a solo and duet, and short sections are left unscored for improvisation. With its nonchalant, edge-of-the-envelope chic and its high-speed slamming attack, *in the middle, somewhat elevated* offers a work in which a strong company can really cut loose, as well as – more generally – an exciting forward path for bravura pointe-work classicism.

∿ View from the Wings

In 1991, when Forsythe came to look at The Royal Ballet to cast *in the middle, somewhat elevated*, I had no idea that I might be involved. He watched a rehearsal of the second cast in Balanchine's *Agon*, and I milled around at the back of the studio as the first cast do, 'marking' sections and trying out different shoes. Impressing the visiting choreographer couldn't have been further from my mind. I was genuinely surprised when the message came back the following week that he would like me to dance in *middle*.

The piece was taught in the first instance by a repetiteur who spent several weeks with us in the studio, teaching the steps and trying to familiarise us with the style before Forsythe himself arrived for the stage calls. I remember very clearly the first rehearsals, and how alien it felt. The whole cast, crowded into the large studio, learnt each of the movement modules in the opening section, two long and complex phrases, even though some of us would, eventually, be using only tiny fragments of them when we came to perform the piece. Immediately I was torn between my two selves: the dancing sponge who thought it was all fascinating, and little Miss Practical who thought it rather a waste of time to be learning steps I wouldn't need to know.

Pretty soon the sponge won out, and I was hooked. Next, I had to get over the initial hurdle of any new work, those early attempts at an unfamiliar style which feel like the first steps of a newborn foal. This period of guaranteed failure makes braving new work a step some dancers are unwilling to take. We are generally so insecure about our achievements that once we've succeeded in getting one style under our dance belts, the temptation to stick to what we know is huge. Starting over may present a challenge, but it's also terrifying.

Right from the very beginning, I was keenly aware of the contradiction which is at the heart of Forsythe; the need to let go whilst still maintaining control. This is, in fact, the essence of all good dancing, as vital in *Sleeping Beauty* as it is in *middle*. It's just that we achieve it so infrequently. For classical dancers, the control is usually there but, terrified into total rigidity by the peculiar challenges of the classics, *Swan Lake*'s thirty-two *fouettés* or the Rose Adagio balances, the letting go rarely happens. In *middle*, a ballet I'd never seen, there were no ghosts of previous performances to haunt my present and I very early on found a courage to dare which I couldn't always sustain throughout the rest of The Royal Ballet's repertoire. Little by little, through constant repetition and clever corrections, I gradually found my way from awkward novitiate to some level of competence. As the rehearsal period progressed, I started to speak Forsythe. Not fluently, but at least my grammar was good.

When the choreographer himself arrived, a few days before the premiere, there was another hurdle to jump. I've worked with enough choreographers and their assistants to know that however good the relationship between them, there is no guarantee that all the work you've put in with the assistant will meet with the choreographer's approval. Choreographers are mercurial creatures, liable to change their minds on a whim. I was nervous about showing *middle* to Forsythe, but when I came to rehearse my solo, a fiendish little number with particularly tricky turns, I decided there was nothing for it but to trust in the work I'd already done and, in dancers' parlance, 'go for it'. I don't remember the exact response when I finished, but I knew somehow that I'd done the right thing. There were plenty of corrections – there always are – but I knew the intention had been right. And that realisation was my first real lesson in Forsythe.

'Still Life' at the Penguin Café

One act. Choreography by David Bintley, music by Simon Jeffes, designs by Hayden Griffin.
First performed by The Royal Ballet at the Royal Opera House, Covent Garden, 1988.

The Penguin Café Orchestra was an ensemble whose work drew its inspiration from an imaginary café, a surreal place whose strange inhabitants and 'paradoxical and metaphysical undercurrents' were much written about by Simon Jeffes, the PCO's founder. At the time of this ballet's creation, David Bintley was The Royal Ballet's resident choreographer.

∾ Outline

The theme of *'Still Life' at the Penguin Café* is man's destruction of the environment, and the threat that this poses to various animal species. To make his point, which he does with wit and charm, Bintley has created a series of dance numbers for creatures at risk (or in the case of the Great Auk, who opens and closes the ballet, actually extinct). He gives us, in order, a ballgowned Longhorn Ram, a dungaree-clad Texan Kangaroo Rat, a Hog-Nosed Skunk Flea on pointe, a despotic Cape Zebra, and a top-hatted Brazilian Woolly Monkey. For their dances, set to Jeffes' appealingly quixotic score, Bintley draws on a wide variety of styles, including charleston, ballroom, jazz, folk, and Latin American. The ballet's pièce de résistance is the White Mischief dance for the Cape Zebra and his harem. Performed by a kind of semaphore – all black-gloved forearms and imponderable freezes – this is one of contemporary ballet's funniest and most poignant set pieces.

∾ View from the Wings

While David Bintley was Resident Choreographer at The Royal Ballet, I danced in most of his ballets: *Galanteries*, *The Trials of Prometheus*, *Cyrano*, *The Planets* and more. My first progression out of the chorus and to my own, named, role was in *'Still Life' at the Penguin Café*. It was a big moment for me when the call sheet appeared on the board, as it did every Friday, and there was my name, alongside Guy Niblett's, called to our own private rehearsal. My big break, I thought, as I stitched new pointe shoes and decided which leotard to wear. It was right at the beginning of the creative process and I had no idea, at that point, what *Penguin* was about. The day before the call, I passed David in the corridor. 'Oh hello. You got any Ginger Rogers shoes?' Ah. So not a classical *pas de deux* which would establish Guy and me as the next Sibley/Dowell or Makarova/Baryshnikov. Oh well. At least we might be the next Fred and Ginger. Over the next few weeks, David created a gorgeous romp of a number in which I could indulge all my dance fantasies: six handsome men in black tie and tails to frame my every move and a long satin skirt which magically unravelled as I spun towards the front and revealed a cutely fringed leotard toning nicely with my golden heels.

The biggest challenge in *Penguin* was, undoubtedly, performing in an animal mask. Some animals were luckier than others: a monkey's head does relate, at least approximately, to the shape of a human head. I was a Ram. A Utah, long-horned ram. My ram nostrils were sited around a foot away from my forehead. The ram's eyes, being situated on either side of the head, were not much use as peep holes, so I was forced to look out of the nose instead. The net effect of all this was that I had to learn to dance the whole number with my chin on my chest. Any use of the head to portray character – a coy glance or a questioning tilt – had to be adjusted accordingly. In order to make it look as if I was tilting my head to one side whilst still seeing out of my nostrils, I had to contort my neck at a bizarre and painful angle. You get the picture. But nevertheless, *Penguin* was always a joy. Because it was essentially a 'show' number rather than a ballet duet, I could just get on and dance without the normal paranoia around pointe shoes and technique.

A complete contrast to *Penguin*, *Tombeaux* was a ballet I picked up 'second-hand' as an alternative cast to the Italian ballerina, Viviana Durante. As dancers, Viviana and I could not be more different: she is tiny, fleet, lyrical and beautifully proportioned with exquisite line. I was relatively tall for a dancer, intensely physical and with strength and dynamism amongst my greatest assets. Normally, the alternative casts are similar in style to the first choice, but from time to time, choreographers like to see the work in a totally different way and cast against type. It's always a challenge to take on roles which have been created with a different dancer's specific skills in mind.

Still, I was delighted and flattered that David wanted me to dance *Tombeaux*, his homage to Ashton and the historic classicism of The Royal Ballet. The choreography took advantage of all Viviana's innate qualities and posed a huge challenge, its serene solos and poetic duets masking real technical complexities. The ballerina's first entrance, for instance, is a smooth, gliding variation of perpetual motion which ends, surprisingly, with a brief burst of energy, all darting leaps and as many changes of direction as a helicopter's whirling blades. Switching, in an instant, from the languorous control of the slow section to the frantic speed of this mini-*coda* required an abrupt gear change which never seemed smooth – like trying to jump without bending your knees first.

Swan Lake

(see page 49 for the original Petipa–Ivanov version)
**Four acts. Choreography by Mats Ek, music by Pyotr
Ilyich Tchaikovsky, designs by Marie-Louise Ekman.
First performed by the Cullberg Ballet at the Royal
Opera House, Stockholm, 1987.**

∾ Outline

Prince Siegfried lives an isolated life with his mother, a
devouring, skinheaded bitch-queen. Bitterly jealous of his
mother's lover, uninterested by the girl she wishes him to
marry, he finds refuge in hallucination. He has visions of a
flock of male and female swans – powerful, androgynous,
bald-headed creatures whose choreographic *leitmotifs* include
a hefty waddle and a randy shudder. With one of these,
Odette, he falls in love.

To escape his mother, armoured by his fantasy, the Prince
turns to travel. His journey, which takes in Russia, Israel and
Spain, becomes a search for male identity. In its course he
meets men who treat women like livestock, and toreadors who
subdue them as if they were bulls. He also meets the sullen,
black-feathered Odile. Mistaking her for Odette, he is over-
joyed. They dance, and she vacillates between tenderness and
whorish crassness. At one point in a dazzlingly inventive *pas de
deux* she takes a running jump and slides down his back. Too
late, as joy turns to horror, he realises his mistake.

The Prince searches for his lost love. Eventually he returns
to the place of his dreams and rediscovers Odette. To his
amazement, however, he discovers that she and Odile are
one and the same creature, neither black nor white.
Empowered by this knowledge, he is able to face the future
with equanimity.

Le Spectre de la Rose
One act. Choreography by Angelin Preljocaj, music by
Carl Maria von Weber, costumes Dominique Gay.
First performed by Ballet Preljocaj at the Paris Opéra,
1993.

∽ Outline

A woman stands alone in an empty room. She is wearing a
brief but expensively cut silk shift, suggesting that she has
attended a fashionable soirée of some kind. She seems dis-
tressed, weary, possibly in shock. The woman falls to the floor,
raises herself, falls again. Behind her, Weber's *Invitation to the
Dance* begins to play, and two more women appear. On the
musical phrase which was once Nijinsky's entrance, two
toreadors in suits of lights leap down onto the stage to join
them, and the two couples dance an ersatz flamenco
sequence.

The Weber music fades. A figure in a costume similar to the
original Spectre's, but with a rose-petalled raincoat on top,
approaches the original woman. As the music restarts this
Spectre gently reassures her, lifting and embracing her, and
it becomes increasingly clear that she has suffered some
traumatic event. Behind them, the toreadors and their partners stamp and swirl.

The music fades, to be replaced by the sounds of dripping
water and weeping. In a bruising metaphor for the sex act, the
principal couple crash repeatedly against each other, chest
to chest. Lifting the Woman, the Spectre whirls her repeatedly
around himself. He bears her urgently to the floor, and their
embraces become crude and uncontrolled. Finally the Spectre
collapses on top of her. In contrast to his earlier tenderness
and solicitude, he now seems indifferent. Looking down at
the recumbent woman, he lays a rose casually across her
throat and exits.

～ Notes

For Preljocaj, *Le Spectre de la Rose* is 'une porte du temps' – a gateway to dance history. But things have changed since Nijinsky leapt through the window. The flirtation that was so blissful all those years ago, and was recalled in such sweet reverie in that Biedermeier bedroom, has evolved into anonymous sex, and perhaps rape. Many of Fokine's original steps are echoed but transformed – the Spectre's airy leaps, for example, are now his jarring crashes against the woman, and the dreamy waltzes are the couple's loveless bumps and grinds. The Spectre is both sinister and sad as he comforts the woman for the violence that he himself will visit on her. The ritual, eternal nature of their exchange is underlined by the calculated foolishness of the choreography for the two secondary couples, who stamp and pose in self-important counterpoint to the principal couple's more organic moves.

Bella Figura

One act. Choreography by Jiri Kylian, music by Giovani-Battista Pergolesi, Alessandro Marcello, Antonio Vivaldi, Giuseppe Torelli, Lukas Foss, decor by Michael Simon, costumes by Joke Visser.
First performed by Netherlands Dance Theatre in The Hague, 1995.

～ Outline

In the opening moments of *Bella Figura*, a near-naked female dancer is carried across the stage wrapped in a black velvet curtain. The image is both lush and unexpected, and signals the moment when, to quote Kylian, 'dream and reality unconditionally come together as one'. In the sequences that follow – duets and double duets, trios, obliquely spaced groupings – the stage curtains play a significant role. Kylian uses them to manipulate his dancers' performance space, sometimes widening it panoramically, sometimes shuttering it down to a close-cropped black square. In one of many extravagant images, a frieze of bare-chested men and women in scarlet skirts lift the dropcloth in their arms, offering themselves facelessly to the audience (the colours of the piece, saturating the women's crinolines and corselettes, are black, vermilion and flesh).

Musically, the piece is set to a nine-part montage of baroque and contemporary compositions. Kylian's concerns here are primarily visual; the music is little more than a backing-track, and washes over the performers like an adjunct to the lighting. The dance itself is a series of flicker-book images with every page impeccable – upper bodies sharply torsioned, arms cleaving space, leg-lines racily hyperextended. The highlight of the ballet is a sensual duet for two women. Bare-breasted, and with their lower bodies concealed beneath cascading, peony-like skirts, they crouch and sway in mesmeric opposition, alternately probing and withdrawing like sea anemones, never quite touching.

∾ Notes

Exquisite, non-specific, unburdened with meaning or consequence, this is an archetypal Kylian ballet. For all that the choreographer keeps step with the avant-garde, he delivers very few rough edges; all is Kylianised – rendered into the language of the upscale European art event. In a typically opaque manifesto accompanying the piece, Kylian describes *Bella Figura* as 'a journey in time, light and space, addressing the ambiguity of aesthetics, performances and dreams'.

V

One act. Choreography by Mark Morris, music by Robert Schumann (Quintet in E flat for piano and strings, op. 44), designs by Martin Pakledinaz.
First performed by the Mark Morris Dance Group at Sadler's Wells Theatre, London, 2001.

∿ Outline

The ballet's name – *V* – is the formation in which we discover fourteen dancers on curtain-up. The quintet is one of Schumann's most Romantic compositions, and from the opening moment, when the allegro brillante bursts into life, the mood is one of joy. The lighting suggests azure skies, and the blue- and green-clad dancers seem to leap through colliding motes of sunshine. They describe circular motifs, linking their arms as if they were in a Matisse painting, and perform open-armed runs across the stage – the runs' momentum trailing off with the music. This, they seem to be proclaiming, is the morning of the world.

The uneven tread of the second movement – not so much melancholy as simply mysterious – is given strange and original form by Morris, who has his dancers creep flat-handed along the green-lit stage like Max Escher lizards. Their passage is interrupted by a wistful interlude for first violin to whose ebb and flow a series of lyrical, male–female, classically based partnerships unfold. A gradual return to the floor sees a continuation of the inexorable reptile progress. As the movement draws to a measured close, dancers are being carried to their first positions like Komodo Dragons.

What does Morris mean by all of this? Has he identified some dark narrative thread in Schumann's work, or are the dancers merely expressing the music's watery ebb and flow? The untroubled runs and collapses of the third movement suggest the whirl of the *scherzo* rather than any more literal interpretation, and by the time that the fourth movement ends, with dancers pouring onto the stage in wave after wave of jetés, the issue has been left behind.

There is no such thing as a 'typical' Morris work, but the lyrical, elegiac *V* is a good example of the sort of crossover piece which classical companies are now taking into their repertoires. The crossover works both ways, and working with classical companies has resulted in a broadening of Morris's more contemporary choreographic style. If there are enigmatic elements in his ballets, Morris says, he is not about to provide arbitrary meanings. 'I could explain in great detail the reasons and logic of all the compositions, but who cares? I don't tell people what to think. Wouldn't it be awful if everybody thought the same thing about everything?'

Tryst

One act. Choreography by Christopher Wheeldon, music by James MacMillan, designs by Jean-Marc Puissant.
First performed by The Royal Ballet at the Royal Opera House, Covent Garden, 2002.
Christopher Wheeldon is a former Royal Ballet dancer who in 1993 joined New York City Ballet and in 2001 became Resident Choreographer there. He is one of the most successful of the younger, classically based dance-makers.

∼ Outline

Wheeldon's ballet takes its structure from James MacMillan's musical composition. Abstract in nature, as almost all his ballets are, it begins with a lone female dancer crouching on stage, and grows into an extended company piece for four couples and a twelve-strong ensemble. Puissant's set, skilfully lit, evokes changeable weather, the backdrop morphing in the blink of an eye from delicate rose-pink to rain-charged oyster-grey. The same volatility is evident in the dances: as clouds slide across the sky, so a sombre note touches the choreography. Wheeldon draws long, calligraphic lines with his dancers, inscribing them like winged birds or cursive verticals against Puissant's skies. At times the shapes he makes are cryptically stylised, suggesting an ancient language of signs, at times they become almost entirely abstract.

As the stage darkens, the ballet's focus narrows to a single couple and a reverberant *pas de deux*. The woman's moves have a sinuous, exploratory character, the man's a dark assurance. The sequence, like almost all Wheeldon's work to date, lies somewhere between pure abstraction and narrative. As a dancer, Wheeldon performed the works of Ashton and MacMillan before switching to those of Robbins and Balanchine. While he has clearly been influenced by all four, his work displays a precisely pitched aesthetic which is very much his own.

Our Top Ten Ballets

Below are our personal favourites from the ballets included in the book. Luke's choice is very much from a spectator's view point, having watched them all and considered them in his role as a writer and critic. I have found it hard to be quite so objective: it is difficult for me to separate my judgement of some of the ballets as 'spectacle' from a deep attachment to them gained in hours of exploration in the studio and on stage. So my list is a mixture of ballets I enjoy watching but have never performed – *Romeo and Juliet* and *Month in the Country*, for instance – and ballets which I lived, breathed and, ultimately, loved: *Steptext*, *The Rite of Spring* and *Swan Lake*.

Deborah Bull

As Deborah says, I've considered all of these ballets as a critic, but I'm not so sure that my impressions are any more objective than hers. All that I can say with certainty is that these pieces have a profound resonance for me, and that I will always return to them.

Luke Jennings

Deborah's Top Ten
Swan Lake
The Rite of Spring
Les Noces
Symphony in C
Agon
Romeo and Juliet
Song of the Earth
Manon
A Month in the Country
Steptext

Luke's Top Ten
Giselle
Sleeping Beauty
Swan Lake
L'Après midi d'un Faune
Apollo
Symphonic Variations
Scènes de Ballet
Agon
La Fille Mal Gardée
Song of the Earth

Index of Ballets